THE OFFICER CORPS OF CUSTER's SEVENTH CAVALRY

Also by the Author
Individual Gear and Personal Items of the GI in Europe • 1942-1945

THE OFFICER CORPS OF CUSTER's SEVENTH CAVALRY

1866-1876

James B. Klokner

Schiffer Military History
Atglen, PA

Acknowledgments

To my wonderful wife, and her commitment to my commitment. She, as always, faithfully supported me as I watched the world go by, tucked into my corner office. To my children, Julian, Gustav, and Eva, who always with good spirits sacrificed many opportunities to play with Dad – I promise to resume, again, "backyard operations." A special thanks to my parents, who as usual were there with love and encouragement – particularly *my* hero, my father, whose strength and sensibilities make me strive always to do better things.

A debt of gratitude go to the many who have helped with this project and without their assistance, contribution and support, this book would have never come to fruition. It has been a luxury of mine to become acquainted with them and thank them again for their help. My sister, Anne and Jeff Gulati; Glen Swanson; John Doerner, Chief Historian at Little Bighorn Battlefield National Monument; Suzanne Christoff, Associate Director for Special Collections and Archives and Alicia Mauldin-Ware, both of the United States Military Academy; Ray Anderson, Proffesor Emeritus; Cliff Hyatt, United States Military History Institute; the Mason County Historical Museum, Mason, Texas; Jeff Bloom; Russ Taylor and the staff at Brigham Young University; the New York State Historical Society; Byrne Photo Imaging of Madison, Wisconsin; Alan Berger; Tom O'Neil at Custer Books; the Massachusetts State Historical Society; Natalia V. Sciarini from the Beinecke Library at Yale University; Rollie and Sharon VanderZyle; Connie Schmeidler from Fort Hays State Historic Site; the Nebraska State Historical Society; Cheryl Goldenstein from the University of Wyoming Library; George Williams, Colorado State Historical Society and the Southeastern Colorado Heritage Center; Cynthia Twing and staff at the Johnson County Library; the University of Oregon at Eugene; Al Johnson, Fort Abraham Lincoln Foundation; the Wilmington National Cemetery, Wilmington, North Carolina; Sara Keckeisen, Kansas State Historical Society; Michael Douglass and Lisa Hinzman, Wisconsin State Historical Society; the Fort Riley Museum; the State Historical Societies of Maryland, New Jersey, Ohio, and Kentucky; and of course Peter Schiffer, Bob Biondi, and Ian Robertson from Schiffer Publishing.

Images for this project came from many varied sources, which I would like to credit and thank: The Glenwood J. Swanson Collection; Western History Department, Denver Public Library; the Little Bighorn Battlefield National Monument; the Kansas State Historical Society; The Spartan Shop, Madison, Wisconsin; the United States Military Academy at West Point; Brady Collection of Photographs, Library of Congress; Yale Collection of Western Americana, Beinecke Rare Book and Manuscript Library; the National Archives, College Park, Maryland; L. Tom Perry Special Collections, Harold B. Lee Library, Brigham Young University; the United States Army Military History Institute at Carlisle Barracks, Pennsylvania and the numerous collections within, including the Civil War Library and Museum MOLLUS, Edward S. Godfrey Collection, Roger D. Hunt Collection, Massachusetts Commandery, Military Order of the Loyal Legion, and the Daniel Potochniak Collection. Also included in the list of sources are the Joel Emmons Whitney Collection, Minnesota Historical Society; Johnson County Public Library, Buffalo, Wyoming; State Historical Society of North Dakota; Fort Abraham Lincoln Foundation, and the Villa Louis Collection, Wisconsin State Historical Society.

Dedication

To my friend, who will be deeply missed, Lt. Commander Eric G. Anderson.

Book design by Robert Biondi.

Library of Congress Catalog Number: 2006937360.

Printed in China.
ISBN: 978-0-7643-2660-8

We are always looking for people to write books on new and related subjects. If you have an idea for a book, please contact us at the address below.

Published by Schiffer Publishing Ltd.
4880 Lower Valley Road
Atglen, PA 19310
Phone: (610) 593-1777
FAX: (610) 593-2002
E-mail: Info@schifferbooks.com.
Visit our web site at: www.schifferbooks.com
Please write for a free catalog.
This book may be purchased from the publisher.
Please include $3.95 postage.
Try your bookstore first.

In Europe, Schiffer books are distributed by:
Bushwood Books
6 Marksbury Ave.
Kew Gardens, Surrey TW9 4JF
England
Phone: 44 (0)20 8392-8585
FAX: 44 (0)20 8392-9876
E-mail: info@bushwoodbooks.co.uk
www.bushwoodbooks.co.uk
Free postage in the UK. Europe: air mail at cost.
Try your bookstore first.

CONTENTS

PREFACE

As a boy, the first time I opened up *The American West* on our family bookshelf, I sat enthralled by the collection of lithographs depicting the exploits of the "taming of the West," particularly the Indian wars and their most celebrated regiment: Custer and the Seventh Cavalry. Thirty years later, my interest hasn't wavered: I continue to be more absorbed by the legend and lore of the period and the colorful but yet somewhat unknown personalities of the Seventh Cavalry. Indulging in the "pulp" legend of the Last Stand, I've often asked myself, "What was it like to be one of Custer's officers?" Craving to learn more, I have collected an extensive library about the legendary Seventh Cavalry during this period. However, battle histories and the existing biographies pertain primarily to the Big Horn participants, which account for only a small portion of the officer corps. The search for information regarding the remainder has yielded very little. My deep determination over the years to learn more has been my inspiration for this project.

This book is not about Custer, nor the famous massacre, but rather about the senior staff officers, the company commanders, and the junior officers who carried his orders through victory and death. Though in some cases their individual histories imparted little to the unfolding of the Indian campaigns and history itself, the consequentiality of their variegated personalities is uniquely relevant and in many ways contributed to the legend of the regiment and the glorious shaping of the American frontier. For further clarification, it is important to explain the numerous references throughout this work to that of *Custer's* regiment. As a Lieutenant Colonel, he was subordinate to another. But for all practical purposes, as one will observe, the absence of a commanding Colonel during this period allowed Custer the opportunity to leave his imprint on the composition and development of the regiment, leading the Seventh Cavalry in their most celebrated achievements and colossal blunders. Also to be noted is the time frame of this research. This book provides a biographical portrait of the leadership core of the Seventh Cavalry for a ten-year span; from the inception in July 1866, through the Seventh Cavalry's so called "glory days" during the war against the Indians. (This statement would be vigorously disputed by the horseless soldiers fighting fiercely on Leyte Island in 1944, or at Ia Drang Valley in 1965).

Something to be said of the biographical section of this writing; first of all, historical data and biographical essay has been outlined in a distinct method. The biographies focus mainly on each individual's military history, both before and after service with the regiment, covering only significant or extraordinary details of personal life. Post-service biographical data was included only if it further defined individual character. In addition, scouring private collections, libraries, national historical institutions, state historical societies, public collections and endless sources of literature, I have endeavored to include a likeness, when available, of the individual to accompany the essay. Lastly, the majority of the biographical data is derived from hundreds of single sources, including journals, articles, government extracts and records, official registers, and their respective supplements, and several core books. All of these indispensable sources are listed in complete detail in the bibliography section, and made this work possible.

James B. Klokner

INTRODUCTION

"... In the Seventh Cavalry, which as I am told by Genl. Hunter, and officers of the War Department, is to be the finest regiment in the service, and "far superior to any of the old regiments"- Maj. Gen. A.J. Smith, who commanded a Corps under Grant, at Vicksburg, and under Sherman, afterwards, is Col. of the regiment, and all the others are equally distinguished ..." — Albert Barnitz to his wife, January 17, 1867

No other regiment in history seems to capture the character, spirit, and imagination like the Seventh Regiment of Cavalry. The Seventh was one of several new regiments formed in 1866 in the wake of the Civil war and the restructuring of the post-war army. The mustering out of the hundreds of state regiments and the wholesale downsizing of the post-war army left few officer positions available within the regular army. As thousands of able-bodied men clamored for political alliances and jockeyed for position, a highly competitive process of social and political selection drew only the top few. Naturally, this drew many colorful and noteworthy characters and encompassed an unusual conglomeration of officers-most of who were connected to some degree of influence or possessed downright astonishing service records.

Before one reads further, it seems in best interest to understand a bit more about post-Civil War army structure. Following hostilities, the mustering out of the volunteer forces left the army with roughly 30,000 troops. Although the Johnson Administration favored a small army, overruling Gen. Grant's proposal for a still sizable army to occupy the south, the challenges to disperse the requirements for reconstruction duties and westward expansion amongst the meager forces spawned the "Act to increase and fix the Military Peace Establishment," signed on July 28, 1866. This act, proposing the creation of several new infantry and cavalry regiments, opened specific vacancies in both new and existing units, creating huge competing claims for limited appointment.[1]

Organizational provisos for appointment in the "new" army limited assignment only to a select few. Junior officers had to have served credibly for two years. These provisos also allotted for only one third of the company commanders (also to have served for two years) to have come from the regular army, while the remainder were to come from officers of volunteer regiments whom had "distinguished themselves for meritorious service during the war." A substantial portion of the appointments were men whom served with the state regiments of volunteers, which were allowed to fill vacancies proportionate to their regiments involved, excluding California, Oregon, and Nevada.[2] Naturally, a regiment with only sixteen Captain vacancies and over a thousand applicants would undoubtedly insure a highly competitive selection. The command appointments of celebrated veterans Andrew J. Smith, and George Custer, whose battlefield accomplishments even today are unparalleled in the annals of contemporary military history, alone exalted the resplendent status of the regiment. And favorable endorsements from such notable names drew an exceptional group of men and an added element of elitism and "espirit de corps." A slew of decorated cavalryman who had shined under Custer's eye or previously served in Sheridan's corps, including Sheridan's own brother, reveal a fair amount of handpicking and political patronage.[3]

Cast as "the finest regiment in the service," the officer corps of the new Seventh United States Regiment of Cavalry came from various backgrounds: Adventurers, career soldiers, foreigners, mercenaries and opportunists. Command of the new regiment was given to Colonel Andrew J. Smith, the popular and charismatic "Hero of Tupelo" and a distinguished cavalry veteran of both the Mexican War and the Rebellion. Lieutenant Colonel George A. Custer would be second in command. This dashing former cavalry general had bolted to glory and fame as one of Sheridan's youngest, most accomplished and colorful divisional commanders, in addition to holding the honor of being one of the youngest generals in the War. Others were teachers and intellectuals, some were (or would later be) prominent in politics, and some were born deeply steeped in military lineage, descended from America's founding fathers and veterans of the Revolutionary war. And throughout their lives, each one enjoyed moments of either astonishing greatness or resounding failure. Many hoped for glory and promotion within the rank's of the nations most prestigious military arm. Although some were unscrupulous and dubiously irresolute, all were hearty and rugged adventures. They knew the hard life of the soldiering, as well as the reputation of their commanding Lt. Colonel. Most were boldly aggressive and fearless, matching Custer's own legendary zeal and lust for battle. Most had command experience. Over twelve of the officers on the initial rosters of the Seventh Cavalry had at one time worn General's stars on their shoulders, and fifteen had been Colonels and Lt. Colonels; most were brevetted for gallantry under fire or meritorious service. Several held the nation's highest honors and some of the regiment's "junior" officers went on to become future military policy-makers, shaping the army for a new kind of war in Europe. As the appointment provisos intimate, most had seen battle during the Civil War, (with a handful sharing experience against Gen. Santa Ana in the Mexican War) with some seeing in excess of thirty engagements. Moreover, of the original rosters of the new regiment, the large percentage of officers wounded in action during the Rebellion was sound testament to the fearless and courageous character of the leadership corps of the new Seventh Cavalry.[4]

These young leaders entered a service of unconventional life in an undiscovered country, where natural selection and hardships prevailed. Few could comprehend the harsh conditions, desolate loneliness, and unforgiving climate in the cruel and remorseless open frontier much less fight the hours of idleness and boredom. Crippling snowfall, stifling heat, and torrential downpours, which turned the landscape into seas of mud, were all too commonplace in the new field of operations. Even more confounding was the introduction to plains warfare and the complexities of the enemy. Few brought with them any experience at all against defeating their adversary. Gone were the chivalrous niceties of Christian "Victorian" warfare, even by standards of the carnage of eastern battles such as Antietam or Bull Run. Indian tactics were baffling at times, and their savage and inexplicable treatment of their enemies, particularly to white non-combatants was easily construed as nothing short of "beastly." These guardians of westward expansion and Manifest destiny were introduced to a savagery and brutality almost unfathomable. To further compound these difficulties, army tactics employed against the Indians often fell under scrutiny and criticism as excessive. The army often found themselves constrained by an unpopular opinion of a public repulsed by the nature and conduct of war: The very same public whom had earlier been passionate proponents of Indian eradication.

The initial officer corps filtered into Ft. Riley, Kansas in early 1867, following their successful entrance examinations and congressional approval (several of whom would not pass on their first attempt). These incoming officers replaced the officers on temporary assignment from Major John Davidson's 2nd Cavalry, who had been charged with staffing the roster and organization of the companies. Seventh Cavalry Major Alfred Gibbs, who was third in line of tenure and another experienced veteran of cavalry warfare, assisted Davidson's staff with training, organization, and protocol; thoroughly embraced the merits of the regimental band. As conspicuous as the talent of these new officers was, the combined experience in regards to plains warfare was acutely limited. It was said that at one time, half the new-arriving officers could not even ride a horse.[5] With few officers of experience on the frontier against the Indians, Gibbs' proclivity for detailed training doctrines provided a firm foundation in the development of the embryonic regiment. The bleak and crowded outpost of Ft. Riley was a difficult introduction to military life on the frontier. The challenge of molding the officers whom served in infantry regiments or came from post-war civil appointments into a smooth cohesive unit was left primarily to the advice and tutelage of the "veterans."[6] All, particularly the company commanders, were held to high expectations as they prepared themselves to lead their men against the Indians, who Custer himself would call the finest "cavalrymen" in America. Those who knew not of Custer's reputation, specifically the year before in Texas, were unceremoniously indoctrinated into his concept of discipline. For the men who had only known service in the state regiments, discipline in the regular army was vastly different and unfamiliar. These veterans of the war, accustomed to volunteer service, paid little attention to the pedantics of formal military etiquette, while Maj. Gibbs, a stern disciplinarian and a firm believer in military protocol, emphatically drilled the men. The task was made even more difficult by the resulting indignant bitterness of the rank-and-file, which was speckled with the more undesirable types of the career criminals and malingerers as well as a dozen different nationalities.[7]

Although certainly not exclusive to the Seventh Cavalry, professional rivalries developed immediately among the assortment of backgrounds of the commissioned ranks-most friendly enough, limited to chides and general teasing. In the summer of 1867, the first of the new commissions directly from the Academy arrived, with more to follow by the end of the decade. Veterans ranking these rigid newcomers were quick to "haze" and criticize the "quality" of their education. Conversely, the West Pointers, considering themselves exclusively of "gentlemanly etiquette," were naturally scornful.

Also arriving were the numerous commissions by appointment from enlisted ranks, former volunteer officers of the many state regiments, and civilians-turned-officers. These officers arrived with little or no knowledge of traditional military life, and confounded attempts at a heterogeneous amalgamation of soldiers. The diversity in arms and friendly rivalries made rank and promotion (and higher pay) highly desirable. Reminiscent of the pre-Civil War army, promotion was agonizingly slow, where stagnation and the monopoly of older officers remained. One could expect promotion only with vacancies by death, sickness, resignation, dismissal, or retirement (which happened at 62) of a senior rank. Even then, men with political influence could circumvent the seniority-based system to reach the "lofty" rank of Captain within a regiment. The process of attaining rank and promotion only became more complex with the arrival of the Grant administration in 1869, when the flaws of the current structure of the army prompted reorganization and further scaling back.[8] The appropriation acts of 1869 again whittled down the numbers, reducing the army from over 50,000 to roughly 37,000, while redefining the existing rank structure. A surplus of nearly a thousand officers forged what became known as "Benzine" or "Hancock" review Boards. Designed to determine qualifications and eliminate sub-standard officers, these reviews effectively encouraged resignation and purged the less-than-desirable army officer corps, although internal strife and political alliances probably fostered some cases of exigent or unfair dismissal. This streamlining of the military, although beneficial in principle, left field units heavily depleted. The regiments felt the deepest pinch, suffering skeleton rosters as qualified field officers rotated through the now vacant jobs of instructors as well as the signal corps and quartermaster and commissary departments. At the same time, stagnation of senior officers continued and shortcomings of the system prompted later proposals amending service retirement. Maximum service length was raised from thirty to forty years after 1882, and mandatory retirement age became sixty-four. Officers under this provision were placed on "unlimited" inactive list while disabilities were placed on "limited" lists. The acts also instituted a new method of promotion in 1890, in which one received a promotion to a specific arm, versus a particular regiment.[9]

A classic characteristic of military duty is the significant amount of idle-time; life on the remote outposts was certainly no exception. The monotony of winter garrison during those first years proved the undoing of many officers. During the war, infractions were often forgiven or simply overlooked due to an individual's accomplishments or success on the battlefield. However, since sporadic engagement of an elusive "enemy" made battlefield distinction difficult to obtain, disciplinary measures were commonplace, and orders of arrest, referred to as being "sick with the measles," were handed out with frequency.[10] The consumption of alcohol was the most prevalent infraction. Although Custer was not unfamiliar with the problem from his service in Texas, he probably never truly experienced the debilitating effects and in the early years would be constantly plagued with drunkenness and insubordination. Somewhat curbed during summer field operations, officers drank freely and save some exception, drunkenness was overlooked, providing they were sober on duty. Nevertheless, Custer, abstinent himself, worked tirelessly to control drunkenness in the regiment and in one case, a new officer guilty of drunkenness, was transferred out of the regiment the very next day after his arrival.[11] In fact, drunkenness on duty, absence without leave, and objectionable behavior while intoxicated, exaggerated on payday, were common charges among the officers and men and attributing to most of the dismissals during the first ten years of the regiment. Capt. Albert Barnitz in a letter to his wife in November 1867 wrote that a total of eight officers were under arrest at one time. Custer and his commanders also faced the enormous but futile task of controlling desertions, which could be a nightly occurrence. Disagreeable military life and the harsh existence of a man on the edge of civilization lured many soldiers into temptation to escape to easier money making professions. Indeed by 1867 alone, the desertion rate in the regiment reached over fifty-two percent. As one company reported, "as the captain woke up one morning, found forty of his sixty troopers and his senior NCO gone towards the mines of the Platte Valley."[12]

Following a period of inactivity while on reconstruction duty in the south, the officers of the Seventh Cavalry reassembled in Memphis in 1873, with orders to proceed to the Dakotas. Happily reuniting with one another, they looked forward to resuming field operations on the frontier. By the time the regiment marched with Stanley's expedition through the Dakotas, the regiment had matured into a cohesive military unit. Most of the "problem" officers, including the malingerers, malcontents, and habitual drunks, had been weeded out of the ranks by the 1869 competency boards, pressure from their own fellow officers, or left on their own volition. Custer would write during the expedition, "...not an officer in my command has been intoxicated since we left Ft. Rice." (E.B. Custer, *Boots and Saddles*)

Fort Lincoln was a vast improvement over the dilapidated Kansas posts or Spartan "mud huts" of Forts Reynolds and Ft. Morgan in Colorado Territory. Social life was significantly better, and barring both the torment of the mosquitoes to man and animal and the intensity of Dakota weather, a general contentment existed, aided by the many marriages, which turned the bachelor ranks into the minority. Despite the well-known "rifts" and internal division between the "pro" and "anti-Custer" factions, the officer corps of the Seventh Cavalry regiment enjoyed a time of veritable tranquility throughout operations in the Dakotas from 1873 to 1875. Author Katherine Gibson-Fougera (wife of Seventh Cavalry officer Francis Gibson) writes, "There was also the very solitude of their mutual existence-just a handful of people, so to speak, afloat upon an uncharted sea of desolation, miles and miles from civilization-and the shared hardships of a bleak climate with it's privations and the daily perils they faced together. These were the factors that brought these army pioneers closer to each other in some instances than many brothers and sisters and forged ties of friendships that neither time not circumstances could sever...." (Fougera, *With Custer's Cavalry*). In the spring of 1876, the officers and wives of the Seventh Cavalry assembled at Ft. Lincoln from various other surrounding stations in preparation for another campaign-this one towards the Big Horn Mountains, and as history records, much further.

CHAPTER ONE

OPERATIONAL HISTORY 1866-1876

"Oh, it was a fine Regiment, right enough. And there wasn't a man in it who didn't believe it was the greatest cavalry outfit in the entire United States army." — Sergeant Charles Windolph, *I was with Custer*

Formation

Following the Civil War, the mustering out of the volunteer forces left the army with a limited number of troops. Requirements for the occupational and judicial duties of reconstruction and westward movement during a time of railroad expansion and urban development in a vast country required the greatest need for permanent military forces. The "Act to increase and fix the Military Peace Establishment"[1], outlined the creation of numerous forces to specifically fill these gaps. Over two-dozen new infantry regiments to the then meager nineteen were added. In addition, the vast geographical (and geopolitical) expanse of the west and the Great Plains, obviously more suited to mounted units, brought about the increase of cavalry forces from six to ten, adding four new regiments designated the Seventh, Eighth, Ninth, and Tenth Cavalry Regiments. Both the Seventh and Eighth were organized along the same guidelines as traditional cavalry units, whereas the remaining Ninth and Tenth Regiments were designated colored regiments and differed slightly in structure.[2]

As a product of the Act of 1866, orders were issued for the organization of the Seventh Regiment of Cavalry. It read: "*Under the act of July 28, 1866, the designation and organization of regiments by which the military peace establishment is increased and fixed will be as follows. The provisions of this order are in accordance with the conditions of the Army on, and are of effect from, the 21st day of September 1866. The two additional regiments of Cavalry, composes of white men, will be the Seventh and Eighth Regiment of Cavalry. (War Dept. G.O. 56, August 1, 1866, War Department G.O. 92, Sept. 1-Dec 22, 1866)*. The regiment was organized in the summer of 1866 at Fort Riley, Kansas, under the auspices of the Department of the Missouri, commanded by General W.S. Hancock, which was overseen by the whole Military Division of the Missouri, commanded by Gen. W.T. Sherman (see appendix). Organizational development and training was charged primarily to elements of the 2nd Cavalry Regiment under Major J.W. Davidson, whose officers would staff the various company vacancies throughout the first winter.[3]

Under the able command of Bvt. Maj. Gen. A.J. Smith, and Bvt. Maj. Gen. G.A. Custer, officers and men trickled into Fort Riley by early September. Newly appointed Seventh Cavalry Major Alfred Gibbs, assisted Davidson's staff with organization and protocol. Custer, Maj. Gibbs, and Davidson immediately set about developing training curriculums and doctrines. By the years end, the command nucleus was firmly established, and as the regiment approached a full compliment of over 900 officers and enlisted men, companies left Ft. Riley for deployment to the frontier forts in Kansas and Colorado Territory. In February 1867, Col. Smith went on detached duty and regimental field command went to Lt. Col. Custer, who would for the most part act in this capacity throughout duty in Kansas.[4]

Hancock Expedition, 1867 and Pursuit of Hostiles

Throughout the preceding years, hostile bands of Indians, principally the Southern Cheyenne, Comanche, Kiowa and Arapahoe bands, had been routinely committing acts of aggression against the white population in the region; attacking overland mail route stations, sacking property and killing the personnel, and murdering civilians. The savage nature of these deplorable attacks outraged the local population. The army, attempting to avoid outright war, sought only to halt the attacks and seek out and bring to justice the perpetrators of this continuous "treachery." In the interest of previous regional agreements, their aim was to establish peaceful council with the hostile bands, forcing upon them the agreement to again retire south, remaining well clear of the Smokey Hill River. Moreover, they indicated they were prepared to act against hostilities and non-compliance. The government, acting through the Department of Missouri, ordered an expedition aimed at intimidating the Indian population to cease aggression by show of force, utilizing the newly formed Seventh Cavalry on it's maiden campaign. The expedition, under the command of Maj. Gen. Winfield Scott Hancock, commander of the Department and already an experienced and accomplished officer, was organized at Fort Leavenworth in spring of 1867, and would include a substantial base of cavalry, infantry, and artillery units.[5]

By springtime, communications between agents and the Comanche, Kiowa, Cheyenne, Arapahoe, and Apache bands had been established, and Hancock's column left Leavenworth. The expedition, delayed initially by poor weather, marched toward Ft. Larned in the Arkansas River Valley, picking up the remainder of the consolidated forces. Accompanied by Hancock, Col. A.J. Smith and Maj. Davidson, Companies A, D, H, and M of the Seventh Cavalry left garrison at Fort Riley in late March, marching through Fort Harker to Ft. Larned, where they picked up additional companies F and G, as well as E and K, which had come from Ft. Dodge and Ft. Hays. The tactical column of the expedition totaled over 1380 men, including eight companies of the Seventh Cavalry under Custer. It also included seven companies of the 37th Infantry

Above: With an impressive service record in both the Mexican War and the War of the Rebellion, Major John Wynn Davidson, detached from the 2nd Cavalry, was charged with organization of the regiment in August 1866. Later, he was assigned to the board of Custer's 1867 court martial, but other orders fortunately excused him from duty. *USMHI*

Below: Fort Riley, Kansas, photographed in the late 1860s, saw the origin of the Seventh U.S. Cavalry in late 1866. After the regiment left in the spring of 1867, it did not garrison there again until after the Yellowstone campaign of 1876. *Library of Congress*

regiment under Capt. J. Rziha, and elements of the 4th Artillery Regiment with a detachment of engineers, both under the command of Lt. M.R. Brown and Capt. C.C. Parsons.[6]

Representatives from the Indian encampment located just north of Ft. Larned, along the Pawnee River Fork, met the column and dialogue began between the Expedition's command and a formidable body of warriors. Communications were ambiguous and inconclusive, as the Indians remained suspicious of Hancock's objectives. Further negotiations were requested, but yielded nothing, as council was rebuffed with the Indians feigning delay. Hancock was unsatisfied with the lack of "cooperation" and continued his march toward the Indian village to reconvene communications and reinforce his message. Arriving at the site of the encampment and proposed council, they found the village deserted. The Indians, having no intention to wait for the arrival of the army and another "Sand Creek Massacre," fled the village again thus permanently deflating the prospect for negotiations.[7]

Camped near the Pawnee Fork for several days, reports arrived bringing news of further hostilities and malicious acts by the same bands of Indians. The exasperated Hancock, ordered the village burned, breaking down all hopes of potential success the campaign may have had. On April 15, the regiment returned north going into camp on the outskirts of Ft. Hays to await forage and supplies. Hancock's column, also short on supplies and forage, returned north. Frustrated at the failure of his expedition, he disbanded the column and ordered the Seventh regiment to proceed in the direction of the fleeing band of Indians-to seek them out and alert the civilian population of potential hostility.

On June 1, Custer and six companies set out, accompanied by a pack train and group of Delaware Indian scouts, with orders to march to Fort McPherson, then proceed to an area near Fort Sedgwick where it would resupply, continue south to Fort Wallace, then back to Fort Hays. Their aim was to search for the hostile bands that fled during Hancock's expedition and to locate an obstinate and dangerous band of Cheyenne, known as "Dog Soldiers,"(Referring to the group of Indians led by Roman Nose, whom wholeheartedly embraced open warfare against the whites). Elements of company I, under Capt. Keogh, departed Ft. Wallace with Gen. Hancock's staff to Denver. Company F was dispatched to Monument Station to scout the Smokey Hill route, and company G remaining camped near Fort Hays.

After the column reached Ft. McPherson, they scouted the area of the Republican River. Instead of halting momentarily at Sedgwick to await further orders, Custer' column marched toward the south fork of the Republican River. While camped near the north and south forks, a small detachment of ten men under Maj. Elliot was ordered to retrieve dispatches awaiting them at Ft. Sedgwick. With supplies rapidly diminishing and rations inadequate from the start, orders were also given for the pack train and company D under Capt. Robbins to proceed to Fort Wallace for supplies. Accompanied by an escort of West's K company, whose orders were to scout the trail, the train left camp on the Republican River on June 22.

Winfield Scott Hancock commanded the failed expedition in the summer of 1867. Although his Civil War record was above reproach, his arrogant and seeming naïve approach in dealing with the plains Indians ultimately cost him his position commanding the Dept. of Missouri. *Library of Congress*

On June 24, while the main portion of the regiment was camped near the headwaters of the Republican, they were attacked by hostiles. Reduced in force by the separation of the column, a detachment under Capt. Hamilton pursued the band, which soon dispersed. Fearing the wagon train would be under similar assault, an additional escort of company E under Capt. Myers was dispatched to link up with West's command as additional reinforcements, which were bivouacked at the Beaver Creek area.

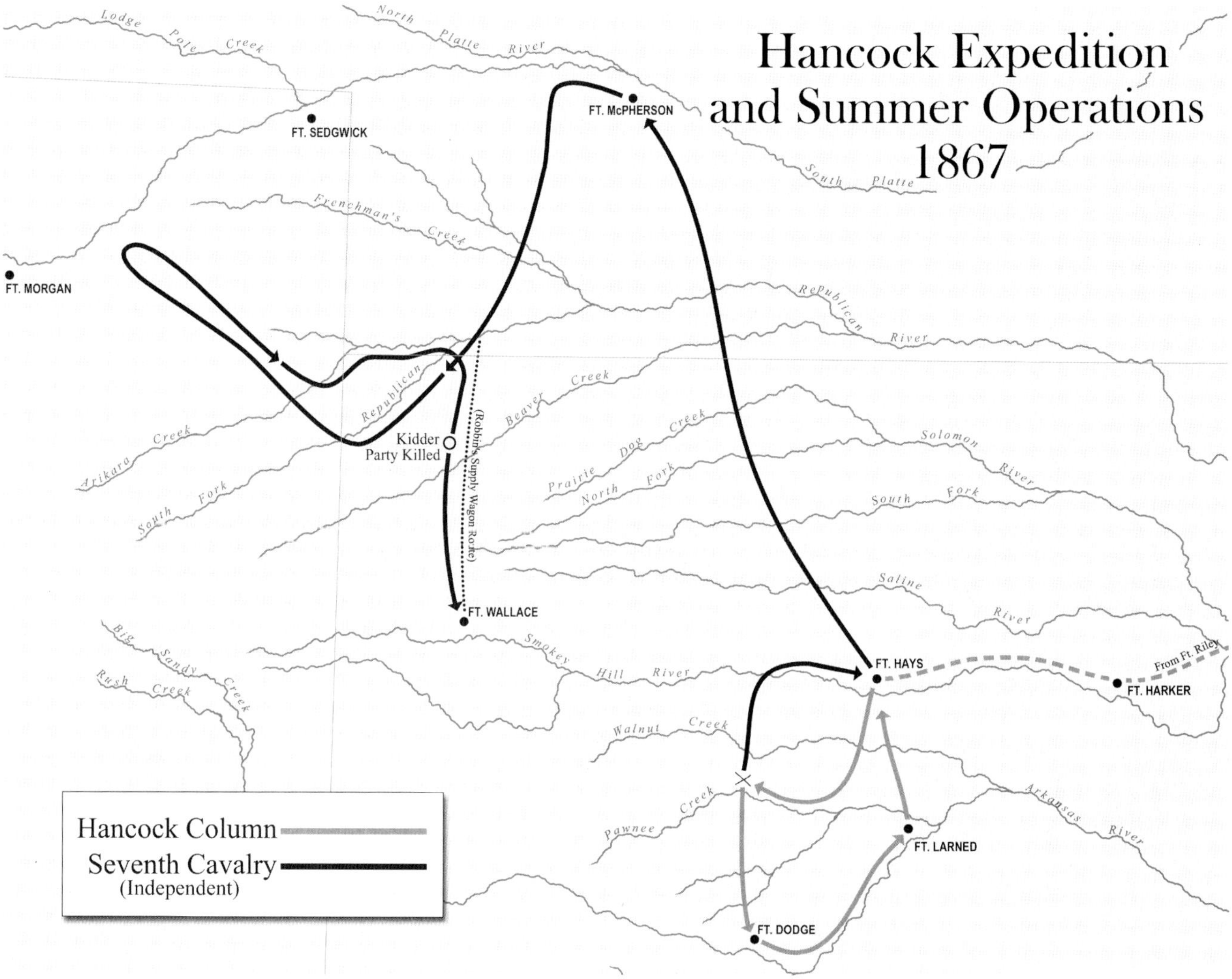

Map of the Hancock Expedition and the Seventh Cavalry's subsequent summer scouting campaign. *TSS*

Without incident, the supply train arrived at Ft. Wallace on June 24, where elements of company I under the command of Lt. Bell had been defending the garrison from Indian pressure throughout the previous several days. The train re-supplied and departed the following morning. On June 26, the post was again under siege; attacked by a large body of Indians. The small garrison of company G, which had returned from escort duty of the Wright Party two days before, and elements of company I, both commanded by Capt. Barnitz, bore the brunt of the Indian attacks and repulsed several attempts to overrun the fort. During the return trip north from Ft. Wallace, the pack train was attacked by the same Indians that had pressed Ft. Wallace. The train was organized into two parallel columns with both Robbin's and Lt. Cooke's detachments covering each flank. Dismounted skirmishers repulsed several attempts to encircle the perimeter and breach the lines until finally being relieved by West's arriving escort, which had been scouting the area during the supply-train's journey to and from Ft. Wallace. The train eventually arrived back to the main command on June 27.[8]

While Elliot was en route back to the main command, further orders from Ft. Sedgwick were unknowingly dispatched with a small detachment under the command of Lt. Kidder, company M, 2nd Cavalry, which was massacred en route. The lost dispatches, eventually received later by way of a telegraph station, had ordered Custer to Fort Wallace. Ragged and hungry from hard marching and limited and inadequate rations, the entire command finally reached Ft. Wallace in mid-July, finding the stores depleted from both the continuous attacks on the fort and Robbin's pack train.[9]

Above: Seventh Cavalry officers James Bell, seated far left, and Albert Barnitz, seated center, in garrison at Fort Wallace on the afternoon of the attack on the fort. *Yale Collection of Western Americana, Beinecke Rare Book and Manuscript Collection.*

Below: An engraving from Harper' Weekly depicting the heroic defense of the Capt. Robbin's besieged Wagon train-enroute from Ft. Wallace. *Library of Congress*

516 HARPER'S WEEKLY. [AUGUST

SIOUX INDIANS ATTACKING A COMPANY OF THE SEVENTH CAVALRY, JUNE 24, 1867.—SKETCHED BY T. R. DAVIS.—[SEE FIRST PAGE.]

The conclusion of the summer operations were highlighted only in failure. The operations of the regiment, the dubious Hancock expedition of the spring, and the Kidder massacre, which the regiment had discovered on their return to Ft. Wallace, served only to exacerbate hostilities with the Indians. This first campaign, in addition to introducing the regiment to Indian tactics, also served as the beginning of events that would fractionalize the regiment. In July, Lt. Col. Custer was placed under arrest for numerous charges leveled against him, some by his own officers, including absence without leave and "Conduct to the prejudice of good order and military discipline."[10] Unsuccessfully citing "military and tactical considerations" in his defense, court marshal in September found him guilty and he was relieved of his command and suspended rank for one year. Further schisms between the regiment developed as officers were called to give testimony during Custer's trial.[11]

In August 1867, Hancock was removed from command of Department of Missouri. "Banished" to the Department of the South, he was succeeded by General Phillip Sheridan. During the time of Custer's absence and subsequent court martial, most of the regiment's companies, now under the field command of Maj. Elliot, assumed routine scouting of the Saline and Republican River valleys from Ft. Wallace and surrounding posts. Companies G and M would provide escort for the Indian Peace commission at Medicine Lodge Creek. Following operations, the regiment went into winter garrison: Companies A, D, F, G and K went to Ft. Leavenworth and companies H and M went to Ft. Harker. The remaining companies were garrisoned along the Kansas Frontier with Company B at Fort Dodge, C at Fort Lyon, I at Fort Wallace, and L at Fort Reynolds.[12]

Lt. Lyman Stockwell Kidder, 2nd Cavalry, left Ft. Sedgwick with dispatches for Custer's regiment. He haplessly mistook the trail left by Robbin's wagon train for that of Custer's command and was attacked and overrun by Indians. His small detachment of men laid mutilated beyond recognition, only identifying Kidder by the peculiar material in his collar. *Joel Emmons Whitney, Minnesota Historical Society*

Sully Expedition, September 1868

In the spring of 1868, the regiment resumed field operations of scouting and escort in the region, mostly performed by the companies stationed at Fort Leavenworth, including a detachment of company F under Capt. Yates escorting an Indian Peace commission in early summer. Discontent began again as annuities (chiefly weapons) promised from the Medicine Lodge Treaty were withheld, prompting reprisals and further aggression against whites along the frontier. Upon Sheridan's arrival to the Department, he dispatched companies A, D, E, G, and K from Leavenworth to scout the region, showing the presence of force in the area. In July, joined by companies H and M from Ft. Harker and company B from Ft. Dodge, the regiment left camp for Ft. Larned. Nevertheless, these continued Indian hostilities against civilians prompted a new campaign to curb the incidents and again seek to bring justice against the guilty parties. An expedition under Bvt. Brig. Gen. Alfred Sully, acting Lt. Col. of the 3rd Infantry Regiment, was organized at Fort Dodge for this purpose. It included three companies of the his own 3rd Infantry, under

Panoramic view of Fort Leavenworth, photographed in 1867. Home to the regiment in the late 1860s, the fort also served as the headquarters for the Dept. of Missouri. *Library of Congress*

Brig. Gen. Alfred Sully was a distinguished and capable commander and recognized as an experienced Indian fighter. Yet the failure of his expedition in September 1868 to seek out and punish the hostiles blemished his reputation. It did, however, as many historians claim, prove to be the catalyst for the winter campaign later that year. *National Archives*

Former Kansas Governor and Bvt. Brig. Gen. Samuel Crawford organized and commanded the 19th Kansas Volunteer Cavalry in October 1868 to assist the Seventh Cavalry on campaign and safeguard the homesteaders on the prairie. *Library of Congress*

the command of Capt. J.H. Page, and eleven companies of the Seventh Cavalry, temporarily commanded by Maj. Elliot during Custer's suspension. Seventh Cavalry companies A, D, E, G, and K left Fort Larned in preparation for the campaign, and joining company B stationed at Fort Dodge, acquiring the remainder of companies C, F, H, I, and M. Company K would provide bodyguard detail for the expedition.[13]

Under cover of nightfall, the expedition began on September 1, 1868, marching south across the Arkansas River to the area of the Cimarron River Valley. As opposed to Custer's energetic leadership style, Sully opted to travel by ambulance, befuddling his command with his seemingly lethargic pace. As the column moved slowly south, hopes of surprise were lost when they stumbled upon an Indian hunting party. For several days, the column continued south along the Cimarron River, frequently hampered and harassed by small bands of Indians that endeavored to remain out of range nor engage in force. Sully and his increasingly despondent command grew more and more frustrated. Several men from company F lagged behind as the column broke bivouac one morning despite warnings from Hamilton's rear guard company. The stragglers were overtaken and captured by Indians hidden behind the ridges, killing one and wounding the other. Captain Hamilton and Lt. A.E. Smith attempted to pursue the fleeing Indians, which in their haste had dropped one trooper, but were ordered by Sully to break off the chase. As the expedition prodded forward, Indian harassment increased in size and frequency. As the expedition continued its march toward Beaver Creek, continuous Indian engagement and rough sandy terrain proved too much for Sully. To the surprise of his command, he abruptly announced a termination of further forward movement and intention to retreat back to Fort Dodge for further reinforcements; citing difficulties the dismounted infantry and pack train were having traversing the inhospitable terrain. The column reluctantly turned back northward, eventually arriving at camp near Bluff Creek (near the future site of camp supply), terminated the futile and hopeless expedition. Sully's return to Ft. Dodge met with sharp criticism from Sheridan, who, among other things, accused him of lacking "aggressive spirit." A dismal failure, the expedition had served only to antagonize the Indian population. The loss of several troopers; one to hostile fire and the other to accidental shooting, compounded by the frustration of failure created dissention in the ranks and discipline waned. As dismal as it was, it did however serve to reinforce the need for definitive action against the "incorrigible" natives (and as many historians agree, prompted the forthcoming winter campaign).[14]

In October, at the request of both Sheridan and Sully, Custer was reinstated, cutting short his suspension and rejoining the regiment in October. With Custer's arrival early in the month, the regiment resumed scouting operations from the vicinity of Fort Dodge in October along the Arkansas River and Medicine Lodge Creek, completing their duties and finally arriving at Camp Forsyth at the end of the month.[15]

The Winter Campaign and the Battle of Washita, 1868-69

The need for effective countermeasures against the troublesome bands of Cheyenne, Kiowa, Arapahoe and Comanche along the frontier prompted a new offensive operation. Keenly aware of the advantages of winter operations, Gen. Sheridan favored a winter campaign. Drawing from the success of previous late-season campaigns against the Shoshones and Navajo in 1863 and 1864, the Indians would be particularly vulnerable and tactically disadvantaged, as they would typically progress southward as the cold season set in, settling in their lodges along the riverbeds for the season. The campaign would be an operation of three separate columns, each exploring the southern regions where the Indians would likely migrate for the winter. The first column, consisting mainly of the 3rd Cavalry under Col. A.W. Evans, would march from Ft. Bascom in New Mexico to Monument Creek, scouting down the Canadian River and portions of the Red River Valley. The second Column, consisting of companies of the 5th Cavalry under Gen. E.A. Carr, would march from Ft. Lyon to the north fork of the Canadian River, scouting near the Antelope Hills. The third column, again under Sully and five companies of his 3rd Infantry, would march south to operate from an established base and supply post. Accompanying Sully's infantry would be all but one company of the Seventh Cavalry, which including an added unit of sharpshooters under the command of Lt. Cooke, Osage scout-trailers, a large supply train, and Kansas volunteer cavalry.[16]

The column left camp near Ft. Dodge on November 12 towards Beaver and Wolf Creek to Camp Supply, a remote post established as a supply depot for the campaign. When Sheridan arrived, accompanied by two companies of the Kansas Volunteers a few days later, he found Custer and Sully at odds over questions of command. Replacing Sully, he gave the command of the column to Custer. The regiment (column) left Camp Supply on November 22, during terribly inclement weather, marching through the Wolf Creek area southward.

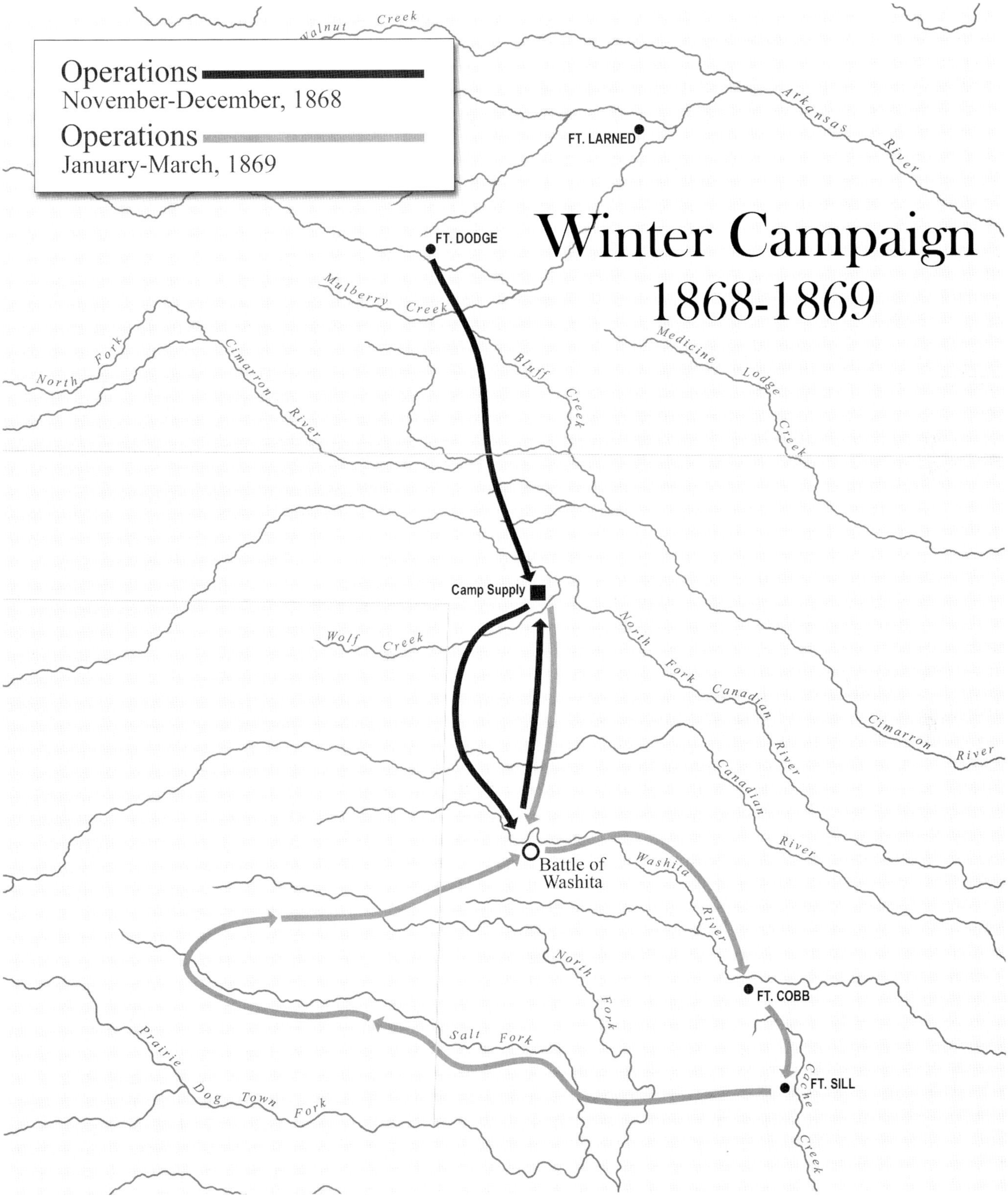

Map of the Seventh Cavalry's winter campaign and route to the Washita River Valley. *TSS*

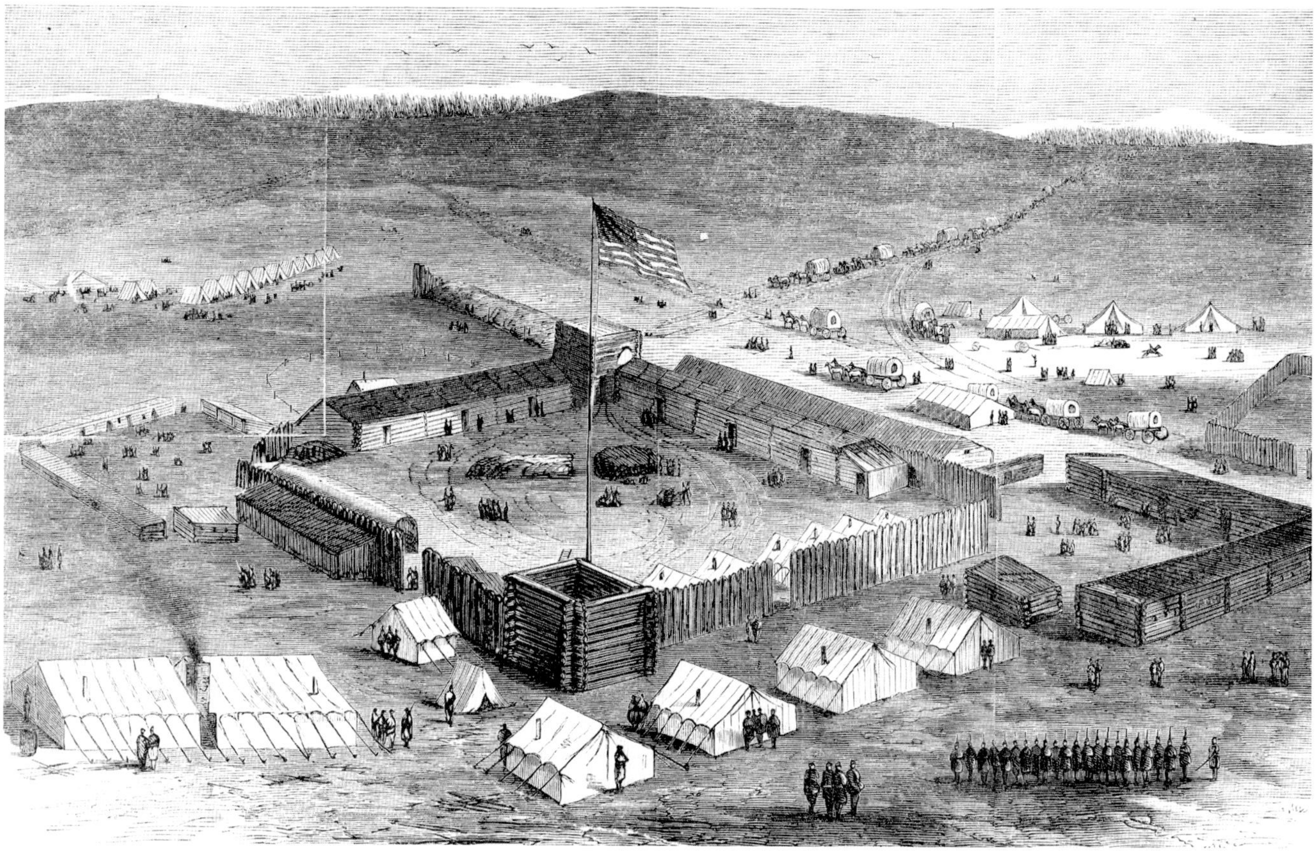

An engraving of Camp Supply, Indian Territory, from *Harper's Weekly*, February 27, 1869. *Library of Congress*

On November 26, Maj. Elliot and companies G, H, and M were dispatched from the main column up the Canadian River to scout for a trail, with the main force continuing toward the Canadian River. After locating the trail and sending a scout back to report, Elliot' detachment proceeded forward with orders to strike the trail until late evening and halt to wait for the remainder to catch up. Leaving the wagon train behind to follow with a detachment of men, Custer and his command continued ahead, eventually linking up with Elliot's advanced party. Several miles ahead, scouts located the enemy encampment along the banks of the frozen Washita River. The plan initiated by Custer was to split up his attacking companies in a typical coordinated converging-column assault at daybreak. Companies G, H, and M, under Elliot, would approach from the northeast. Companies B and F, under W. Thompson, would approach from the southeast. Companies E and I, under Myers, would approach from the south. The main thrust, including the Osage scouts and accompanied by Custer, consisted of Companies A and C under Hamilton, who were posted on the left with Cooke's dismounted sharpshooters on the far left of their line, and Companies D and K, under West. The accompanying pack train, under Lt. Mathey, was halted in the rear, while the remainder of company M as well as Benteen's company H, which was detailed with the pack train, joined Elliot's squadron. When the troops deployed in line, they waited quietly for the morning.[20]

At daybreak, the column advanced toward the river, and the charge was sounded. The battalions rushed through the village from various sides, attacking and stampeding horses to prevent escape. Bewildered Indians poured out of their lodges amidst the charging troopers. Hostiles that fled to the nearby ravines were engaged and cut down by the detachment of sharpshooters in the tree line. Near the center of the village, the Indians began to organize in body, threatening Custer's group with encirclement as troops began to run low on ammunition. Skirmishers were deployed, exchanging heavy fire. It was not until the timely arrival of Lt. Bell, through heavy enemy fire with a wagonload of ammunition to the beleaguered troopers did they rally, eventually dispersing the hostiles with a cavalry charge. Fierce, close quarter fighting went on roughly an hour before the assaulting force had completely taken the village. Some small bands, which fled into the valley, offered sporadic resistance throughout the morning until eventually subsiding, at which point only isolated pockets of fighting ensued. In the village, Arapahoe, Kiowa, Cheyenne, and Comanche prisoners, mostly women and the elderly, were rounded up and all lodges, weapons, and horses were destroyed. Over one hundred warriors of Black Kettle's band were killed, including Black Kettle himself as he fled across the river. Casualties among the regiment totaled thirty, including two officers and nineteen enlisted men killed. Capt. Hamilton was killed during the initial assault, as was Major Elliot, who with a small body of troopers pursued a group of fleeing Indians down into the valley. In addition, Capt. Barnitz was severely wounded and Lts. T.W. Custer and March received slight wounds.[21]

Throughout the battle and into the late afternoon, hostiles coming up from the valley below were observed massing on the ridges above. Fearing another encirclement and a coordinated counter attack against the meager protection of the wagon train and all the winter supplies, Custer, in a bold gamble, ordered his men to assemble in the early evening, with captured Indian women in tow, and proceed down the valley toward suspected encampments. When they regiment arrived at the neighboring encampments, they found them vacated, presumably at the onset of the attack on the village. Naturally presuming the advancing column was still heavily reinforced, the Indians dispersed into the valley. The column began their return march north, picking up the pack train several miles in the rear, which to their relief had been unmolested. By the first days of December, the Regiment arrived back at Camp Supply, thus ending the Washita offensive.[22]

With the swift and decisive victory at Washita behind, Sheridan, wanting to keep pressure on the reeling hostiles, ordered the regiment to resume operations, using the effects of the bitter winter to press Indian compliance and return to reservations. The regiment, accompanied by Sheridan and the

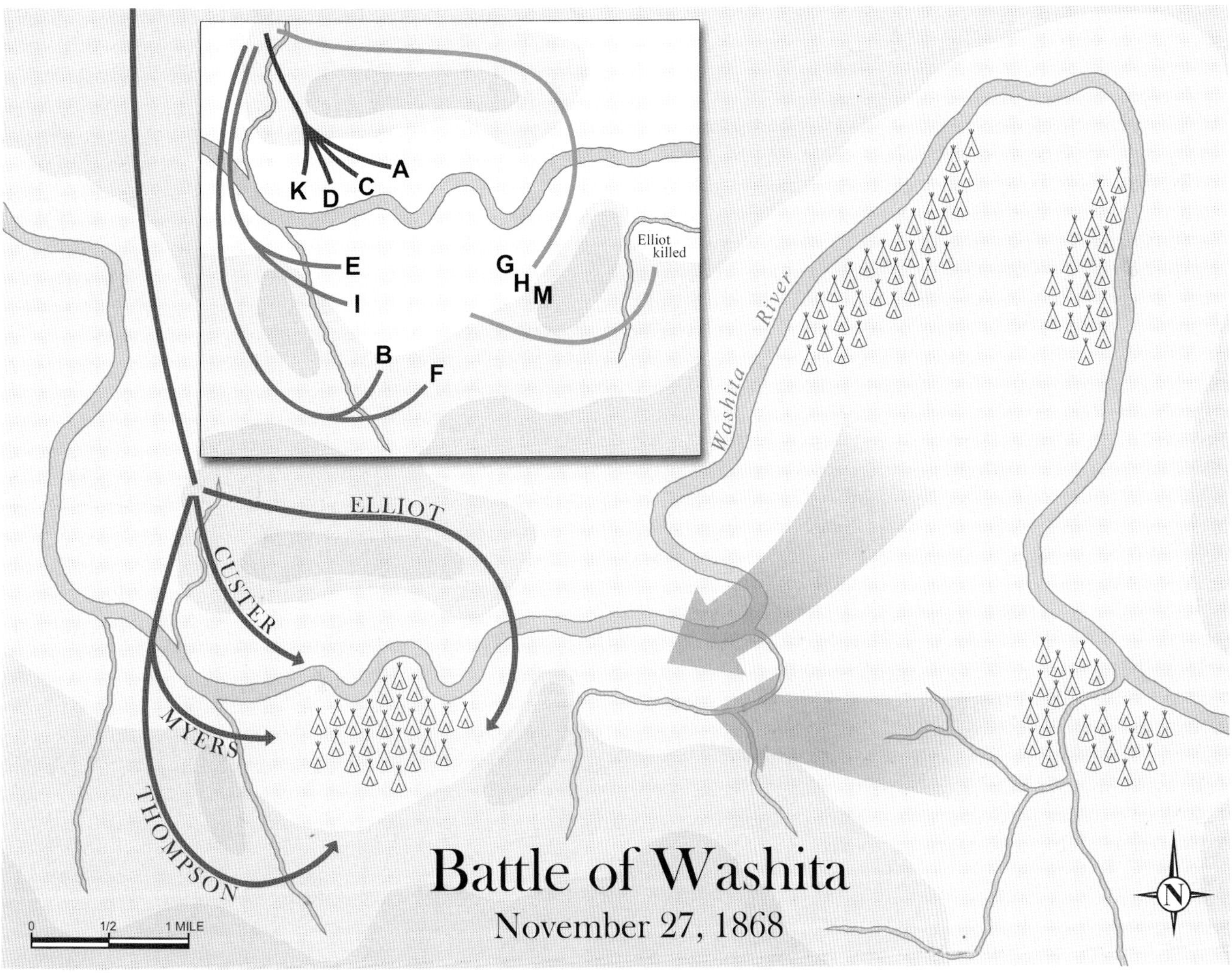

Map of the Battle of Washita, November 27, 1868. *TSS*

THE SEVENTH U.S. CAVALRY CHARGING INTO BLACK KETTLE'S VILLAGE AT DAYLIGHT, November 27, 1868.—[See Page 811.]

Harper's Weekly engraving of the Washita Battle, depicting the initial early morning charge into Black Kettle's sleeping village. *Library of Congress*

19th Kansas Volunteers again left Camp Supply, marching south toward the Washita River Valley in pursuit of the remaining Indian bands and to locate Elliott's still-missing party (which was found several miles down the valley from the battle.) As they continued on, the command was met by Kiowa Indians under a flag of truce near Medicine Bluff Creek. Through negotiations and threats of further army force, the Indians acquiesced and within days, began to filter into Ft. Cobb. Negotiations with both the Arapahoe and Comanche bands yielded similar success. Only the defiance of the Cheyenne Indian remained, who were now even more reluctant to be brought in.

In early March, the regiment marched further south, near the Red River in search of the Cheyenne bands. Again the command was split with one column under Myers and the pack wagon moving north toward the Washita River to await orders, and the other under Lt. Col. Custer, marching west striking the trail. Arriving at the Cheyenne encampment after several days, a detachment under Custer, including Cooke, Robbins and T.W. Custer, went forward to the Indian camp. Through threat of force, they successfully negotiated both promises to surrender at Ft. Cobb, and the release of two white captives without bloodshed. The Regiment's return to Camp Supply in late March 1869 and the arrival at Ft. Dodge concluded the winter campaign. The column was disbanded and the Kansas volunteers, who needed to be reigned in to prevent retribution for the atrocities committed on the their frontier, were mustered out of service. The campaign had dealt a substantial blow to organized resistance, particularly to the Kiowa, Arapahoe, and Comanche bands, effectively bringing moderate stability to the frontier. After the success of the winter campaign and closure of hostilities by the various Indian bands, officers and men of the Seventh Cavalry enjoyed a respite of light duty throughout the summer of 1869 and for the rest of the year, performing field duty, escort, and mail delivery. By October, the majority of the regiment, now under the command of Col. S.D. Sturgis, took winter quarters at Ft. Leavenworth, while the remaining companies assumed winter garrison at Fort Hays, Fort Wallace, Fort Harker, and Fort Lyon.[23]

Occupation and Reconstruction duty in the South

The following year the regiment was stationed along the frontier, again on scouting and escort duty from Forts Leavenworth, Harker, and Hays. In March 1871, with little Indian activity remaining on the plains, the Seventh Cavalry was relieved of duty in Kansas and the Department of Missouri. Ordered to take up various postings in the southern states under the auspices of the Dept. of the South, they would join the occupational forces in the reconstruction of the former Confederacy. In conjunction with the Department of Justice and the U.S. Marshals Service, companies were scattered throughout the southern region policing illegal distilleries, revenue collecting, suppressing Klan operations and assisting U.S. Marshals in upholding law and order. Custer's headquarters along with company A were stationed in Elizabethtown, Kentucky and the rest of the companies served at various posts in Kentucky, Mississippi, Georgia, Alabama, and Tennessee. The regiment remained under the Department of the South in 1872, with the exception of company L, which moved operations to Louisiana under the Department of the Gulf in December of that year.[24]

Department of the Dakota and the Yellowstone Expedition

Development of a northwest railroad route, which meandered through the region allotted by treaty to the Teton Sioux in the Northwest, was problematic for the government. Undoubtedly, the rightful claims of the Indians would hinder progress and threateningly impede construction. Officials of the Northern Pacific Railroad applied for military assistance in exploring urban sites of the northern route, prompting an escort expedition for protection of the engineering and survey parties. In January 1873, the regiment was ordered to the Department of the Dakota, at that time under the command of Gen. Terry, to serve in this capacity. The majority of the Regiment left their posts in the south and reassembled in Memphis, Tennessee in March. Traveling north by steamer and railroad, they arrived in Yankton, Dakota Territory in April.[25]

In May, the regiment left Yankton for Fort Rice, and following an exhausting 350-mile march, arrived in June to prepare for the expedition. The remainder of the regiment, including Sturgis' headquarters and one squadron of companies D and I under Major Tilford, (later joined by Major Reno,) were dispatched to Fort Snelling, Minnesota to serve as escort for the International Boundary Commission. Using Fort Rice as a jumping-off point, the expeditionary escort force was organized. Under Maj. Gen. D.S. Stanley, the large column consisted of the remaining ten companies of the regiment, ten companies of the 8th and 9th Infantry Regiments under L.P. Bradley, six companies of both the 17th and the 6th Infantry Regiments under R.E.A. Croften, artillery from elements of the 22nd Infantry Regiment under J. McAdam Webster, and a detachment of Arikara Indian scouts, under D. Brush, 17th

David Sloane Stanley commanded the Yellowstone Expedition of 1873. During the Civil War, he served as Maj. Gen., Vols. and was awarded the Medal of Honor for his actions at the Battle of Franklin. Both capable and highly regarded, he initially clashed with Custer, partly due to his alcohol indulgences, over operational use and command of the regiment during the expedition. *Library of Congress*

Infantry. In addition, the column also included a team of engineers, scientists, and surveyors.[26]

The column began its movement westward, with the Seventh regiment divided into two Battalions; one commanded by Capt. Hart, and the other by Capt. Benteen. In July, the expedition marched to a Junction of the Yellowstone River, receiving supplies by steamer. The column moved slowly westward as progress was hindered by poor weather. Eventually, with the terrain becoming increasingly difficult to traverse, Custer, allowed independent command of his officers and men, forged ahead in his customary fashion with a small detail to scout suitable passage and campsites. Joined by companies A and B, including T.W. Custer, Lt. Varnum, Lt. Calhoun, and Capt. Moylan, they bivouacked on the north bank of the Yellowstone and Tongue River junction. On August 4, while awaiting the arrival of the main column, the small detachment of roughly eighty men was harassed by a small band of hostiles. Custer, ordering Moylan's men to stay in reach of support, split his forward detachment in two, and accompanied by T.W. Custer and Lt. Calhoun (acting adjutant), pursued the baiting Indians. This typical "ruse" tactic was followed by a larger more spirited attack of several hundred hostiles suddenly emerging from the tree line. T.W. Custer, repulsing the attack by a dismounted defense, was soon joined by Moylan's forces, which also provided a dismounted defense. The small command managed to move toward the riverbank to protect the horses and establish a more suitable defensive position. Through prolonged exchange of gunfire and repeated attempts of the Indians to steal cavalry horses and burn the unwieldy prairie grass, a mounted charge finally ended the skirmish and the Indians fled. Shortly thereafter, elements of the main expeditionary column arrived and relieved Custer's forward group.[27]

For the next several days, Indians harassed the expedition as it traveled along the river. After several days, the column came across the remnants of an Indian village, having since been hastily vacated. Custer and his regiment left Stanley's main column, pursuing the Indian trail towards the Yellowstone River. On August 10, Custer's command halted on the banks of the river and bivouacked. The following morning, the outlying pickets were attacked by a large number of hostiles. Deployed into squadrons, one company of the first squadron on the left moved to the bluffs and formed skirmish lines, while the remainder deployed with elements of the fourth squadron. As concentrated fire from positions on the bluff and dismounted skirmish lines kept the Indians at a distance, a cavalry charge dispersed their attempts to encircle the command. Several rounds from artillery from Stanley's arriving column broke up all coordinated assaults and the Indians fled. During the fight, one trooper was killed and Lt. Braden and several other troopers were wounded. By mid-August, the column had reached its furthest point west, and

Officers on the steps of Custer's house at Ft. Abraham Lincoln, 1874. Left to right: Lt. Nelson Bronson, 6th Infantry, Lt. George Wallace, Lt. Col. G. Custer, Lt. Benjamin Hodgson, Elizabeth Custer, Capt. T. McDougall, Lt. Wiliam Badger, 6th Infantry, Mrs. Yates, Capt. Yates (with saber), unidentified, Mrs. Calhoun, unidentified, Capt. John Poland, 6th Infantry, Lt. Charles Varnum, Lt. Col. William P. Carlin, 17th Infantry, Mrs. Moylan, Capt. T. Custer, W. Thompson, Lt. J. Calhoun, Mrs. McIntosh, Capt. Moylan, Lt. Donald McIntosh. *National Archives*

soon turned toward the Musselshell River and back down the Yellowstone. The regiment departed from the main expedition at the arrival at Mussellshell, eventually arriving back at Ft. Lincoln for winter garrison in early October 1873. Later that month, the command of Maj. Tilford and Reno arrived at Ft. Lincoln from escort duty, enroute to winter garrison at Ft. Totten, Dakota, Territory.[28]

The Black Hills Expedition, 1874

In late spring, an expedition was formed to the Black Hills to survey the region and investigate rumors of gold. As far as the military was concerned, increasing Dakota Indian raids south into Nebraska were becoming difficult to control. Pressure on the government to allow purveyors access to the Black Hills intensified the need for permanent military station. Sheridan in his annual report recommended the establishment of a large military post at the base of the Black Hills, stating his objective to, "secure a strong foothold in the heart of Sioux Country, thereby exercising a controlling influence over these war-like people."[29] An expedition, flanked by accompanying geologists, paleontologists and other scientific fields, would be aimed at surveying the topography and assessing the region. However, the Black Hills were allotted to the Indians under treaty of 1868, and free encroachment by whites fell in direct discord with the agreements. However, the government and particularly Sheridan, was aware that if in fact gold was discovered in an area in close proximity to Indians, it would bring an unavoidable climactic clash between whites and natives.[30]

In May, the majority of regiment joined near Fort Lincoln in preparation for the expedition. Companies D and I, under Maj. Reno, again left garrison at the end of May to rejoin the International Boundary Commission and would not return to Fort Totten until September. The remainder of the Seventh Cavalry, also consisting of company I of the 20th Infantry, company G of the 17th Infantry, a battery of several Gatling guns, sixty Arikaree scouts under Lt. Wallace, and a small engineering team under the command of Capt. W. Ludlow, U.S.C.E., would take part in the expedition, and left camp in early July, slightly behind schedule.[31] They moved southwesterly across the Heart River, over the Belle Pierre Hills, crossing the Belle Fourche. Ludlow's team of engineers, botanists, topographers, anthropologists, and mineralogists mapped the route and surveyed the region: The first authorized exploration of the Black Hills. Custer and Companies E and C along with the scouts under the command of Wallace,

Capt. William Ludlow accompanied the Seventh Cavalry as the ranking engineer during the Black Hills Expedition and served as chief Engineer, Department of Dakota. Later, he commanded a brigade in Cuba, and rose to the rank of Brig. General. *National Archives*

forded ahead of the column, encountering only small bands of Indians who left them unhampered. No "hostile" Indians were reported and after completing their objectives, returned to Fort Lincoln in late August. With no significant engagements with hostile bands and at the loss of four men during the sixty-day expedition, three from sickness and one from a dispute with another trooper, the expedition was considered a success. The scientists had indeed discovered gold in the region, (as per the report of findings by Custer) and upon public word of the reports, the rush of miners naturally began.[32]

Realizing the resources within the region, both militarily and economically, the Government made repeated attempts to purchase the land from the Indians. All were rebuffed or not taken seriously. Up until that point, the army had offered sincere effort in attempts to keep the rush of white civilians at bay; seizing property and arresting and prosecuting encroachers. However, as hopes for a negotiated settlement withered, along with the futile endeavor to bar entrance, the

Grant administration realized that the region could be only accessed through force, and eventually pulled the military presence at the entrance of the Black Hills.

In September 1874, three squadrons of cavalry stationed at Fort Rice, including companies A, B, E, G, H and K under the command of Maj. Tilford, were ordered to the Department of the Gulf to perform constabulary duty; serving warrants and policing illegal distilleries from various stations in Alabama and Louisiana. Through 1874 and 1875, companies stationed in the Dakotas performed typical garrison and field duties of scouting and escort detail from their respective garrisons, including the arresting of illegal miners in the Black Hills region, and serving arrest warrants to known Indian criminals at the Standing Rock Indian Agency. In May 1875, Companies A, E, and H returned from duty in the Gulf, and by the end of 1875, most of the regiment had assumed winter garrison at Fort Lincoln, except companies B, G, and K, who would remain at stations in the Gulf until early 1876.[33]

Yellowstone Campaign, 1876

For a variety of reasons, unrest among the Indian population had grown continuously, prompting many to leave the confines of the reservation and return to their hunting lands and former way of life. These disillusioned Indians, many whom had willingly complied with reservation resettlement, had endured seasons of corrupt Indian agencies that would knowingly deprive them of food and other necessities for their own profit. They also witnessed an enormous influx of miners encroaching on the sacred burial grounds of the Black Hills; operating freely and without impunity, since military units no longer actively policed illegal mining activity.[34] In addition, increased railroad construction and civilian inhabitance as well as the destruction of buffalo herds by white hunters necessary to the survival of the natives, forced many Indians to join roving hostile bands. By the end of 1875, after fruitless negotiations with representatives of the Teton Sioux, the government became determined to reign in the unyielding and defiant Indian population. Agencies reported the strong presence of Indian resistance, who were "well armed, well fed, and lofty and independent in their attitudes."[35] With recommendations from the Indian Bureau for removal of the threat, a proclamation was issued to the various bands, imploring them to return to the reservations by January 31 or be subject to military action.[36]

As the deadline for compliance came and went, the Secretary of Interior turned the matter over to the military.

Above: Frederick Dent Grant accompanied the regiment to the Black Hills in 1874 as advisor. Joining the expedition for little more than merely "something to do," he served no real purpose during the expedition other than to later dispute Custer's claim of a substantial presence of gold. The son of President Ulysses S. Grant and a graduate of the Military Academy in 1871, he held mostly obscure and inconsequential positions in the Grant administration but did rise to Brigadier General, U.S.A., commanding a brigade in numerous battles and operations in the Philippines in 1899. *Library of Congress*

Opposite

Top: Seventh Cavalry officers at camp during the Black Hills Expedition, August 1874. Left to right: William Ludlow, Capt. Yates, Lt. McIntosh (standing), Lt. T. Custer, Lt. Wallace, Lt. Calhoun (silhouette), Capt. French (stretched out), Lt. Harrington, unknown standing, unknown sitting, unknown standing, Lt. A.E. Smith, Paleontologist G.B. Grinnell, Maj. Surgeon John Winfield Williams, Maj. Forsyth, 9th Cavalry, Lt. Col. G. Custer (stretched out), Botanist A.B. Donalson, Capt. McDougal, Bloody Knife, Maj. Tilford, Geologist N. H. Winchell, Col. F.D. Grant, Unknown sitting, unknown standing, Lt. Varnum (stretched out), Capt. Moylan, unknown sitting, Capt. L. Wheaton, 20th Infantry, unknown standing, unknown sitting, Lt. Hodgson (stretched out), Capt. Hart, Lt. G.H. Roach, 17th Infantry (standing), Capt. Benteen, unknown standing, Lt. Godfrey, Lt. Gibson. *LBHNM*

Bottom: View of the 1874 Expedition. *National Archives*

Sheridan immediately set about organizing a three-pronged winter offensive to encircle and destroy the hostile forces. The force consisted of three main columns, all under the overall command of Gen. A. Terry. The first column, commanded by Gen. G. Crook, consisted of elements of the 2nd and 3rd

Officer's quarters at Ft. Lincoln during the winter of 1874. *Library of Congress*

Officers and guests on afternoon excursion at the Heart River near Fort Lincoln, July 1875. Left to right: Lt. James Calhoun, unidentified, Stephen Baker, 6th Infantry, Boston Custer (nephew), Lt. Winfield Edgerly, unidentified, Capt. Miles Keogh (standing), Margaret Calhoun, Elizabeth Custer, unidentified, Lt. Col. George Custer (standing), unidentified, Dr. G. Lord, Capt. Thomas Weir, Lt. William Cooke (with white hat), Lt. Richard E. Thompson, 6th Infantry, unidentified, unidentified, Lt. Tom Custer, Lt. Algernon E. Smith. *LBHNM.*

Cavalries, as well as units from the 4th and 9th Infantry.[37] The second column, commanded by Gen. J. Gibbon, consisted of units from Gibbon's own 7th Infantry as well as the 2nd Cavalry. The third column, directly under Terry, consisted of the Seventh Cavalry regiment, elements of the 17th Infantry, the 6th Infantry, a battery of Gatling guns under the command of the 20th Infantry, and a detachment of Arikara and Crow scouts.[38]

The campaign, delayed by heavy snow and muddy, impassable terrain, turned from a winter strategy into a spring offensive. Only Crook was able to take to the field, kicking off the campaign in March. This southern column, under the command of Gen. J.J. Reynolds, located and attacked the Indian village on the Powder River on March 17. They succeeded in destroying a large portion of the village, but under heavy fire from Indians on the bluffs, the excited Reynolds sounded a retreat-which turned into a route. The column returned to Ft. Fetterman to refit and reorganize.[39]

By April of 1876, as the weather improved, planning for the campaign resumed. Companies of the Seventh Cavalry left garrison at Fort Totten, Fort Rice, and stations in the Gulf, and assembled near Fort Lincoln in early May 1876. On May 17, Terry's column from Ft. Lincoln was underway. With Gibbon's column already in the field from Ft. Ellis in the west, Terry marched west, arriving at the Powder River in early June. Crook's column, which had reorganized after the debacle at the Powder River, left Ft. Fetterman on May 29, comprising the third spearhead of the campaign. On June 8, Terry left camp on the Powder River for the steamer ship, which had anchored downstream on the Yellowstone, and met with Gibbon's forces camped several miles up the Yellowstone River the following day. Conferring with Gibbon, Terry returned by steamer to camp near the mouth of the Powder River, where a new supply base had been established. On June 10, Terry ordered the right wing of the Seventh, including companies B, C, E, F, I, and L under Maj. Reno, to scout up the Powder River in search of hostiles. The following day, the remainder of the regiment left camp on the Powder River and marched west along the banks of the Yellowstone. Leaving the wagon train with a detachment of Infantry, the column left the supply depot and marched toward the Tongue River, arriving on June 18. During this time, Reno's troops,

Brig. Gen. Alfred Terry, photographed in 1865, commanded the Dept. of Dakotas at its organization in 1866. Heading the eastern column from Ft. Lincoln, he was responsible for Custer's inclusion on the Yellowstone campaign in 1876. *Library of Congress*

Major General Phillip Sheridan commanded the Department of the Missouri and later succeeded Sherman as Military Division head. "Little Phil" was a die-hard proponent of Cavalry and utilized the Seventh Cavalry to spearhead operations during his successful winter campaign. *Library of Congress*

Officers and families stationed at Ft. Rice, Dakota territory, 1875. *Courtesy of Glen Swanson*

who had discovered the presence of Indians in the Rosebud River valley, arrived back north, where they reunited with the remainder of the regiment at the junction of the Rosebud and Yellowstone on June 21. Later that day, the steamer arrived carrying Gibbon and Terry, and the three met to determine the strategy for the offensive.[40]

The columns were to be split, with the Seventh regiment, acting independently, marching up the Rosebud valley toward the Big Horn valley arriving from the south. Gibbon's command, with Terry marching from the Yellowstone River up the Big Horn River, would approach the area from the north. Their purpose was to drive the hostiles into one another's forces, where coordinated attacks would be made on June 26. The regiment left camp on the mouth of the Rosebud River on June 22 and marched upstream toward the valley. During their two-day march, they discovered numerous sites of previous Indian encampments and a trail leading west, across the divide between the Rosebud and Big Horn Valley. On June 24, the regiment forded the Rosebud River in the late evening under cover of darkness, arriving at the Wolf Mountains in early morning. Shielded by the mountain defilade, Custer announced his intention to wait through the next day, where they would be in position for operations on June 26.[41]

Halting in a ravine among the bluffs on the morning of June 25, a broad view of the Big Horn River valley could be seen from the summit. From a vantage point known as the "Crows Nest," scouts observed evidence of an Indian encampment within fifteen to twenty miles. It soon became obvious that the presence of the column was detected, as both rear elements reported observing Indians looting supplies left behind and along the neighboring bluffs. Custer, with surprise compromised, feared the sighting of his approaching column would alarm the Indians into flight and gave the order to attack.[42]

Battle of the Little Big Horn June 25, 1876

The regiment crossed the divide in late morning. Committed now to action, Custer divided his regiment into battalions for the attack. Capt. Benteen's battalion, with companies D, H, and K, was ordered to proceed southwesterly, scouting the bluffs with orders to prevent an escape route and "pitch into anything he came across."[43] Both Maj. Reno's battalion, with Companies A, G, and M, and Yates' battalion, accompanied by Custer and the remaining companies, would follow a tributary up the valley towards the village. Company B under Capt. McDougal, would escort the train, which followed in

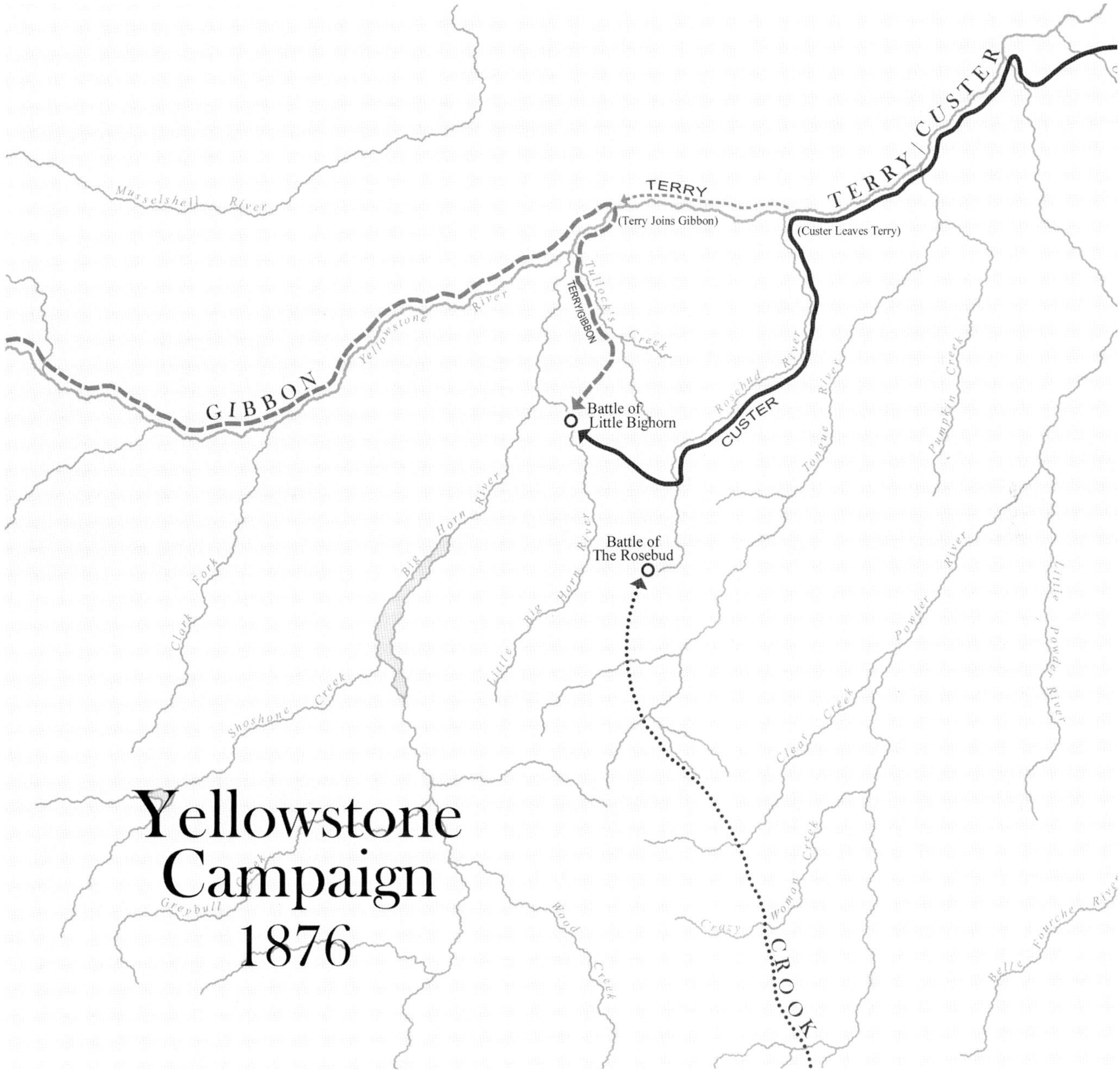

Map of the Yellowstone Campaign of 1876 and the route to the Big Horn Valley. *TSS*

the rear. When the battalions came to within about three miles of the southeast portion of the village, Custer, whose battalion paralleled Reno's command on the northern side of the creek, ordered Reno to ford the creek and attack the village, and would be "supported" from the converging columns from the northeast. Yates' battalion, with Custer, charged up the bluffs to find a location in which to ford the river and support Reno's frontal attack.[44]

Reno's battalion, with the detachment of scouts on the far left, charged forward toward the village, soon encountering sporadic fire. The fire intensified as more Indians began to spring from the trees and gullies. Closing on the village, which was just becoming visible past the tree line at the river bend, the Arikara scouts broke ranks, leaving Varnum's handful of Crows to join the other companies. At this point, Yates' battalion was still visible on the bluffs to Reno's troops. About a quarter mile from the edge of the southeastern portion of the village, now in full view, Reno abruptly ordered a halt to the advance, dismounting his troops and deploying skirmish lines. The Indians took advantage of the loss of

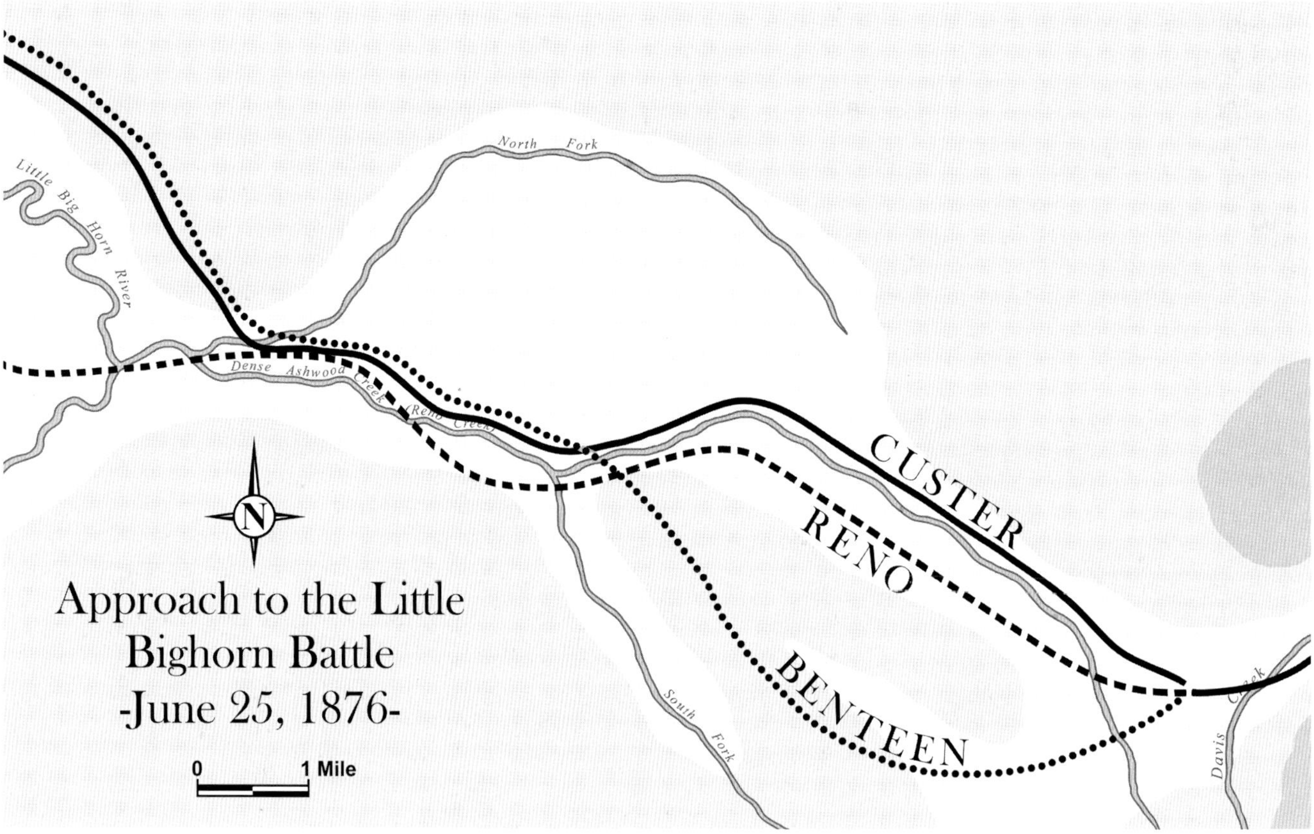

Map of the approach to the valley from the southeast. *TSS*

momentum, and began to envelope his command. As the line of skirmishing troopers began to suffer casualties, Reno gave the order to displace toward the tree line on the riverbank. Rear protection from the river and relative cover from the trees offered Reno and his men a respite, at least temporarily, from being overrun. After a few minutes in the treeline, their position again became questionable as more Indians massed for counter-attacks. Reno ordered a retreat from the cover of the trees back across the river, toward high ground, but ambiguity of commands and confusion from noise prevented a timely or organized retreat.[45] As the battalion whole hastily retreated across the river, the Indians, closely bearing down on the panicked mob, simply fired into the disorganized masse, overtaking and shooting down many troopers, including Lts. Hodgson and McIntosh.[46]

Benteen's battalion moved slowly westward along the bluffs and ravines, traversing rough terrain without contact. Further information from Lt. Gibson, whom was dispatched ahead earlier, also reported nothing. Paralleling the path of both Reno and Custer, Benteen swung northward, eventually merging into the previous route of the other commands (slightly ahead of the lagging pack train). At this point, he was intercepted by dispatches from Custer's detachment, carrying the famous message, hastily scribbled by Lt. Cooke: "*Benteen. Come on. Big village. Be quick. Bring packs. P.S. Bring packs.*"[47] Moving toward the direction of where the dispatches had come, they came upon bluffs, where fighting could be seen from several areas in the valley below. Met by Crow scouts who relayed news of fighting, Benteen's column marched in the direction toward the bluffs on the northeastern side of the river, where Reno's beleaguered command had taken position.

Troops at Reno's hilltop defense fought doggedly from their makeshift positions. With Benteen's arrival bolstering their ammunition supply, the Indian attacks slackened. With sporadic fighting still visible in the valley, the Indians abruptly turned and started up the adjacent valley, where firing could be heard beyond the ridges. Shortly afterwards, two volleys of fire were heard from the direction of Custer's command. As Capt. Weir and Lt. Edgerly took off west toward high ground to ascertain a position, they were confronted by overwhelming Indian forces and retreated back to Reno Hill. By mid-afternoon the pack train arrived, and Indian fire had withered. By late afternoon (approximately five o'clock),

Reno ordered his command to proceed toward Custer's position. Moving only a mile west, the command halted in the face of heavy opposition and deployed skirmish lines. Under fire, the command independently fell back, leaving only Lt. Godfrey's company to hold the line until they too were forced to withdraw back to their original defensive position. Fire began to taper off in the early evening and by nine o'clock pm, Indian fire subsided.[48]

By early morning, the Indians had resumed their assault on the entrenched position. As the morning attacks grew in

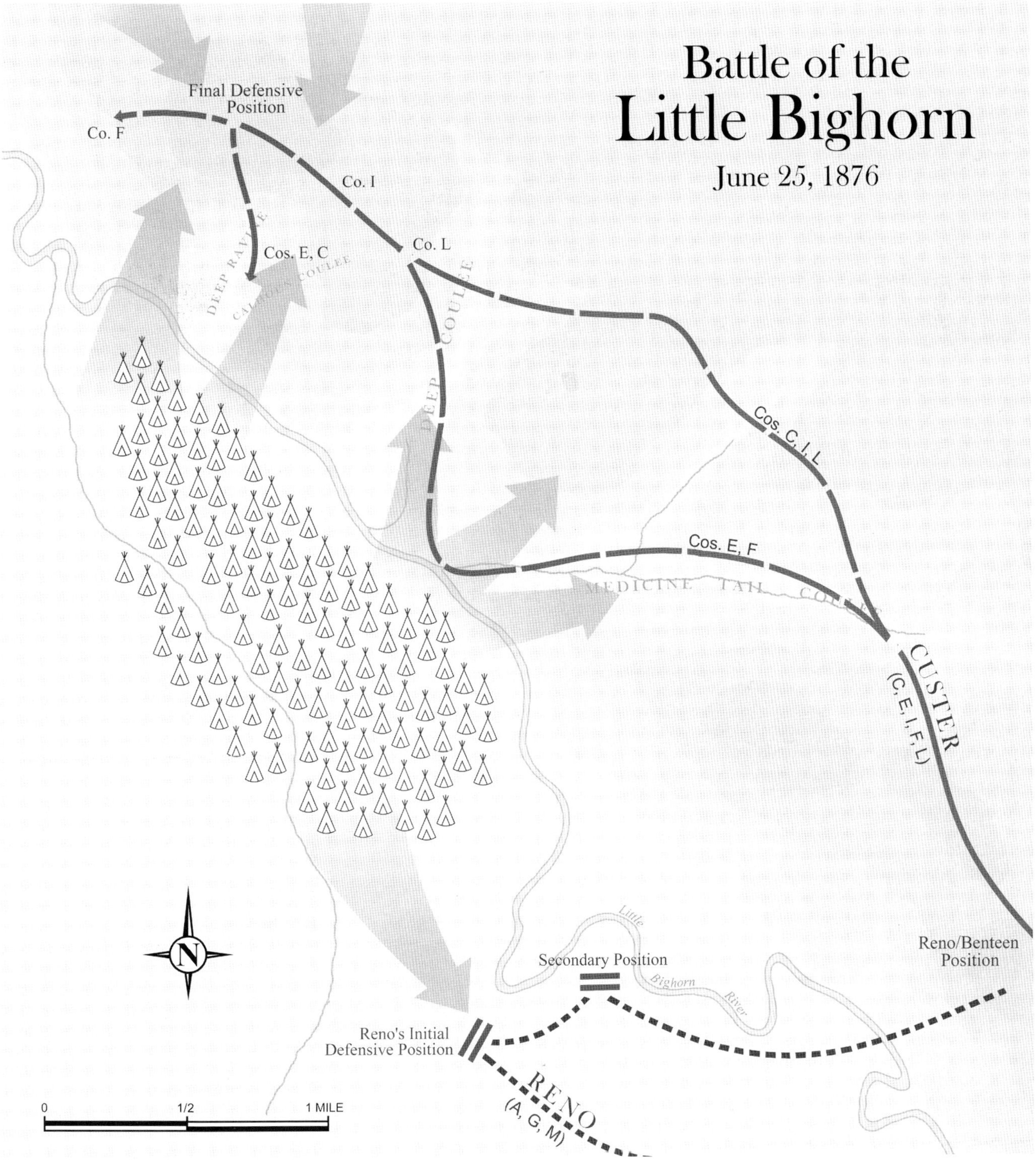

Map of the Battle at Little Big Horn. *TSS*

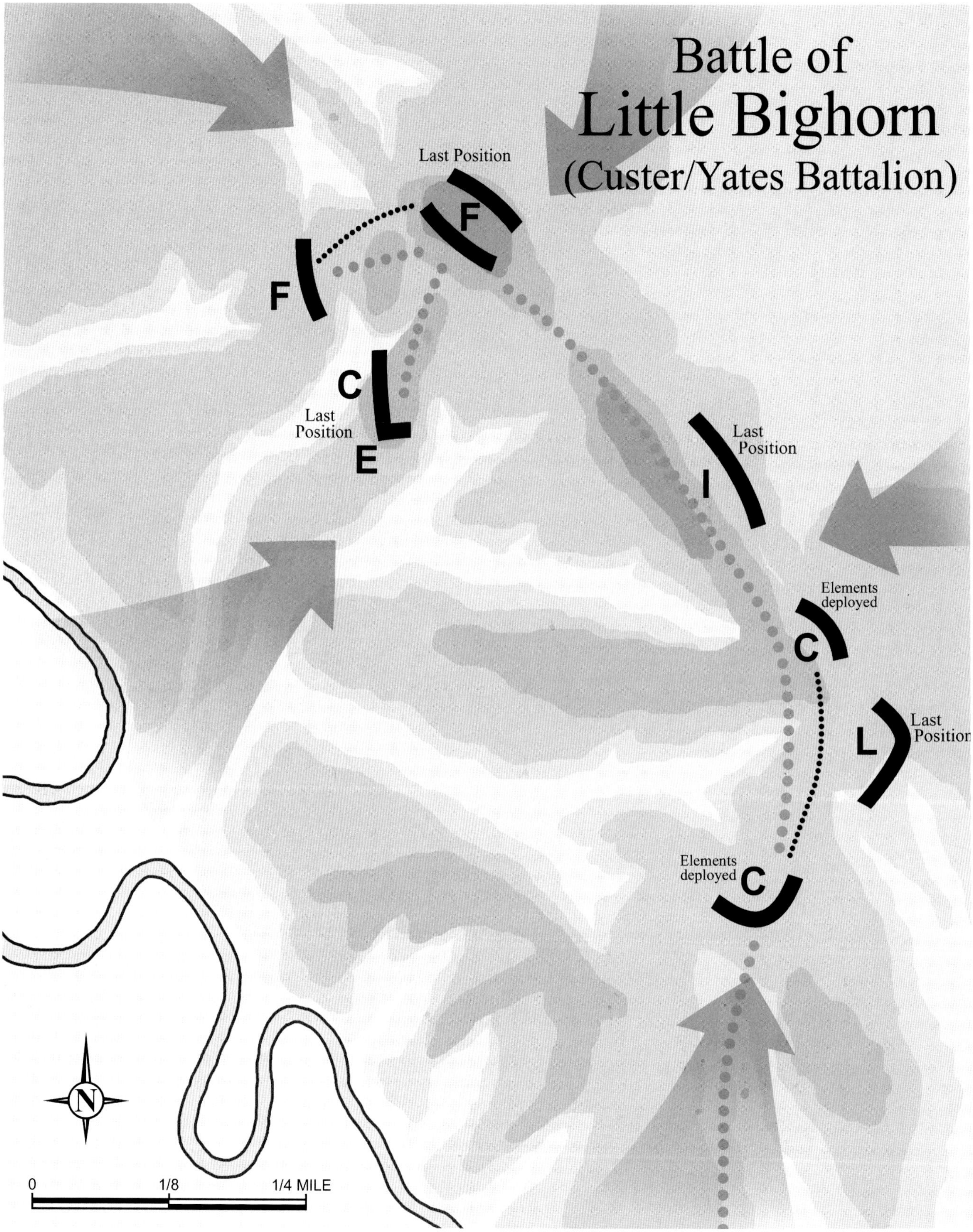

Above and opposite: Diagram of the battalion positions during the Battle of Little Big Horn. *TSS*

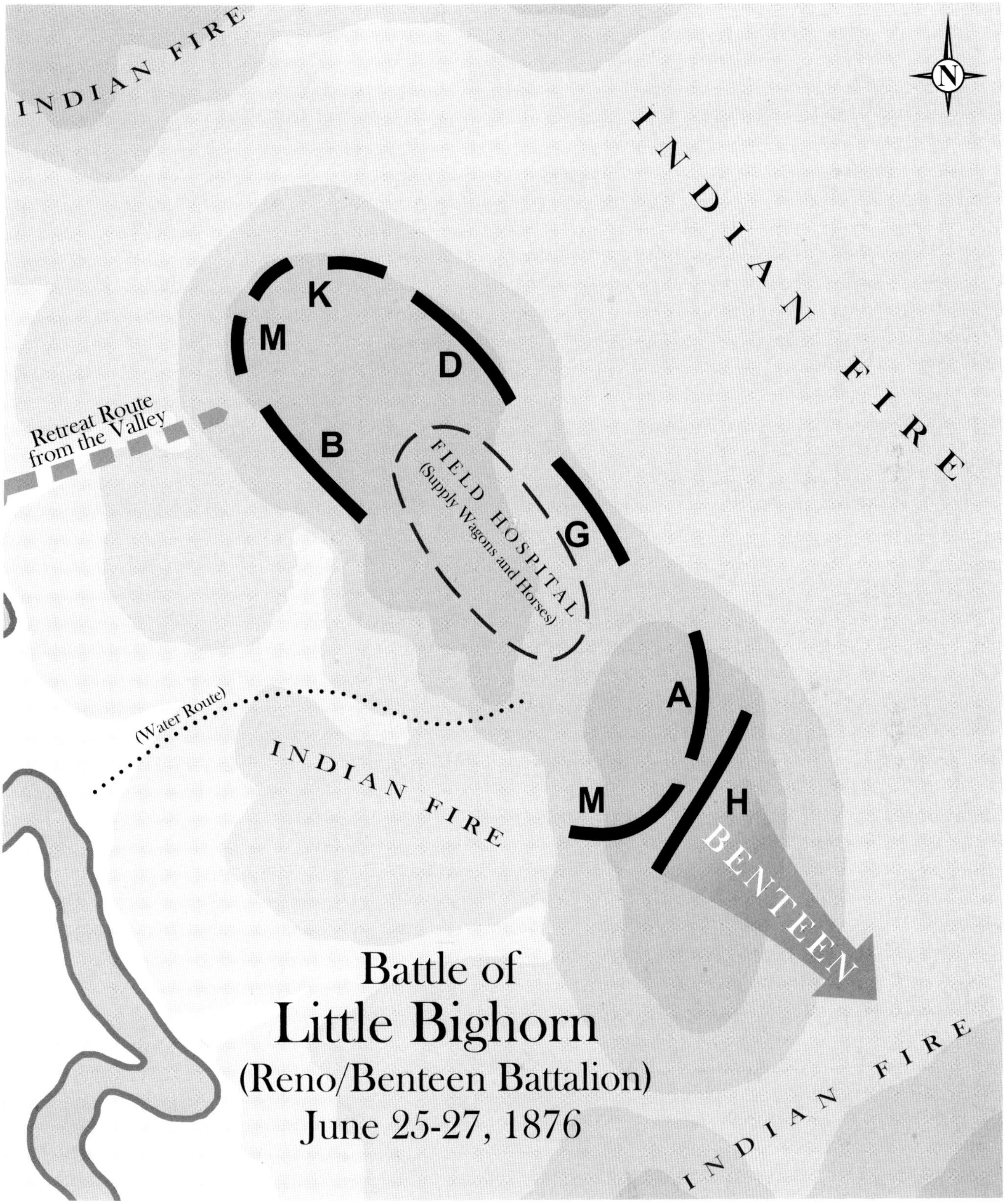
INDIAN FIRE
INDIAN FIRE
INDIAN FIRE
INDIAN FIRE
N
K
M
D
B
G
A
M
H
FIELD HOSPITAL
(Supply Wagons and Horses)
Retreat Route from the Valley
(Water Route)
BENTEEN
Battle of
Little Bighorn
(Reno/Benteen Battalion)
June 25-27, 1876

ferocity, Benteen's troops, absorbing the brunt of casualties from exposure to long-range sniper fire, were reinforced by elements of Company M, under Capt. French. As a pocket of Indians organized for the attack on the southeast side, Benteen ordered a charge, which dispersed the attack. In late morning, several troopers volunteered to go to the river to pick up much needed water for the wounded, taking several casualties during the process. Indians continued to press smaller, independent attacks and long-range fire throughout the morning. By early afternoon, on June 26, Indian fire finally subsided. The troops remained on the hill, dug-in throughout the rest of the day, and by evening, watched curiously as a large body of Indians, partially concealed by smoke from burning prairie grass, crossing the western side of the river valley, disappearing on the horizon toward the Big Horn Mountains.[49]

The arrival the next morning (June 27) of troopers of Gen. Terry's column, relieved the weary defenders still entrenched on the hill. Destroying discarded property and surplus equipment and tending to the many wounded, the column left their tiny hill-top garrison toward the west the next morning, where they eventually came across the remains of Yates' and Custer's battalion. Just a few miles from their position, the troops lay scattered along the bluffs and coulees. Thus began the unfortunate process of burial detail of the hacked and disfigured bodies, putrid and whitened in the hot summer sun.[49]

By August, the regiment had begun its return trip to the east, with the wounded transported by steamer down the Yellowstone. On August 8, while near the Rosebud River, Terry's column, along with the depleted ranks of the Seventh Cavalry, met with Crook's command and marched toward the Powder River. Arriving at the depot on the Yellowstone, Crook's command departed to the south, in search of the retreating Indians. After scouting the Yellowstone River region for several days, the Regiment continued eastward, along the banks of the Missouri River, eventually arriving at Ft. Lincoln on Sept. 26. The majority of the regiment, under the field command of Col. Sturgis, who joined the regiment from St. Louis, left camp just near Ft. Lincoln towards Standing Rock agency, to disarm the Indian population. Elements of the regiment, including companies A, C, D, and G under Maj. Reno, joined Sturgis' command at Standing Rock, and from there, returned to garrison for the winter at Ft. Lincoln. Sturgis' remaining companies continued on to the Cheyenne Agency, to disarm the population, returning north in early November. From there, the companies were deployed to their respective winter stations of Forts Abercrombie, Ft. Rice, Ft. Totten, and Ft. Lincoln.[50]

Aftermath and Reflection

There are literally hundreds of writings on the last battle, from the reputable, the novice, and the "fanciful." It is well known that Custer's movements and subsequent actions at the point of departing up the bluffs are conjecture. The record of the battle on June 25, 1876 is based on both reasonable assumptions from white and Indian testimony and over one hundred and thirty years of battleground analysis. For these reasons, the end in which Custer's battalion faced is consciously omitted from the "Operational History" of the Seventh Cavalry. Describing only the last known actions of the missing battalion until it's gruesome discovery three days later, my approach to explain the actions of the "Last Stand" was left enigmatically undetermined, as it was to the very participants, who exclaimed with bewildered curiosity, "What happened to Custer?" Due to speculative nature and the hypothetical supposition of the events surrounding the battle (as well as the tens of thousands of pages of literature devoted to this epic fight), the account of battle at "Last Stand" Hill is covered only in summary and brief reflection of my own personal thoughts.

It is commonly believed that Custer further divided his command into smaller sub-battalions: Capt. Keogh command of companies C, I, and L, and Yates' command of companies E, and F. By the time Reno's besieged battalion had made its way back across the river toward their defensive position on the bluffs, Custer's battalion had already commenced the action. While Keogh's battalion moved along the ridge providing fire while in search of a support approach, it is assumed that Yates' battalion had charged down the ravine of Medicine Tail Coulee, attempting to ford the river in support of Reno's offensive, but was cut off and repulsed by a large force of warriors still racing to meet Reno's fleeing troops. Retreating up the slopes and turning to make a defensive stand, skirmishers were deploying from company C in rear guard defense, until their line fell apart forcing a retreat back up the ridge. Reunited at the crest of the hill, north of Deep Coulee, the column shifted northwesterly. Company L, under Lt. Calhoun was deployed along the crest of the bluff, on the northeastern side, remaining until overwhelmed. Further up the crest, company I, under Capt. Keogh, with elements of company C were deployed in skirmish lines. Protecting the northern approach and covering the movement of the remainder of the battalion, they too fought until overwhelmed.

Col. Sturgis with officers of the Seventh Cavalry at Ft. Lincoln, late 1876. By August, replacement officers began filtering in to fill the numerous vacancies in the regiment. *Villa Louis Collection, Wisconsin State Historical Society*

Company E, under the command of Lt. Smith, and Yates' company F, with Custer, as well as elements of company C moved along the crest until deploying at the northwestern edge of "Last Stand" Hill. It is suggested that at this time, a second attempt was made at fording the river, but overwhelming opposition thwarted further forward movement. As Yates' position farthest north crumbled, they retreated back towards the crest of the hill and held until all were killed. The remainder of Company C and Company E had moved down the slope of Deep Ravine, where some troopers of Company E succeeded in breaking through the lines toward the river but were cut down near Cemetery Ravine. Forming defensive lines against the onslaught of Indians from the west, the remaining companies along Deep Coulee were eventually overrun and wiped out.

In the end, over 250 soldiers of the Seventh Cavalry were overwhelmed and killed on the bluffs at Little Big Horn, not to mention Reno's losses, which although tragic, were comparatively minimal. The arrival of Terry and Gibbon on June 27 prevented what could have been a much greater loss, and they along with Reno's veteran besieged shared the unpleasant duty of identifying and burying their comrades. But no matter how many times one reads about how that battle unfolded that day, new emotion is stirred and the natural question is raised. How did this happen? Or who is to blame. Obviously, so dramatic a legend with such ironic tragedy invites reflection and "armchair" criticism. The sad loss of life and the seemingly infinite "what ifs," exist on multiple levels. It is the tragedy of battle when young soldiers are killed brutally in such a lonely desolate place. The mere notion of two young comrades bound together in a suicide pact, as the tide of battle shifted to an unforgiving and brutal enemy is depressing to say the least. The subsequent ramifications of this Indian victory at Big Horn, which effectively defined and prolonged the Sioux wars of 1876 and 1877, on Native American life and culture, also incur speculation. The Indian's victory indirectly served as a springboard for later campaigns, galvanizing the army into a total war of destruction during the 1870s and 1880s and eventually culminating into the final defeat of the Plains Indians in 1890 at the terrible massacre of Wounded Knee. From a historical standpoint, there is a monumental sense of curiosity about the possibilities if Custer had been victorious. As young America prepared for the Centennial in the East, who could speculate as to what the political future would have held for such an individual, rumored to be a prospect groomed by the Democratic Party.

Popular conception portrays Custer at fault for this great debacle, attributed mostly to his impetuous nature, arrogance and insubordination. Actually, however, as most scholars have endeavored to highlight, there seem to exist too many complexities and intriguing variables to solely place blame on him alone. Custer sent his men to their doom, possibly with his knowledge, although he probably did not see it that way. Surely his young troopers, save a few, with the Kidder and Fetterman Massacre lingering in their minds, did not share his zest for action nor his aspirations and ambitions, and undoubtedly wished they were elsewhere. The fault simply couldn't rest on Custer that day. That withstanding neither was he blameless. In reality, the government's principle position towards the Plains Indians led to an inevitable clash, lending the euphemism, "wrong man, wrong place-it was just a matter of time" sort of explanation. A string of untimely occurrences, some coincidental, establishing "links" of a chain of events, where only one interruption would break the continuity of the chain and alter the outcome, led to the events of that day. Moreover, so much hinged on elements as intangible as destiny and fortune, where that nebulous attribute of "Custer's luck," simply ran out.

The essence of criticism of the defeat of the regiment at the Battle of the Little Big Horn circles around a resounding premise: The blatant disobedience of orders, and the senseless charge with a fractionalized regiment, without benefit of intelligence or heavy weaponry, in which both were vainly dismissed, into an overwhelming number of hostiles, ending in annihilation. In dissecting that premise, however, for the sake of scrutiny, one can see the incongruity and questionability of that assessment. It is fair to say that the number of hostiles was a surprise-but probably would have been to Terry, Gibbon, or anyone else for that matter. During conference aboard the steamer, the command concluded an expectation of around fifteen hundred hostiles; an engagement well within the limitations of a mobile and well-armed Cavalry regiment. These figures were drawn both from Reno's assessment from his previous scouting, and reports from shamelessly corrupt Indian agencies that would deliberately falsify the number of Indians in order to pocket their allotments. In addition, many of the Indians who had previously fought Crook's command on June 17 at the Rosebud River migrated north to join the larger force.[51]

A force of hostile Indians larger than expected would have not been so decisive in their favor had a coordinated attack between commands been made, which Custer both disregarded and disobeyed. But what exactly were the regiment's orders? Terry's orders seem to be as specific as one wants to interpret. With Custer's regiment already detected and fearing a missed opportunity to catch the hostiles, an attack was commenced with no support of any of the coordinated elements of the offensive. Although this was not the desired strategy, it appeared to *not* be out of limits of the standing order, which ambiguous as it was, allowed for commander's individual initiative as "do as you see fit." Although written orders indicate a desired course of action, an excerpt from the letter indicates the ambiguity, but apparent autonomy: *"The Brigadier General commanding directs (sic) you will proceed up the Rosebud in pursuit of the Indians (sic). It is of course impossible to give you any definite instructions in regard to this movement, and were it not impossible to do so the Dept. Commander places too much confidence in your zeal, energy, and ability to wish to impose upon you precise orders which may hamper your action when nearly in contact with the enemy. He will however, indicate his own views of what your actions should be, and he desires that you should conform to them unless you shall see sufficient reason for departing them."* (Of Garryowen in Glory, pp. 50-51)[52] Custer simply found the trail and pursued it, attempting later to comply with the timeline set by Terry's plan.

Much reprehension and criticism lay in his decision to split up his command, attempting a coordinated attack against the Indian encampment as one can naturally reason the disadvantages of lesser numbers. However, to better comprehend his haughty impertinence, we must consider cavalry tactics as a whole as well as Custer's nature. Similar tactics, which had been successfully deployed at the battle of Washita years earlier (and the fight on the Yellowstone in August 1873) undoubtedly fostered a favorable impression on the validity of converging assaults, which were typical of the Cavalry doctrine. However, the strategy employed during the battle of Washita, the regiments only real coordinated engagement, had achieved success through the element of surprise, and the Indians were seasonally disadvantaged. Despite skirmishing against the hostiles for eight years, however, the regiment as a cohesive element was never really afforded the opportunity to understand the complex dynamics of Indian warfare in a classic pitched battle. Again, there at Washita, that aphoristic "luck" remained. The outcome could have been completely different as Black Kettle's village was on the edge of a much larger encampment. Had the scenario been shifted slightly, Custer's last stand could have been seven years earlier in Oklahoma instead of Montana. So, the question should be "Why would he?," but more, "So why wouldn't he?"

Nevertheless, the principle rationale for the success of the division of his battalions was of course based on coordinated pressure during the initial charge, and the fact that Reno's wing floundered. They were stopped as they neared the outskirts of the village, redeployed, and eventually pushed back across the river in a disorganized and panic-stricken rout. Benteen's forces were useless-unopposed as their orders drew them away from the action to scout south. (This, followed by a slow return pace, provided insufficient opportunity to arrive for any support). Regardless, the converging attack required support, which was simply not there. Whether that support came in the form of a simultaneous attack or with the hostiles averting attention to Reno's south assault allowing the gap for Custer's command to ford across the river to attack, one can only speculate.

The leadership of Custer and his officer corps is, by far, the most intriguing variable in the equation and has been vigorously lamented over for thirteen decades. As mentioned before, by the time the regiment was deployed to the Dakotas, it had been purged of the "incompetents," and most of the drunkards and other undependable sorts had long since been removed. With several successful campaigns behind them, the regiment had surely achieved some degree of fighting unity. But despite that, the fractionalization, which began so many years before, was securely entrenched in the officer ranks, and certainly impacted the outcome of the day. Custer and Yates' battalion was staffed with confidants of unquestionable loyalty-with the majority of them counted among Custer's "Royal Family." Custer, an arch autocrat certainly had no aversion to giving orders, but was not without sense. He did confer with his officer's prior to battle; soldiers whom he respected and deemed capable of getting the job done. True, he had no love for Reno or Benteen, but as far as we know, never had sufficient reason, at least that day, to question their commitment or bravery, particularly with Capt. Benteen. Both had distinguished service records, and certainly Custer knew of the popularity and devotion Benteen enjoyed amongst his men. If he had any misgivings regarding Reno's abilities, it apparently either never went further than privately, or is not recorded that day. It is easy to assert blame and rebuke Reno's actions and failed charge, but without seeing through their eyes, a wall of screaming hostiles bent on their very destruction one can only sympathize. Testimony from several officers under Reno's command unequivocally stated, "Had he not ordered the final withdrawal from the tree line, all would have been lost."[53] Then again, subordinate support for his actions are voiced from grateful survivors thankful for their own "skins," as well as perhaps surely being aware of even the slightest innuendos of cowardice from their own actions. In addition, the social fractionalization of the regiment by this time-had climaxed, which naturally had a profound impact on personal loyalty and devotion to dutifully carrying out Custer's orders.

Looking finally at the command structure of Custer's wing, marble markers on the bluffs map out the fall of troopers along the way, inadvertently documenting the last routes taken. If we analyze the peculiar location of bodies on "Last Stand" Hill, it offers many intriguing questions about the possibilities of who actually commanded the doomed troopers on the hill, or who died first. Calhoun and Keogh, and their lieutenants, as well as Harrington, were deployed in skirmish lines along the route, rallying their men until the end. As was Smith and Sturgis, deployed further down the slope. Custer, Yates, Tom Custer, and Cooke were all on the hill until the end. The possibility even exists that Custer was not effectively commanding the hilltop. He may very well have been killed, or at least incapacitated fairly early on, as some Indian testimony indicates. Perhaps wounded in the upper side as he first attempted to ford the river with Yates further down the valley, his exceptional endurance and solid fitness may have carried him until he reached the final hill. The nature of his life-ending wounds are also of interest. Benteen's report stated that in addition to the wound to the side of the chest, the shot to his temple (the other of Custer's two wounds) had "bled."[54] This, medically speaking, indicates he had received the wound before death or immediately following his heart ceasing to pump, which would seem to preclude a wound administered by post-battle non-combatants milling about the carnage. In all probability, his life was either ended by one of his own men as he lay dying against his horse, or by the proverbial "lucky" shot of an adversary. At any rate, although an enduring legacy immortalizing Custer and the Seventh Cavalry, the image so often fostered in popular culture of Custer falling amidst his slain troopers as he expended his last round from his "Webley" pistols is improbable.

CHAPTER TWO

OFFICER BIOGRAPHIES 1866-1876

Henry Harrison Abell
Born in Bazetta, Ohio in 1841. Enlisted in Co. C, 19th Ohio Infantry, in May of 1861 for a ninety-day enlistment. He enlisted again in Co. L, 6th Ohio Cavalry in October and served for the remainder of the year. In December 1861 he received a commission as 2nd Lt. 6th Ohio Cavalry, taking part in numerous campaigns and engagements in the Shenandoah Valley including the battles at Cross Keys, Bull Run, Beverly Ford, Upperville, and Five Forks. At the battle of Aldie, Virginia, he led a cavalry charge against Col. T. Munford's Confederate forces and was cited by Gen. Kilpatrick himself for gallantry. He was mustered out of the volunteers in October 1864.

His conspicuous war record won him an appointment from the civilian ranks to the Seventh Regiment as Second Lieutenant, Company L, on July 28, 1866, at the date of initial organization. Joining the regiment in February 1867, he was posted to Ft. Morgan and promoted to 1st Lt., effective February 21, 1867. In June his company was posted to Ft. Reynolds, Colorado, where he remained most of the year on scouting duty and as adjutant to the company commander at that time, Capt. Gillette. Following Gillette's reposting, he commanded company L in the absence of Capt. M.V. Sheridan. Abell went on leave of absence to attend personal affairs, during which time he tendered his resignation on December 15, 1870. He died on September 14, 1883.
Highest rank achieved: 1st Lieutenant, U.S.A.

William Stretch Abert
Born in Washington, D.C. on February 1, 1836. The influence of his father, Brig. Gen. John J. Abert helped enable him to secure an appointment as 2nd Lt., 4th Artillery in June 1855. After promotion to 1st Lt. in March 1857, he applied for a position in the Cavalry as they prepared for war and was appointed Capt., 3rd U.S. Cavalry in May 1861. Abert transferred to the 6th U.S. Cavalry in August and took part in numerous engagements during the Peninsula Campaign including Hanover Courthouse, where he was brevetted Major in May 1862 for gallantry. His actions caught the eye of Gen. George McClellan and was appointed to his staff in June. Distinguished service in various engagements during the Maryland Campaign followed with a brevet promotion to Lt. Col. in September 1862 for gallantry at Antietam. Shortly afterwards, he transferred to the staff of Maj. Gen. N.P. Banks, serving as Assistant Inspector General and later as Assistant Inspector General in the Dept. of Gulf. In October 1864, he was appointed Colonel, 3rd Massachusetts Volunteer Heavy Artillery Regiment, attached to Hardin's Division, XXII Army Corps. Following duty in Washington, D.C., and a brevet promotion to Brig. Gen., Volunteers, in March 1865 for meritorious service during the war, he was mustered out of service in September 1865.

Abert petitioned for appointment as Colonel in the new post-war regiments but as still an active officer, he was declined on the basis of seniority. His achievements, however, during the war landed him a promotion to Major on June 8, 1867 in the Seventh Regiment. Awaiting his orders to the Department of Missouri after he was relieved of duties in the south with the 6th Cavalry, he contracted yellow fever and

died in Galveston, Texas on August 25, 1867 before he could join his new regiment.
Highest rank achieved: Brevet Brigadier General, Vols.

***Abert**. Massachusetts Commandery, Military Order of the Loyal Legion Collection*

Richard Henry Lee Alexander
Born in Louisville, Kentucky on February 15, 1851, the son of Col. Thomas Ludwell Alexander, 5th U.S. Infantry. His father's influence and close personal friendship with General and future president U.S. Grant helped secure an appointment for his son "Lee." Commissioned in the Seventh Regiment as Second Lieutenant, Company M, on December 12, 1872, he joined the regiment in February 1873 as it assembled in Tennessee for deployment to the Dakotas. Suffering from poor health, Alexander went on sick leave in 1874 with a certificate of disability and remained there until his death from Pulmonary Tuberculosis in Sacramento, California on February 9, 1875.
Highest rank achieved: 2nd Lieutenant, U.S.A.

John Aspinwall
Born in Springfield, Vermont in 1846, the son of a Methodist Minister. Enrolled at the United States Military Academy in July 1865, graduating class of 1869. Among his classmates were fellow Seventh Cavalrymen Charles Rea, James Porter, and William Craycroft.

Left
***Alexander**. Villa Louis Collection, Wisconsin State Historical Society*

Following graduation, he was appointed Second Lieutenant, Company K, Seventh Regiment on June 15, 1869, joining the regiment in July in the field near the Saline River. Serving on duty at Ft. Harker and Ft. Leavenworth, he accompanied the regiment to the south for occupation duty, posted in Yorkville, South Carolina. Upon deployment to the Dakotas, he took part in the Yellowstone Expedition of 1873, where temporarily attached to company E, participated in the fight on the Yellowstone River August 11. After winter garrison at Ft. Rice, he went on leave of absence in April 1874 and never returned. In July, he was listed as a deserter and dropped from the roster effective July 12, 1874. Aspinwall drowned on December 26, 1881 in Toronto, Canada.
Highest rank achieved: 2nd Lieutenant, U.S.A.

Albert Trorillo Siders Barnitz
Born in Bedford County, Pennsylvania on March 10, 1835. A formed student of law at Cleveland Law College, Barnitz volunteered in the 13th Ohio Infantry at the outbreak of the war. After expiration of his enlistment, he again enlisted in Co. G, 2nd Ohio Cavalry in August 1861 and received a commission as 2nd Lt. in June 1862, serving in Missouri and Kansas. Following promotion in February 1863 to both 1st Lt. and Capt, he took part in numerous engagements attached to the Dept. of Ohio and the Army of the Potomac including Ashland Station, where he was wounded. Later participating in operations in the Shenandoah Valley, he served with distinction under Custer's command. In March 1865, he was promoted to Major and again fought with distinction at Sayler's Creek and Appomattox, commanding his regiment. He was mustered out in September 1865. He later received a brevet to Maj. for action at Ashland Station and Lt. Col. for action at Sailor's Creek in March 1867.

Barnitz won appointment to the Seventh Regiment as Captain, Company G, effective July 28, 1866 at the formation of the regiment. Joining the regiment at Ft. Riley in February 1867, he was posted to Ft. Harker with his company and later that year served on escort duty to the Wright survey party while the regiment was in the field with Gen. Hancock's expedition. Upon his arrival back at Ft. Wallace in June, he found himself engaging in heavy Indian attacks near Pond Creek

Top right
***Aspinwall**. Courtesy of Glen Swanson*

Right
***Barnitz**. Yale Collection of Western Americana, Beinecke Rare Books and Manuscript Collection*

Station commanding company G (and elements of Company I) after which he was commended for gallantry. During the winter campaign the following year, he again distinguished himself at the battle of Washita (under Elliot's wing), where he was severely wounded by a bullet to the abdomen in what he describes as a dramatic dual with an opponent. He was rewarded for his actions with a brevet promotion to Colonel and placed on light duty until application for disability, retiring from his wounds on December 15, 1870. Despite his wound, he lived until old age, dying in Asbury Park, New Jersey on July 18, 1912. Barnitz' correspondence to his wife, complied and published by author Robert Utley describes in colorful detail life in the Seventh Cavalry, including his own observations and perceptions of Custer's officer corps.
Highest rank achieved: Brevet Colonel, U.S.A.

Bradford S. Bassett

Born in Pennsylvania in 1836, the son of Col. O.A. Bassett, 2nd Kansas Cavalry Regiment. Enlisted in company D, 1st Illinois Cavalry in July 1861, attached to the Dept. of Missouri. He took part in the capture of Lexington where he himself was captured in September 1861 and later released. With the aid of his father, he received a commission as 2nd Lt., 2nd Kansas Cavalry. Regimental shortages resulted in elements of his unit being organized into the 3rd Kansas Battery (Hopkins Battery) in May 1862. There he took part at the battle of Old Fort Wayne, Prairie Grove and Cane Hill, where he was again captured and released. Following a promotion to 1st Lt. in January 1864, he remained until January 1865, after which he accepted appointment as Capt., 16th Kansas Cavalry in May 1865. Before mustered out in December 1865, he took part in the Powder River Indian Expedition and the battle of Powder River operating around the upper Arkansas River.

Bassett sought a position in what was then being called the "new army" and secured appointment to the Seventh Regiment as Second Lieutenant, Company B, on June 18, 1867. Joining the regiment in August 1867, he replaced Lt. H.M. Bragg, 3rd Cavalry, who was among the last of the original officers to temporarily staff the position. Detailed to Company M, he was assigned escort duty for the Indian Peace Commission from Ft. Harker to Medicine Lodge Creek in October 1867. Following winter garrison at Ft. Dodge with his company, he was promoted to 1st Lt., Company G on July 31, 1868, to occupy the vacancy created by the absence of J.T. Leavy. Bassett applied for leave-of-absence, citing poor health in September 1868, during which he died from chronic dysentery on March 11, 1869 in Galesburg, Illinois.
Highest rank achieved: Captain, Vols.

***Bell.** Yale Collection of Western Americana, Beinecke Rare Books and Manuscript Collection*

James Montgomery Bell

Born in Williamsburg, Pennsylvania on October 1, 1837. A graduate of Wittenberg College in 1862, he enlisted in Co. B, 86th Ohio Infantry in the summer of 1862 remaining until September of that year. The following year, he organized "Bell's Independent Company of Pennsylvania Cavalry," in Altoona, serving as Capt. in June 1863. Commanding his company at the engagement at North Mountain, his unit was absorbed into the 13th Pennsylvania Cavalry in October 1863, where he took part in numerous other engagements including Mine Run, Spotsylvania, North Anna, White Oak Road, Coggin's point, where he was wounded, and Hatcher's Run, Raleigh, and Bentonville. He was mustered out of the Volunteers in July 1865. In March 1867, he was brevetted 1st Lt. and Capt. for gallantry at Wilderness and Maj. for gallantry at Ream's Station.

Bell won appointment to the Seventh Regiment as Second Lieutenant, Co I, at the formation of the regiment on July 28, 1866. Solidly built and ruggedly dependable, he was the quintessential cavalryman. Promoted to 1st Lt. on

March 2, 1867, he was posted to Ft. Wallace, where he both commanded the company during Capt. Keogh's absence and took part in engagements and defense of the garrison against hostile Indian attacks. From November 1867 to March of 1869 he served as regimental quartermaster and during the Battle of Washita in 1868, he proved his worth and dependability bringing ammunition and ambulance on his own initiative into the thick of battle and which he was cited for gallantry. After serving again as regimental quartermaster from October 1869 to December 1870, he accompanied the regiment on occupation duty in the South, posted to Bagdad, Shelbyville, and Lebanon, Kentucky. In 1873, as the regiment took to the field on campaign, he joined his new company (D) on escort duty with the Northern Boundary Survey Commission. In March 1876, he applied for leave of absence until September, thus missing the 1876 campaign. Bell was promoted to Capt., Co. F, as of June 25, 1876, to occupy the vacancy created by the death of George Yates. With the regiment short on officers and still on leave at the time, urgency of orders to report immediately for the conclusion of the campaign resulted in his being listed as absent-without-leave. Consequently, he and several other officers were somewhat unfairly criticized of undeserving of the position of company commander, being referred to as what Benteen called "Coffee Coolers" or "stay-at-home-officers." After rejoining the regiment in September and the conclusion of operations against the Sioux, he took part in the Nez Perce Campaign, commanding company F in Merrill's battalion at the battle at Canyon Creek, Sept 13, 1877. He served throughout the next decade on frontier duty, participating in the capitulation of Gall's band of hostile Indians in 1881 and protection duty for the Railroad. With a brevet promotion to Lt. Col. in February 1890 for gallantry at Canyon Creek, he remained on frontier duty with the regiment until he was promoted to Major, 1st Cavalry on May 23, 1896. During the Spanish war, he accepted appointment as Colonel, 27th Volunteer Infantry in July 1899 and was posted to the Philippines, during which time he was advanced to Brig. General, USV, and Lt. Col., 8th U.S. Cavalry. Following his discharge from Volunteer service, he was promoted to Col. in March 1901, and Brig. Gen., U.S.A. before his retirement from active duty on October 1, 1901. Bell died in Hermosa Beach, California on September 17, 1919.

Highest rank achieved: Brigadier General, U.S.A.

Benteen*. L. Tom Perry Special Collections, Harold B. Lee Library, Brigham Young University*

Frederick William Benteen

Born in Petersburg, Virginia on August 24, 1834. At the outbreak of war, he was appointed 1st Lt., Co. C, "Bowen's" Cavalry Battalion in September 1861. Promoted to Capt. in October serving under the District of Southwest Missouri, he took part in numerous engagements including Wet Glaize, Wilsons' Creek, Salem, Batesville, Springfield, Sugar Creek, Cotton Plant, Kickapoo Bottom, Pea Ridge, Greenville, Bolivar, Millikin's Bend, and Helena. In October 1862, his unit was absorbed into the 9th Missouri Cavalry and the 10th Missouri Cavalry the following month. Promoted to Maj., he participated at the siege of Vicksburg and the battles of Florence, Cane Creek, Iuka, Brandon, Jackson, and Pleasant Hill. Following promotion to Lt. Col. in February 1864, he participated at Montevallo, Little Osage Crossing, Big Blue, Mine Creek, Chariot, Selma, and the raid on Columbus. Later in March 1867, he was brevetted Maj. for gallantry at Osage, and Lt. Col. for gallantry at Columbus. After being mustered out of the volunteer service in June 1865, he was appointed

Colonel 138th Colored Infantry in July 1865, until the regiment was disbanded. Application for a post-war position offered little more than a staff position in the then, less prestigious colored cavalry regiments, which he declined.

Eventually, his creditable war record yielded a Captaincy in the Seventh Regiment on July 28, 1866, assigned to company H at the formation of the regiment. Benteen was one of the more vocal personalities in the regiment and from the start, thought little of Custer personally. Like Barnitz and Godfrey, many of his observations and viewpoints have been recorded offering a unique but pessimistic history of the early years of the regiment. Missing Hancock's summer campaign in June 1867 as he remained in garrison at Ft. Hays, he got his first taste of actions against Indians in the engagement near Saline Creek in August 1868 while stationed at Ft. Harker, in which he was brevetted Colonel. He took part in the Winter Campaign of 1868 and the Battle of the Washita (under Elliot's wing) serving with what later became known as characteristic cool-headedness and charismatic bravery. Following the battle and the events regarding Elliot's disappearance, he began to outwardly display his contempt for Custer and became a vocal anti-Custerite. In June, he accompanied the regiment on reconstruction and occupation duty, posted to Huntsville, Alabama. Upon return north to deployment in the Dakotas, he commanded a battalion in the Yellowstone Expedition and the Black Hills Expedition of 1874. Benteen joined the regiment from Ft. Rice in the Yellowstone Campaign and the Battle of the Little Big Horn commanding a battalion. By many accounts, much of the success at Reno's hilltop defense was credited to his gallantry and stalwart leadership. Following the conclusion of the Sioux Campaign, he took part in the Nez Perce campaign the following year and the engagement at Canyon Creek, Sept 13. Commanding a battalion during the battle, his actions and leadership again were noteworthy, leaving his earlier adversary Chief Joseph, after his own surrender, to inquire as to who was the courageous officer with "trout rod and pipe in his mouth." Eventually, his temperament and fondness for alcohol led to deterioration of his performance, landing him in arrest for drunkenness in October 1879 while at Ft. Meade. On December 17, 1882, he was promoted out of the regiment to Major, 9th Cavalry, where he spent the majority of his time on frontier duty in Nebraska and Utah, commanding the garrison at Ft. Duquesne. By this time, he was often intoxicated, and found himself charged with drunkenness and inappropriate conduct. Court martial found him guilty and suggested dismissal. Fortunately, his service record was considered and was graciously permitted instead to retire on disability, which he did in July 1888. In February 1890, he was brevetted Brig. Gen. for gallantry at Little Big Horn and Canyon Creek. Benteen's antagonism and intense dislike for Custer is well documented. He had his own peculiarities but was nevertheless supremely courageous and highly respected, even idolized, particularly by his beloved Company H. He died of heart disease in Atlanta, Georgia on June 22, 1898.

Highest rank achieved: Brevet Brigadier General, U.S.A.

Mathew Berry

Born in Ireland in September 1835 (other records show 1837). After immigrating to the United States in 1854, he enlisted in Co. H, 2nd U.S. Cavalry in May 1857. He accepted the opportunity for commission as 2nd Lt., company D, 5th Pennsylvania Cavalry at the beginning of the war and with promoted to 1st Lt. in December 1863, he took part in numerous campaigns, including the Peninsula Campaign, serving on staff of Gen. Smith, the Pope Campaign, the Shenandoah Campaign of 1862, and Valley campaign, participating at the battles of Malvern Hill, Manassas, and Fredericksburg. In February 1864, he was appointed Capt. 20th Pennsylvania Cavalry, taking part at the battle of White Post and Rude's Hill against Imboden's Brigage. He took part in the Shenandoah Campaign of 1864, engaging at numerous battles including New Market, Lynchburg, Manchester, and Cedar Creek. He served until mustered out in January 1865, and was brevetted Capt. in March 1867 for gallantry at Antietam.

In October 1866, he applied for a post-war position but despite an enviable combat record with the volunteers and years of faithful service, he was rejected by the examining board for deficiencies in tactics and geography. He eventually passed, and with a recommendation by Gen. Sheridan won appointment to the Seventh Cavalry as First Lieutenant, Company C, effective July 28, 1866, at the formation of the regiment. Joining his company at Fort Lyon, Colorado in February 1867, he remained there for the duration of the year, and in the absence of the company commander, commanded his company through several engagements against hostile Indians near the Arkansas River. After a brief assignment on detached service in March 1868, he took part in the winter campaign and the battle of Washita, serving under Hamilton's squadron. On December 5, 1868, he was promoted to Captain to fill the vacancy created by the death of L.M. Hamilton. Enroute from

Camp Supply to Ft. Cobb in December 1868, his open disdain for Capt. West led to an altercation of insubordination and disobedience of orders, resulting in his arrest, after which he left confinement. Following court marshal in June 1869, he was sentenced to a three-month suspension (During this time, news reached him that West had died, which probably resulted in few tears shed by Berry). While serving his sentence, he negotiated a trade with Capt. S. C. Plummer, who at that time was stationed in New Mexico with the 26th Infantry. Plummer did eventually transfer, but Berry resigned instead, effective August 9, 1869. He refutably died in Essex County, Massachusetts.

Highest rank achieved: Captain, U.S.A.

John Williams Biddle*

Born to an affluent family in Philadelphia, Pennsylvania in 1856, the son of Capt. Henry Jonathan Biddle who was mortally wounded at new Market Crossroads in 1862. Graduating from Princeton University in June 1875, he was commissioned Second Lieutenant.

Following the losses at Big Horn, he was assigned to the Seventh Regiment, Company K, on August 31, 1876 to fill the vacancy left by the promotion of Luther Hare. (The position was originally filled by Lt. E.P. Andrus, but he never joined the regiment.) Following the regiment's return from the field, Biddle joined his company at Ft. Lincoln. The following year, he took part in the Nez Perce Campaign of 1877, where he commanded Company K in the absence of Capt. Hale, who commanded the battalion. An intelligent and promising young officer, Biddle's army career was untimely short. Bearing the brunt of the Indian defenses on the far right wing of a classic cavalry charge, he was killed in action while during the battle of Snake Creek on September 30, 1877.

> *"(Owen) Hale shouted "Charge Boys!" and at the same instant received his first wound, but leaped with the others over the edge of the embankment down among the Teepees, as he alighted, a bullet pierced him in the throat. He stopped, staggered, and raised his right hand over his head, again shouting feebly, "Charge Them!" He fell dead, and Lt. Biddle, mortally hurt at almost the same moment, reeled backwards and fell across his body."* (4898 ACP 1876, Records Group 94, National Archives, Washington, D.C.)

Highest rank achieved: 2nd Lieutenant, U.S.A.

***Biddle**. Courtesy of Glen Swanson*

Charles Braden

Born in Detroit, Michigan on November 23, 1847. Enrolled at the United States Military Academy in 1865, graduating class of 1869. Among his classmates were fellow Seventh cavalrymen Charles Rea, James Porter, William Craycroft, and John Aspinwall.

Appointed Second Lieutenant, Co. L, Seventh Regiment on June 15, 1869, to fill the vacancy created by the promotion of Charles Brewster, Braden joined the regiment in August. Following garrison at Ft. Leavenworth, he took part in Colonel Dodge's Expedition of 1870, afterwards being posted to Ft. Wallace. Nicknamed "Old Gothic," for his solid build and reliability, he accompanied the regiment to the south, posted in Columbia, Winnsboro, and Yorkville, South Carolina. Following a leave of absence during the summer of 1872, he was posted to New Orleans until March 1873. With the regiment's deployment north in the Dakotas, he took part in the Yellowstone Expedition of 1873. During the engagement on the Yellowstone River on August 11, 1873, fighting on the skirmish line with the far left wing while under the command of Capt. V.K. Hart, he received a serious bullet wound in the thigh. Custer later wrote, *"... Lt. Braden received a rifle ball through the upper part of the thigh, passing directly through the bone, but he maintained his position with great gallantry and coolness until he had repulsed the enemy."* (Official report regarding the engagement on August 11, 1873. E.B. Custer, *Boots and Saddles*, p.245). After a tediously long and painful journey in ambulance back to Lincoln, he remained hospitalized until October, afterwards assigned light duty. In March 1874, he applied for sick leave, during which time he received promotion to 1st Lt., Co. F, on December 9, 1875. Remaining on leave and a brief detached duty with the recruiting Dept., Braden eventually retired on disability from his wounds on June 28, 1878. After service, he went into teaching, appointed Professor of Military Science at the New York Military Academy. In February 1890, Braden was brevetted 1st Lieutenant for gallantry at the skirmish at the Yellowstone River and awarded the Distinguished Service Cross, "for extraordinary heroism in action against the Sioux Indians near the mouth of the Big Horn River, Montana, August 11, 1873." His citation read: *"Lt. Braden, with twenty men, having been attacked by nearly two hundred Indians, although severely wounded in the encounter, by his personal gallantry with splendid leadership, so inspired his small command as to enable it to repulse the attack by overwhelming superior numbers." (*Annual Reports of Graduates, United States Military Academy, 1919). He died in Highland Falls, New York on January 15, 1919.

Highest rank achieved: First Lieutenant, U.S.A.

Edwin Parker Brewer

Born in New Lisbon, Ohio on April 16, 1854. Brewer suffered the loss of both his father, Paymaster Major Anson Brewer, a prominent Ohio Lawyer and Republican, and brother to an explosion of a Mississippi River steamer in 1866 as well as an older brother, killed in action at Dallas, Georgia in 1864. He enrolled at the United States Military Academy in July 1871 but was dismissed for deficiencies in November of that year. However, with influential family connections, he was accepted for examination and subsequently commissioned 2nd Lt., assigned to the 2nd Cavalry.

Following the aftermath of the Battle of Little Bighorn, Brewer was reassigned to the Seventh Regiment, Company K, on August 31, 1876, filling the vacancy created by the

Brewer. *Edward S. Godfrey Collection*

promotion of W.S. Edgerly (The position was originally filled by Lt. Pearson, but he never joined the regiment.). Joining the regiment at Ft. Lincoln at the conclusion of the Sioux campaign, he took part in the Nez Perce campaign of 1877 and the engagement at Canyon Creek on Sept. 13, 1877, temporarily serving with Company I in Merrill's battalion. With promotion to 1st Lt., Company G on September 23, 1885, he served at various posts in Dakota Territory, Kansas, and Arizona Territory where he took part in several engagements against hostile Indians. He was again promoted to Captain, Company B on December 8, 1896, while stationed at Ft Huachuca, Arizona Territory as acting Quartermaster and Commissary of Subsistence. In 1898, he was appointed Capt., 3rd U.S. Volunteer Infantry, serving in Cuba. At the request of his widowed and ailing mother, a personal friend of President McKinley, Brewer was posted east on recruiting duty. After returning to Cuba, he was later promoted to Major on January 6, 1905, serving with his regiment in Luzon, Philippines. After posting to New York City with the Quartermaster Dept. and a return to the Philippines, he was promoted out of the regiment to Lt. Col., 14th Cavalry on June 30, 1911. With promotion to Colonel of Cavalry in Sept. 1912, Brewer retired after thirty-seven years of active service in November 1913 and died in 1925.

Highest rank achieved: Colonel of Cavalry, U.S.A.

Charles Brewster

Born in New York in March 1836. Leaving employment in a law office in Minnesota, he received appointment as Capt., Commissary of Subsistence, serving from November 1862 through the end of the war. He assisted in recruiting New York volunteers, and was awarded a commission as 1st Lt., 13th New York Cavalry in July 1863. Brewster's regiment took part in anti-guerilla operations and in action against Confederate Col. J.S. Mosby's men, he was captured near Cedar Creek in a dramatic incident:

> "These, with prisoners brought in by others, made up a total of 27 men – all belonging to Custer's cavalry. It was decided that seven of them should be taken and executed, in retaliation for the six men of our command hung or shot at Front Royal, after the fight with Custer's Division ... One being Captain Brewster, commissary of subsistence, of Custer's command. Twenty-seven pieces of paper, seven of which were numbered and the remainder blanks, being put into a hat, and the hat shaken up, each prisoner was required to draw. The numbered pieces meant death by hanging, and the blanks meant Richmond and Libby Prison." (Account by James J. Williamson, *Mosby's Rangers.*)

Brewster*. Yale Collection of Western Americana, Beinecke Rare Books and Manuscript Collection*

Eventually escaping, Brewster returned to his duties in the Commissary and was assigned to the staff of Brig. Gen. Custer in 1864 as Captain, C.S. while attached to the 1st Brigade, 1st Cavalry Division, Army of the Potomac. There he distinguished himself at numerous engagements including Wilderness, Spottsylvania, Dinwiddie Court House, Yellow Tavern, Cold Harbor, Waynesboro, Cedar Creek, Five Forks, and Southside Railroad Station. Brevetted Maj., Vols. in March 1865 for meritorious service, Brewster remained with Custer until he was mustered out in July 1865, forging a loyalty to him he carried throughout his career. Later in March 1867, he was brevetted Capt., U.S.A. for gallantry and meritorious service at Trevillian Station.

Brewster sought an appointment in post war organization, requesting service under his old commander. Custer's recommendation won him an appointment to the Seventh Regiment as Second Lieutenant, Company K, effective July 28, 1866, at the formation of the regiment. He joined his company at winter garrison at Ft. Riley in February 1867 and after promotion to 1st Lt., Company E on February 24, 1867, he was posted near Ft. Hays in May 1867 and appointed acting regimental quartermaster while the regiment was in the field. Among Brewster's shortcomings, like so many others, was alcohol, which landed him in arrest during winter garrison at Ft. Leavenworth. The following year, he took part in the winter campaign and the battle of Washita, serving with Company I. Although a courageous soldier, he was considered by many of his peers to be "unfit" to be an officer. When Sturgis took command of the regiment and army reorganization competency boards came bearing down, he was ordered before what became known as the "Hancock" board; referred by Col. Sturgis, charging him with being "constitutionally inefficient." With few to lend encouraging testimony on his behalf, rather than face certain dismissal, he took leave of absence in November 1870 and resigned effective November 18, 1870. Brewster tried for years unsuccessfully for reinstatement and to clear his name and died on July 20, 1904 in Milford, Nebraska.

Highest rank achieved: Brevet Major of Volunteers, Bvt. Capt., U.S.A.

James Calhoun*

Born in Cincinnati, Ohio on August 24, 1845. Enlisted in Co. D, 14th U.S. Infantry in January 1864 attached primarily to the V Army Corps. Following the end of action, he applied for a commission but was rejected, accepting a vacancy as a non-commissioned officer. Eventually, his application was accepted and he was commissioned 2nd Lt., 32nd U.S. Infantry, effective July 1867, serving on frontier duty in Oregon and Arizona Territory. In March 1869, during the restructuring of the army, he was left unassigned by 1870 as his regiment was merged into the 21st U.S. Infantry.

He sought position in the Cavalry and at the behest of Custer and a glowing endorsement, he entered the Seventh Regiment as Second Lieutenant, Co. C, January 1, 1871, with simultaneous promotion to 1st Lt. on January 9, 1871 days later. Calhoun joined the regiment in Bagdad, Kentucky and following detached duty in Arizona Territory to attend a court of inquiry, he returned to posting in Kentucky, Chester, South Carolina, and Rutherford, Lincolnton, and Charlotte, North Carolina until March 1873. Unswerving gratitude and loyalty to Custer for his generosity in appointment, and a marriage to Custer's sister during his duty in the south permanently commited Calhoun to what was known to outsiders as the "Royal family."

Upon his posting to the Dakotas, he took part in the Yellowstone Expedition of 1873 as acting assistant adjutant, participating in both skirmishes on the Tongue River and Yellowstone River in August, and the Black Hills Expedition of 1874. "Jimmy" Calhoun joined his new brothers and fellow officers on the Yellowstone campaign, serving with Company L, and at the battle of the Little Big Horn was killed in action on June 25, 1876. His battered body was found on what is now known as "Calhoun" Hill amidst hundreds of empty cartridges.

Highest rank achieved: 1st Lieutenant, U.S.A.

***Calhoun**. Courtesy of Glen Swanson*

William Brittin Clark

Born in Waterloo, New York on March 4, 1838. Enlisted in Co. E, 2nd Massachusetts Cavalry from March 1863. After mustering out, Clark was commissioned 2nd Lt., 14th Kansas Cavalry in September 1863, taking part in numerous engagements including the battles at Aldie and Bentonville. He also took part in the Expedition into Choctaw Station and General Steele's Expedition into Camden, where under Gen. Thayer, he was praised for gallantry at the battles at Prairies D'Ann and Saline River. During that time, Clark was briefly captured at Cabin Creek in September 1864 and released. He rejoined his regiment and took part in the Brice Raid on the Arkansas River. He served until mustered out in June 1865.

Clark secured an appointment in the Seventh Regiment as Second Lieutenant, Co. F on June 18, 1867, and soon after became a "disciplinary" problem. While posted to Ft. Wallace, following an arrest for drunkenness and insubordination, court martial found him guilty and sentenced him to six months suspension in October 1868. He returned to the field in March and resumed his duties. In early April 1869, he was again in trouble, being charged with "Conduct unbecoming an Officer," including drunkenness and fighting with a fellow officer near Ft. Dodge. Rather than face a second court martial and probable dismissal, he tendered his resignation, effective May 1, 1869 and disappeared.

Highest rank achieved: 2nd Lieutenant, U.S.A.

Frank Young Commagére

Born in Lucas County, Ohio on April 18, 1844, the son of Col. Henry Steel Commagere, Col. 184th Ohio Inf. and Bvt Brig. Gen. of Vols. He enlisted in Co. A, 14th Ohio Infantry in March 1861 for a ninety-day enlistment. Commagére won appointment at the United States Naval Academy in the fall semester of 1861, but according to his entrance autobiography, he left on his own accord to "join the war." In October 1862, he was commissioned 2nd Lt., 67th New York Infantry where he took part in numerous engagements including Harper's Ferry, Fredericksburg, Franklin's Crossing, and Salem Heights. In November 1863, he fell ill and after a lengthy sickness, he was dismissed from service, citing poor health. After recuperation, he found ample support on his behalf and received an appointment in the regular army as Major, 6th U.S. Colored Cavalry in January 1865 and was assigned to a comfortable position at Headquarters at the Office of Organization. Following detached service as Assistant paymaster in Kentucky, he was mustered out in April 1866.

Commagére, like so many others jockeyed for a position in the "new" army. Declining an appointment in the 10th Colored Cavalry regiment, requesting an "all-white" regiment, his persistence found appointment to the Seventh Regiment as First Lieutenant, Company F, at the formation of the regiment on July 28, 1866. Transferring to Company K in August 1867, he commanded the company in the absence of R.M. West. Commagére was affable and sociable, but to his senior officers, considered lazy, unmotivated, and seeming disinterested in Military life. As a result, he was punitively reassigned to Capt. Benteen's command, so as to "improve his disposition." In September 1867 at Ft. Wallace, while the regiment was under the command of Maj. Elliot, he was charged with "Conduct Prejudiced to Good Order of Military Discipline" for failure of duty and disobedience of orders, spending a good majority of time under arrest while at winter garrison at Ft. Leavenworth. Shortly thereafter, following an altercation with the post commander at Ft. Leavenworth, he resigned on February 1, 1868. Claiming his resignation was a mistake – done out of necessity to help his ailing father and the need to attend personal business, he petitioned for restoration of his position and reappointment. His unfounded claims were unanimously rejected. Commageré died in Washington D.C., on July 25, 1892.
Highest rank achieved: Major, U.S.A. (Colored)

***Commagére**. United States Military History Institute*

***Cooke**. United States Military History Institute*

William Winer Cooke*

Born to a wealthy upbringing in Ontario, Canada on May 29, 1846, the son of an affluent physician. After enlisting in the 24th New York Volunteer Cavalry at the organization of the regiment in 1863, he was appointed 2nd Lt. in January 1864. At the ripe age of seventeen, attached to Marshall's Provisional Brigade, Army of the Potomac, he took part at Wilderness, Cold Harbor, and Petersburg, where he was wounded. While attached to the 1st Brigade, 2nd Division, Cavalry Corps, Army of the Potomac, he was promoted 1st Lt. December 1864, and distinguished himself in numerous engagements during the Appomattox campaign before being mustered out in June 1865. In March 1867, he was brevetted Capt. for gallantry at Petersburg, Maj. for gallantry at Dinwiddie Court House, and Lt. Col. for gallantry at Sailor's Creek.

His notable service record, particularly during Sheridan's Appomattox campaign won him a post-war appointment, entering the Seventh Regiment as Second Lieutenant, Company D, July 28, 1866, at the formation of the regiment. Following his arrival at Ft. Riley in December, he was appointed both regimental commissary and Adjutant until February 1867, which established the beginning of a close relationship with Custer that would last until their end. During the summer campaign, he was promoted to 1st Lt. on July 31, 1867. Following the wake of Custer's court martial and suspension, Cooke, a devout Custer loyalist, joined his commander in the hot-seat-charged with the murder for the shooting deaths of K company deserters, as he was the one who actually fired the shots. (See biography, G.A. Custer) With Cooke's loyalty and faithful support, Custer's favoritism was plainly obvious, as Cooke was so "honored" with command of a detachment of Sharpshooters during the Winter Campaign of 1868 and the battle of Washita. He accompanied his regiment on duty in the south, posted to Elizabethtown, Kentucky. After deployment to the Dakotas, Cooke, known as "Queen's Own," because of his peculiar facial hair, took part in the Yellowstone Expedition of 1873 and the Black Hills Expedition of 1874. Assigned again as Reg. Adj., a posting he reoccupied since January 1871, he took part in the Yellowstone Campaign and was killed in action during the Battle of the Little Big Horn on June 25, 1876. A supreme athlete and soldier, his scalped and mutilated body was found on "Last Stand Hill," as he had always been: not far from Custer.

Highest rank achieved: Brevet Lt. Colonel, U.S.A.

Wickliffe Cooper

Born in Lexington, Kentucky on October 19, 1831. Enlisted in Co. K, 20th Kentucky Infantry at the age of thirty in November 1861. Accepting a commissioned as 2nd Lt. in January 1862,

Cooper. *Roger D. Hunt Collection*

he took part at Shiloh, the Siege of Corinth, and Richmond. He resigned in April 1863 to accept an appointment as Lt. Col., 4th Kentucky Cavalry in April 1863, attached to the 1st Division, Cavalry Corps, Army of the Cumberland. Promoted to Colonel in May 1863, he took part in numerous engagements including Chickamauga, Triune, Unionville(town), and Franklin, where he was wounded while leading a charge against J.B. Hood's Confederate forces. After mustering out in August 1865, he later received brevet promotions in March 1867 to Lt. Col. for gallantry at Resaca and Col. for gallantry during the capture of Montgomery.

One of the many to receive appointments in the "new" army based on distinguished Volunteer service, Cooper joined the Seventh Regiment as Major, effective July 28, 1866, at the formation of the regiment. Although a brave and probably competent officer, he was a hopeless alcoholic, and the men and fellow officers of the regiment endured his many raging bouts. On June 8, 1867, while in the field acting as second in command during the scouting campaign, during a drunken

delirium, he committed suicide by shooting himself in the head in his tent. Although tragic, his affliction had so deteriorated his capabilities that Barnitz commented upon his death that he was, "not too terribly missed."
Highest rank achieved: Colonel, Vols.

Charles G. Cox
Born in Portland, Maine in 1841. Enlisted in the 40th Massachusetts Infantry in September 1862 and received a commission as 2nd Lt. the following month. Cox took part in the second Peninsula campaign, and both the Siege of Suffolk and Battery Wagner and after promotion to 1st Lt. in September 1863, he served in the campaigns in Florida with the Tenth Army Corps, including Olustee, where he was cited for gallantry against J. Finnegan's Confederate forces. Promoted to Capt. in April 1864, he took part at Drury's Bluff, Cold Harbor, where he was wounded, and the battle at Petersburg. Following a promotion to Major in November, he resigned in December 1864. In January he was appointed 1st Lt., 26th New York Cavalry, in what he referred to as the Massachusetts Contingent until discharged the following month. In March 1865, he was appointed Capt., 3rd Massachusetts Regiment, which had been refitted from infantry to a Cavalry regiment, eventually mustered out of the volunteers in September 1865. He was later brevetted Major in March 1867 for gallantry at Cold Harbor.

His former service as Adjutant General of Colorado under Sheridan secured a post war appointment to the 17th Infantry but he solicited transfer to the Seventh Regiment as Second Lieutenant, effective March 7, 1867. Joining his company I at Ft. Wallace, he was posted as escort to Gen. Hancock's staff en route to Denver. He took part in field operations including the Sully expedition, where he commanded company I during Capt. Keogh's detached absence. He appears to have been, as author Robert Utley points, "highly political. An opportunist motivated by promotion and advancement, after only a few short months, he was promoted out of the regiment to Captain, 10th Cavalry effective June 12, 1867. In 1870, while serving with the 10th Cavalry on frontier duty, he was charged with numerous infractions including drunkenness, absence from duty, breach of arrest, and destruction of property. The court obviously found the charges serious enough and he was summarily dismissed and sentenced to three years in a penitentiary. He died on January 14, 1886 near Miles City, Montana Territory.
Highest rank achieved: Bvt. Major, U.S.A.

Cox. Massachusetts Commandery, Military Order of the Loyal Legion Collection

William Thomas Craycroft
Born in Springfield, Kentucky on January 28, 1847. Enrolled at the United States Military Academy in July 1865, graduating class of 1869. Among his classmates were fellow Seventh Cavalrymen James Porter and Charles Braden.

Following graduation, he was appointed Second Lieutenant, Seventh regiment on July 7, 1869. Assigned to Company F, he joined the regiment after leave at Ft. Wallace in October. Posted to Ft. Reynolds, Colorado through the summer of 1870, he transferred to garrison at Ft. Leavenworth until March 1871. Craycroft accompanied the regiment on duty in the south, posted to Bagdad, Kentucky and both Spartanburg and Unionville, South Carolina. Upon deployment to the Dakotas, Craycroft was posted to Ft. Rice, assembling at Yankton for Stanley's Yellowstone Expedition of 1873. After several sick leaves for poor health; one of several since his arrival, he rejoined elements of the regiment southward. Posted to the Department of the Gulf, he served on duty in

Opelika, Alabama and Shreveport, Louisiana, after which he was promoted to 1st Lt., Co. B, on December 2, 1875. In April 1876, as the regiment prepared for the upcoming campaign, Craycroft went on detached duty, probably attributed to his health and limited capabilities, assigned to a supply board to purchase horses until September 1876 and was spared participation in the debacle of the Little Big Horn during the Yellowstone campaign of 1876. He again applied for sick leave in October of that year and remained there until his retirement from disability on June 28, 1878. He died in Dallas, Texas on October 31, 1906.
Highest rank achieved: 1st Lieutenant, U.S.A.

Craycroft. *Courtesy of Glen Swanson*

Charles Clement Cresson

Born in Philadelphia, Pennsylvania on February 24, 1845. At the young age of 17, he was commissioned 2nd Lt., 66th Pennsylvania Infantry in August 1861. His regiment was absorbed into the 73rd Pennsylvania Infantry and with promotion to 1st Lt. in March 1862, he took part at Bull Run, where during an attack on an entrenched battery, he was wounded in the arm. In August following the battle, he was promoted to Capt., refutably making him the youngest Captain in the service. In 1863 he participated in the campaigns in Virginia and Pennsylvania attached to the XI Corps, distinguishing himself at Chancellorsville, where he was severely wounded under Buschbeck's Brigade, and Gettysburg, including being heavily engaged at Cemetery Hill. Promoted to Major in January 1864, Cresson again served with distinction, participating in numerous campaigns and engagements including Resaca, Chattanooga, Pine Knob, where he received his third wound, Kenesaw Mountain, Atlanta, and Savannah. Following promotion to Lt. Col. in December 1864, he was mustered out of the volunteer service in August 1865. Later in March 1867, he was brevetted 1st Lt. for gallantry at Mill Creek, Capt. for gallantry at Resaca and Maj. for gallantry at Kenesaw Mountain. Post war assignments

Cresson. *United States Military History Institute*

easily landed him a commission as 2nd Lt., 17th U.S. Infantry in May 1866, as the youngest commissioned officer in the service. He transferred to the 35th Infantry in September of that year and was promoted to 1st Lt. in October 1867.

Following reorganization of the army in 1869, Cresson was assigned to the Seventh Regiment as First Lieutenant on December 15, 1870. A nominal assignment only, he transferred out of the regiment after less than a month to the 1st U.S. Cavalry on December 23, 1870 and never joined the regiment in the field. While posted to the frontier, he took part in the engagements against the Modoc Indians at the Lava Beds of California in 1873 and at Camas Meadows in 1877, where he would take part in the capture of "Captain Jack" and was later brevetted Lt. Col. for gallantry in February 1890. After retiring from service, advanced to the rank of Colonel, Cresson died in San Antonio, Texas on March 15, 1906 from complications while performing surgery on the wound he suffered during the War.

Highest rank achieved: Colonel, U.S.A., Ret.

George Armstrong Custer*

Born in New Rumley, Ohio on December 5, 1839. Enrolled at the United States Military Academy in July 1857, attending with notable names Ranald Mackenzie and Judson Kilpatrick, graduating class of 1861. Custer was appointed 2nd Lt., Co. G, 2nd U.S. Cavalry in June 1861 as the Civil war began, serving on various staff detail and taking part at the battle at Bull Run. Eager to fight, he volunteered his services on the staff of Gen. Hancock at Williamsburg and taking part in several other skirmishes, his aggressive lust for action did not go unnoticed. With a promotion to 1st Lt., 5th Cavalry in August 1862, he was promptly plucked for assignment on staff of Gen. McClellan, who commanded the Army of the Potomac. Given the temporary rank of Captain, he distinguished himself during the Antietam campaign. The disappointment of the dismissal of his chief soon gave way to a new springboard for success, with assignment to the staff of Gen. Pleasanton in April 1863. Developing a close relationship, Pleasanton's succession of Gen. Hooker fostered young Custer an appointment to Brig. Gen., Vols., giving him command of the "Michigan" 2nd Brigade in June 1863. Attached to the 3rd Division, Cavalry Corps, Army of Potomac, he took part in numerous engagements during the Gettysburg Campaign. Continuing his affinity for battle with distinguished leadership at Brandy Station, Aldie, Gettysburg, Falling Waters, and Culpepper (where he suffered his only combat wound of his life), prompted Pleasanton to remark, "... Custer is the best Cavalry General in the World." When Pleasanton was replaced, Custer was transferred to the 1st Brigade, 1st Division; his qualities quickly endearing him to Pleasanton's successor. Under Phillip Sheridan, Custer aggressively commanded his brigade at Yellow Tavern and Trevillian Station, against his nemesis Stuart. Attached to the Army of the Shenandoah, he took part at what some historians call the apex of his career, the battle of Winchester, and in September 1864, he was given command of the entire 3rd Division. As a new divisional commander and Major General, he continued to distinguish himself in the field, commanding troops at Cedar Creek. In March 1865, attached again to the Army of the Potomac, he took part in the closing campaign at Appomattox, leading his men at Waynesboro, Five Forks, Namozine Church, Sayler's Creek, and Appomattox Station. A tribute to his achievements, Sheridan would write to Custer's wife regarding Lee's surrender, "... there is scarcely an individual in our service who has contributed more to bring this about than your very gallant husband."(Urwin, *Custer: The Civil War Years*) A slew of brevets followed, including Lt. Col. for gallantry at Yellow Tavern, Col. for actions at Winchester and Maj. Gen., Vols. for actions at Winchester and Fisher's Hill, Brig. Gen, U.S.A. for actions at Five Forks, and Maj. Gen., U.S.A. At the conclusion of the war, Custer was transferred to the Dept. of Texas for occupation duty in June 1865, commanding the Cavalry Division, Division of the South. Transferred again in August to the Division of Gulf, he commanded the 2nd Cavalry Div, and was appointed Chief of Cavalry, Department of Texas. Unfortunately, Custer's duty in the south was marred by friction and insubordination, resulting in a near-mutiny. In February 1866, after his command was relieved of duties in the south, he entertained a generous offer to serve for Maximillian of Mexico, but the army vetoed the notion and he was transferred north to await new appointment.

Custer won the vacancy in the new Seventh Regiment as Lieutenant Colonel, effective July 28, 1866, at the formation of the regiment. Joining the regiment at Fort Riley in October, he took de facto command in the field in the absence of Co. A.J. Smith, commanding the regiment during summer operations of 1867. Wracked with desertions and little success against his new adversary, incidents during field operations in July resulted in his court martial and suspension, but continued failure against the Plains Indians prompted requests for his

G.A. Custer. *Western History Department, Denver Public Library*

early return the following year. Rejoining the regiment in October 1868, he commanded his troops during the winter campaign and led his troops in the decisive victory at the battle of Washita. However, the sound decision to leave Elliot's missing detachment in the field following the battle began the ultimate fractionalizing of his command and discontinuity of his officer corps; an attribute that lingered throughout the rest of his life. In 1871, he took his regiment south for occupation and reconstruction duty, posted to Elizabethtown, Kentucky and following deployment to the Dakotas, commanded his regiment during the Yellowstone Expedition of 1873, including the engagements on Aug. 4 and Aug. 11, and the Black Hills Expedition of 1874. Custer ultimately led his command on the Yellowstone campaign of 1876, accompanying Yates' battalion and was killed in action on June 25, 1876. Surrounded by the butchered bodies of his close associates, "Long Hair" as he was known to the Indians, refutably averted post-mortem mistreatment, sustained only two wounds: One to the chest and the other to the temple.
Highest rank achieved: Major General, Vols., Brevet Major General, U.S.A., Lt. Colonel, U.S.A.

T.W. Custer. *Yale Collection of Western Americana, Beinecke Rare Books and Manuscript Collection*

Thomas Ward Custer*

Also born in New Rumley, Ohio on March 15, 1845. He enlisted in Co. H, 21st Ohio Infantry in September 1861 and attached to the XIV Army Corps, he took part in the Stone's River and Chickamauga campaigns, during which he served on escort duty to Gen. J. Negley and Gen. U.S. Grant. Following reenlistment in his unit in January 1864, he served as escort to both Gen. Palmer and Gen. Thomas and participated in several engagements during the Atlanta campaign. After he was mustered out in October 1864, older brother Brig. Gen. G.A. Custer used his influence to secure for him a commission in Co. B, 6th Michigan Cavalry, which he accepted that same month. Serving as Aide-de-Camp to his brother, he took part at numerous engagements while attached to the 1st Brigade, 1st Division, Cavalry Corps, Army of the Potomac, including Waynesboro, Dinwiddie Court house, and Five Forks and received brevet promotions to 1st Lt., Capt., and Maj., Vols. for gallantry in March 1865. Tom Custer holds the distinction of being one of only a handful of men twice awarded the Congressional Medal of Honor: One from actions at Namozine Church on April 2, and the second from actions at Sayler's Creek on April 6, 1865, where bandaged from a severe shot in the face, he returned to fight only to be arrested by his brother and sent to the rear. (He was later brevetted Capt. for gallantry at Waynesboro, Maj. for gallantry at Namozine Church, and Lt. Col. for gallantry at Sayler's Creek.

> At Namozine Church, Va., 10 May 1863. The *"Capture of a Flag."* At Sailor Creek, Va., April 1865. "2nd Lt. Custer leaped his horse over the enemy's works and captured two stands of colors. Having his horse shot from under him and receiving a severe wound." (Committee on Veterans' Affairs, U.S. Senate, *Medal of Honor Recipients: 1863-1973*).

He remained on the roster of the Michigan regiment until it's official decommission in April 1866, but had earlier joined his brother serving in Texas. Following their duty, he was mustered out of the volunteers, accepting a commission as 2nd Lt., 1st U.S. Infantry.

Custer resigned his commission when he secured appointment again under his brother, entering the Seventh Regiment as First Lieutenant, Company A, effective July 28, 1866 at the formation of the regiment. Arriving at Fort Riley in December, he immediately was appointed regimental

quartermaster, which he occupied until March 1867. In early summer 1867, he took ill, suffering from inflammatory rheumatism, and remained on the sick list for over a year. Following his recuperation and return to duty, he took part in the Winter Campaign of 1868 assigned to company D, where he was slightly wounded in the hand at the battle of Washita. He accompanied the regiment on duty in the south, posted to various stations in South Carolina and Mississippi. Upon the regiment's deployment to the Dakotas, he took part in both the Yellowstone expedition of 1873, including the engagements on Aug. 4 and Aug. 11 near the Tongue and Yellowstone Rivers, and the Black Hills Expedition of 1874. After staffing numerous company vacancies, he was promoted to Capt., Company C, on December 12, 1875. Custer marched with the regiment on the Yellowstone campaign of 1876, acting as Aide-de-Camp to his brother and was killed in action on June 25, 1876; his badly disfigured body, identifiable only by his tattoo, lay on "Last Stand" Hill near his brother.
Highest rank achieved: Bvt Lt. Colonel

John Townsend Daniel
Born in North Hamptonshire, England on September 21, 1839. After immigrating to America in 1860, he was appointed Capt., 36th New York Infantry in June 1861, where he took part in numerous actions during the Virginia and Maryland campaigns including Williamsburg, Chantilly, Fredericksburg, Market Heights, and Salem Church. During the fighting at Fair Oaks (Seven Pines) in May 1862, he was severely wounded in action. After his discharge in April 1863, he accepted a commission in June 1864, as Maj., 10th Maryland Infantry and took part in actions during the Lynchburg Campaign, including New Market, Piedmont, and Lynchburg as well as Ashby's Gap and Winchester. After being mustered out in January 1864, he was appointed Maj., 1st Potomac Home Brigade of Maryland Cavalry in March, organized in Frederick in which he served until mustered out in June of 1865.

Daniel petitioned and received an appointment to the Seventh regiment as Second Lieutenant, effective July 28, 1866 at the formation of the regiment. However, charges of forgery in late 1866 deferred his acceptance, pending investigation. Before he could be assigned to the regiment, his appointment expired on July 20, 1867. He purportedly died in Wakefield England in March 1877.
Highest rank achieved: Major, Vols.

Dayton. *Civil War Library and Museum, MOLLUS Collection*

Lewis Mulford Dayton
Born in Albany, New York on June 20, 1835. In March 1862, he was commissioned 1st Lt. 78th Ohio Infantry. His education as a civil engineer landed him a detail as Aide-de-Camp to General W.T. Sherman where he was present at Shiloh, the Siege of Corinth, and Chickasaw Bayou. Appointed Captain, Aide-de-Camp, Volunteers in March 1863, Dayton took part in numerous campaigns including Atlanta, Savannah, and Carolina Campaigns and participated at the battles of Vicksburg, Mission Ridge, New Hope Church, Kenasaw, Atlanta, and Chattanooga. In January 1865, he was promoted to Major, Volunteers and brevetted Lt. Colonel of Volunteers in March 1865 for service during the Savannah and Carolinas campaigns. Mustered out of the Volunteers in September 1866, he remained with the adjutant general's office on staff with Sherman, and nominally accepted appointment as 2nd Lt., 2nd U.S. Infantry, effective July 1866.

Following brevet promotions in March 1867 to 1st Lt., Capt., and Maj. for gallantry and meritorious service in the Atlanta campaign and Lt. Col. for operations in the Carolinas, he was promoted to Captain, Seventh Regiment on March 6, 1867, filling the existing vacancy in Company M. Remaining on detached duty with Gen. Sherman, Dayton's service in the regiment was purely abstentious, and he saw no operations in the field. Following the conclusion of his lengthy and successful staff detail in December 1870, he applied for leave of absence, and shortly thereafter resigned from service on December 31, 1870. He died in Cincinnati, Ohio, on May 18, 1891.
Highest rank achieved: Colonel, U.S.A.

Charles Camilus DeRudio
Born in Belluno, Austria on August 26, 1832. DeRudio's history is an intriguing apologue and reads like a suspense novel. After attending the Austrian Military Academy, he became "radically" opposed to Napoleon III and was allegedly involved in a failed assassination plot in Paris that landed him a death sentence. Commuted to a life-term of imprisonment at Devil's Island, he made a daring escape, fleeing to England in 1858. After immigrating to America, arriving in Florida in February 1864, he enlisted in the 79th New York Infantry while his regiment was attached to the IX Army Corps, serving until October. In November 1864, he accepted a commission as 2nd Lt., Co. D, 2nd U.S. Colored Infantry, attached to District of Key West, Fla., Dept. of the Gulf and was mustered out in January 1866. DeRudio somehow secured a post war appointment as 2nd Lt., 2nd U.S. Infantry in August 1867. In October 1867, his appointment was reinstated after a brief cancellation and remained until effectively unassigned in April, 1869 during reorganization of the army.

His reassignment landed him a position in the Seventh Regiment as Second Lieutenant, Company H, on July 14, 1869. He accompanied his regiment on duty in the south, posted to Tullahoma, Humbolt, and Nashville, Tennessee. Upon the regiment's deployment to the Dakotas, he took part in the Yellowstone Expedition of 1873. After promotion to 1st Lt. on December 15, 1875, he marched with his regiment on the Yellowstone campaign of 1876 and the Battle of the Little Big Horn, temporarily assigned to Company A under Moylan. During the fight in the valley with Reno's battalion, DeRudio escaped certain death, concealing himself in the tree line and eventually making his way across the river to high ground the following day. At the conclusion of the Sioux campaign, DeRudio accompanied the regiment in the field the next year against the Nez Perce, serving under Lt. G. Doane's scouting battalion. Promoted to Capt. on December 17, 1882, he remained on frontier duty for almost his entire career in the Dakotas and New Mexico. DeRudio retired from active duty on August 26, 1896, advanced to Major, and wholly retired in 1909. One of the more colorful characters of the regiment, "The Count" as he was somewhat unaffectionately known entertained his associates with incredulous tales and his boastful nature purportedly earning him the reputation of a "braggart." Custer evidently thought less of him labeling him both a "confirmed gambler and a natural conspirator", and "the inferior of every first lieutenant in this regiment." DeRudio died in Los Angeles, California on November 1, 1910.
Highest rank achieved: Major, U.S.A., Ret.

DeRudio. *Villa Louis Collection, Wisconsin State Historical Society*

Edwin Philip Eckerson
Born at Ft. Vancouver, Washington Territory on March 8, 1850, the son of Major Theodore. J. Eckerson, Quartermaster Department. (Other records indicate birth on April 9, 1850.)

Eckerson secured a commission as 2nd Lt., Co. L, 5th U.S. Cavalry in December 1872, where he participated in actions against Apache Indians near Maztalan Mountains in 1873 earning a brevet promotion to 1st Lt. for gallantry. Following assignment to the Quartermaster Dept. as acting paymaster, he was charged with "conduct unbecoming an officer and gentleman," while posted to Camp Grant, Arizona Territory. Regarding two peculiarly similar incidents of missing regimental funds under his charge, court martial found him guilty and sentenced him to dismissal in July 1875.

A year of appeals and several influential acquaintances affirmed his reinstatement in good standing, entering the Seventh Regiment by appointment as Second Lieutenant, Company L, on May 19, 1876. Filling the vacancy created by the promotion of Charles Braden, an application for leave and a delay in posting was granted as the regiment took to the field on the Yellowstone Campaign. Eckerson's propitious timing prevented his probable death; as his replacement, temporarily filled by Lt. J.J. Crittenden of the 20th Infantry, perished at the battle. Joining the regiment in August, he was promoted to 1st Lt., Company K, effective June 25, 1876, filling the vacancy created by the promotion of James Bell. The following year, he took part in the Nez Perce Campaign and of battle at Snake Creek on Sept. 30, 1877, where he headed the defense of three companies in the absence of dead or wounded company commanders and was commended for conspicuous duty. During the apex of battle he reported to Gen. Miles, "… I am the only damned man of the Seventh Cavalry wearing shoulder straps who's alive!" (Jerome Green, *Nez Perce Summer*). Unfortunately, after returning to winter garrison at Ft. Lincoln, he found himself under court martial for "conduct unbecoming and officer," including drunkenness and acts committed while intoxicated. As before, inquiry found him guilty and he was dismissed from service on June 30, 1878. Eckerson, employed as a civilian with the Quartermaster Department, died at the age of thirty-five from malaria at Ft. Hays, Kansas on August 17, 1885.
Highest rank achieved: 1st Lieutenant, U.S.A.

Winfield Scott Edgerly

Born in Farmington, New Hampshire on May 29, 1846. Enrolled at the United States Military Academy in July 1866, graduating class of 1870. Among his classmates was fellow Seventh Cavalryman Charles Larned.

Edgerly, at 6'4" and the tallest officer in the regiment, was commissioned Second Lieutenant, assigned to Company D, Seventh Regiment on June 15, 1870, joined his company

***Edgerly**. Courtesy of Glen Swanson*

in September for winter garrison at Ft. Leavenworth. He accompanied the regiment on duty in the south in March 1871, posted to Mount Vernon, Kentucky, Meridian Mississippi, Chester, South Carolina, and Opelika, Alabama until March 1873. Upon deployment to the Dakotas, he served on escort duty to the International Boundary Commission from June to October, afterwards applying for leave of absence. After his return to duty, he again served on escort duty from May to September 1874 and did not join the regiment on campaign. During the Yellowstone campaign of 1876, his company was detailed as escort to the pack train, where he took part in Reno's hilltop defense. Promoted to 1st Lt., effective June 25, 1876, he was assigned acting quartermaster until a transfer to Company C, stationed at Ft. Lincoln and Ft. Totten. After promotion to Capt. on September 22, 1883 and postings to various stations in Montana and Kansas, he took part in the Sioux campaign of 1890, including the battles of Wounded Knee and White Clay Creek (Drexel Mission) and received a commendation for conspicuous service. At the conclusion of the Indian Wars, Edgerly began a series of assignments to

and away from the regiment. After a brief stint as Professor of Military Science at Maine State College, he was appointed Lt. Col., Inspector General of Volunteers, II Army Corps and on July 8, 1898 was promoted out of the regiment to Major, 6th U.S. Cavalry. After rejoining the Seventh again the following year in Cuba, he was promoted to Lt. Col. 10th U.S. Cavalry, but again transferred back to the Seventh Regiment, serving under the Dept. of Havana. Posted to the Philippines, he joined the 2nd U.S. Cavalry on February 17, 1903 as commanding Colonel. Edgerly eventually achieved the rank of Brig. General in June 1905, commanding both the Cavalry and Artillery Schools, and after a long and distinguished career, he retired on disability in December 1909. Edgerly died at home in New Hampshire on September 10, 1927.
Highest rank achieved: Brigadier General, U.S.A.

Joel H. Elliot*

Born in Wayne County, Indiana on October 27, 1840. A former schoolteacher and school superintendent, he enlisted in Co. C, 2nd Indiana Cavalry in September 1861, where he participated in actions at Shiloh, Perryville, and Stone's River, also serving on staff of General A.M. McCook. In June 1863, he accepted a commission as 2nd Lt., 7th Indiana Cavalry at the formation of the regiment, taking part in numerous engagements. Promoted to Captain in October of that year, he was slightly wounded during engagements with Col. Jeffrey Forrest's Confederate Forces at Ivey's Farm. Elliot took part in the Tennessee Expedition in December 1863 under future Seventh Cavalry Colonel, A.J. Smith and Sturgis' Expedition to Guntown where he was severely wounded in action at Brice's Crossroads. After duty in Louisiana in 1865, his regiment was posted in the Dept. of Texas, where he served on Custer's Staff until mustered out in February 1866.

Custer's adulatory endorsement praising Elliot as a "natural soldier," won him an appointment as Major, filling the remaining staff vacancy in the Seventh Regiment on March 7, 1867. Following posting at Ft. Harker commanding the garrison, he transferred to Ft. Larned the following year and as next senior officer, commanded the regiment in the field during summer operations, scouting missions and Sully's failed expedition in the absence of both Lt. Col. Custer and Col. Smith. Elliot was a popular, courageous and capable officer, and his zeal and dedication won him praise from his superiors. Unfortunately, slow progress and inactivity against the Indians during his field command lessened both the effectiveness and morale of the men, overshadowing his attributes. In addition,

***Elliot.** Courtesy of Glen Swanson*

Sully, under sharp criticism himself labeled the young Major somewhat inexperienced, attempting to shift the blame for his own shortcomings and lack of success on the expedition. Upon Custer's reinstatement, he took part in the winter campaign of 1868, commanding the northeast wing. On November 27, during the Battle of Washita, he was killed in action when he and a small detachment of soldiers ventured in pursuit of a fleeing band of hostiles down into the valley. Overcome and massacred, evidence showed after dismounting his men and tying the horses together, he valiantly and desperately fought a short, furious fight: his mutilated body was found in a tight semi-circle with his troops. An extract of the examining doctor's post-mortem report describes the savage treatment he received:

> "*... Two bullet holes in the head, one in left cheek, right hand cut off, left foot almost cut off ... deep gash in right groin, deep gashes in calves of both legs, little finger of left hand cut off, and throat cut.*" (Excerpt from Dr. Lippincott's Report, reprinted in Swanson's *G. A. Custer: His Life and Times*)

Highest rank achieved: Major, U.S.A.

David Fairly

Born in London, England on May 26, 1830. After immigrating to America, he received a commission as 2nd Lt., 3rd New Jersey Infantry in June 1861. In July 1862, he was promoted to 1st Lt., and took part at the battles of Gainsville, where he was wounded, and Spotsylvania. As his regiment was re-designated a cavalry unit, he was commissioned Capt., (3rd New Jersey Cavalry) in October 1864, attached to Sheridan's army of the Potomac, serving under fellow Seventh Cavalryman W.P. Robeson, (both in the Cavalry and Infantry). Under the command of Gen. G.A. Custer, he participated in the battle at Namozine Church on April 3, where he received five wounds during a charge against the forces of Gen. Fitzhugh Lee; one of which required the amputation of his left arm. As a testament to his abilities and spirit, he returned to duty a mere month after his traumatic wound, "showing thereby his zeal for the service." In March 1865, he was brevetted Maj. for gallantry near Richmond and on recommendation from Custer, brevetted Lt. Col. for gallantry at Namonzine Church. He was mustered out of service in August 1865.

With a favorable endorsement from Custer, Fairly won appointment to the Seventh Regiment as First Lieutenant on January 22, 1867. On leave of absence awaiting his posting to the field, he was killed in a train accident on April 2, 1867 while traveling from Washington, D.C., to Philadelphia, undoubtedly cutting short the promising career of a brave and able officer.

Highest rank achieved: Brevet Lt. Colonel, Vols.

French*. L. Tom Perry Special Collections, Harold B. Lee Library, Brigham Young University*

Thomas Henry French

Born in Baltimore, Maryland on March 5, 1843. Enlisted in the 10th U.S. Infantry in January 1864 until accepting a commission as 2nd Lt. in May 1864 and promotion to 1st Lt. the following month. While attached to the 1st Brigade, 2nd Division, V Army Corps, he participated in numerous engagements during the Richmond-Petersburg Campaign, including the siege of Petersburg, Weldon Railroad, where he was brevetted Capt. of Vols. for gallantry in August 1864, and Chappell House, where he was wounded in action against A.P. Hill's Confederate forces. After the war, he declined an appointment in the 44th Infantry at its organization. Following a promotion to Captain in March 1868, he became effectively unassigned during reorganization of the army.

French was reassigned in the Seventh Regiment as Captain, assigned to Company M, on January 1, 1871, joining the regiment at Fort Hays. He accompanied his regiment to the south a few months later, posted to Spartanburg and Unionville, South Carolina. After deployment to the Dakotas, he took part in the Yellowstone Expedition of 1873 including the fight on August 11 and the Black Hills expedition of 1874. French joined the regiment on the Yellowstone campaign in 1876, assigned to Company M. Cited for gallantry and leadership during the hilltop fight with Reno's besieged troops, Capt. Benteen paid him a cryptic compliment, regarding the leadership during the fight, stating, "*... They were all a pack of cowards, Capt. French excluded.*"(Benteen-Goldin Papers). Following the Yellowstone campaign, French took part in the Nez Perce Campaign in 1877 commanding his company under Benteen's battalion and was slightly wounded at Canyon Creek on September 13, 1877. Unfortunately, like so many others, he succumbed to the excesses of alcohol, eventually bringing down his career. In January 1879, he was court marshaled for drunkenness and other associated infractions and sentenced to be dismissed. However, just like his former battalion commander, Frederick Benteen, prior service and recommendations on his behalf spared him the hatchet, and

the court lessened his sentence to suspension and forfeiture of pay. He retired on February 5, 1880, while serving out his sentence, and died a few years later at Leavenworth, Kansas on May 27, 1882.
Highest rank achieved: Captain, U.S.A.

Ezra Bond Fuller
Born in Rockford, Illinois on October 4, 1848. Enlisted at sixteen years old in Co. E, 141st Illinois Infantry in May, serving on garrison duty in Kentucky until October 1864, when his regiment was mustered out. He enlisted again in Co. M, 8th Illinois Cavalry in February 1865, where attached to the XXII Corps, he participated in anti-guerilla operations in Virginia before being mustered out in July of that year. In July 1869, he enrolled at the United States Military Academy, graduating class of 1873. Following his graduation, he was commissioned 2nd Lt., 8th U.S. Cavalry in June 1873, serving in the field in Texas and New Mexico and participating in small skirmishes with Indians at Staked Plains and Muster Creek, Texas.

Following the losses at Little Big Horn, Fuller transferred to the Seventh Regiment as Second Lieutenant, assigned to Company A, effective June 26, 1876, to fill the vacancy created by the promotion of Charles Varnum. Fuller joined the regiment at Ft. Lincoln in September, and took part in the Nez Perce Campaign of 1877 and the battle of Canyon Creek on Sept. 13, 1877, temporarily commanding Company H in the absence of Benteen, the battalion commander. Following a promotion to 1st Lt., effective September 30, 1877 and duty in the Dakotas, he was appointed Assistant Professor Philosophy at the Academy in August 1881 until August 1885. Returning to frontier duty again in the Dakotas, he took part in the Sioux expedition of 1890, serving as Regimental Quartermaster. In February 1890, he was brevetted Capt. for gallantry at Canyon Creek, 1877 and shortly after, promoted to Captain March 22, 1892. After a three-year appointment as Professor of Military Science at Clemson College, S.C., he rejoined his regiment in Cuba in July 1898. While there, he was promoted out of regiment to Major, 10th U.S. Cavalry on May 31, 1901. Fuller retired on disability, advanced to the rank of Lt. Col., in May 1904. He died at Ft. Leavenworth on September 17, 1925.
Highest rank achieved: Lt. Col., U.S.A., Ret.

***Fuller**. Courtesy of Glen Swanson*

Ernest Albert Garlington
Born in Newberry, South Carolina on February 20, 1853, the son of Brig. Gen. Albert Cresswell, C.S.A. He left the University of Georgia to enroll at the United States Military Academy in July 1872, graduating class of 1876. Among his classmates were fellow Seventh Cavalrymen John Gresham, Hugh Scott, Horatio Sickel, and Albert Russell.

Upon graduation, Garlington was commissioned a Second Lieutenant, Seventh Regiment on June 15, 1876. Assigned to Company H, he joined the regiment in August at Ft. Lincoln and was immediately promoted to 1st Lt., Co. G, effective June 25 to fill the vacancy created by the death of Donald McIntosh. He took part in the Nez Perce Campaign of 1877 and the action at Canyon Creek on Sept. 13, 1877, serving as Regimental adjutant to Col. Sturgis; which he occupied until November 1881. He remained on field duty in Dakota Territory until 1883, taking part in the Northern Cheyenne Campaign. After service with the Office of the Signal Corps and in command of a relief expedition in Newfoundland, he returned to the frontier. Taking part in the Sioux campaign of 1890, he was both severely wounded and awarded the Congressional Medal of Honor at the Battle of Wounded Knee:

First Lieutenant, 7th U.S. Cavalry. *For distinguished gallantry At Wounded Knee Creek, S. Dak., 29December, 1890.* (Committee on Veterans' Affairs, U.S. Senate, *Medal of Honor Recipients: 1863-1973*).

Garlington. *Villa Louis Collection, Wisconsin State Historical Society*

Garlington's exemplary record, personifying a model cavalry officer, resulted in steady movement in rank. On February 2, 1895, he left the regiment with promotion to Major, Inspector General's Office, serving in Cuba and the battles of Santiago and subsequent surrender of Spanish forces. After service in the Philippines and promotions through Colonel, he ultimately achieved the rank of Brig. Gen., Inspector General of the Army. As did his son, whom would later also claim similar rank, Garlington enjoyed a successful career in the army, eventually retiring in February 1917. He died in Coronado, California on October 16, 1934.
Highest rank achieved: Brigadier General, U.S.A., Ret.

Alfred Gibbs

Born in Sunswick, New York in April 22, 1823, a descendant of the Wolcott family and grandson of the Secretary of Treasury in both the Washington and Adams administrations. He enrolled at Dartmouth College but left to attend the United States Military Academy, graduating class of 1846. Among his fellow classmates was fellow Seventh Cavalryman Samuel Sturgis. Few vacancies left Gibbs was a brevet Lt. rank, 1st Mounted Rifles in July 1846, engaging in numerous battles in the Mexican war including Vera Cruz, Cerro Gordo, Contreras, Churubusco, San Antonio, Garita de Belen, Chapultepec, and Mexico City. During fighting near the Mimbres Mountains, he was severely wounded. After a full commission the following year and a promotion to 1st Lt. in May 1853, he served on frontier duty in New Mexico, as Aide-de-Camp to Gen. P.F. Smith and saw action against Apache Indians at Cooke's Spring, where he was again severely wounded in March 1857. After taking part in the Navajo Expedition of 1860, he received promotion to Capt. in May 1861. In August 1861, as his unit was re-designated 3rd U.S. Cavalry, he was captured by Texas insurgents at San Augustine Springs, New Mexico. Following his release in August 1862, he returned to his home state, appointed Col., 130th New York Volunteer Infantry in September 1862. In August 1863, his regiment was absorbed into the 19th New York Cavalry, and a month later changed to 1st New York "Dragoons," in which he commanded a provisional

Gibbs. *Library of Congress*

brigade in the operations near Suffolk, Virginia. He took part in numerous campaigns in the Army of the Potomac, including the Peninsula, Richmond, and Shenandoah campaigns. He participated at Todd's Tavern, Spotsylvania, Yellow Tavern, Hanover, Cold Harbor, Cedarville, Opequon, and New Market. In October 1864, he was appointed Brig. Gen of Volunteers, taking part at Cedar Creek, Newtown, Dinwiddie Courthouse, Five Forks, Sailors Creek, and Appomattox, commanding a Cavalry Brigade under Gen. Sheridan. After commanding forces in the Division of the Gulf, he was mustered out of the Volunteers in February 1866. Brevetted 1st Lt. for gallantry at Cerro Gordo in April 1847, Capt. for gallantry at Garita de Belen in September 1847, Maj. for gallantry at Trevillian Station in June 1864, Lt. Col. for gallantry at Winchester in September 1864, and Col. for gallantry at Five Forks and both Brig. Gen. and Maj. Gen. for gallantry and service during the war in March 1865.

Gibbs distinguished service record and command capabilities won him a promotion to a staff position as Major, Seventh Regiment on July 28, 1866, at the formation of the regiment. Forming part of the original cadre, he was the next senior officer under Lt. Col. Custer, working alongside Maj. Davidson in development of the unit. Gibb's administrative abilities and introduction of Cavalry tactics and guidelines nurtured the infant regiment into operational status. Both he and his wife enjoyed a close relationship of shared mutual affection and respect with the Custers and his attention to military protocol and strict discipline earned him the name "General Etiquette." Poor health brought on by heavy drinking and wounds received before the war kept him away from field duty, remaining on staff at garrison. After commanding the post at Ft. Harker, he was posted to Ft. Leavenworth in late 1867, where he remained for the duration of his service. On December 26, 1868, he died of his illness during winter garrison at Ft. Leavenworth, citing "congestion of the brain". *Highest rank achieved:* Brevet Major General, U.S.A.

Gibson. *Courtesy of Glen Swanson*

Francis Marion Gibson

Born in Philadelphia, Pennsylvania on December 14, 1847. Following employment with the Paymaster's Department, he was commissioned Second Lieutenant, Seventh Regiment on October 5, 1867, joining the regiment in December at Ft. Leavenworth. Assigned to Company A, Gibson took part in field operations in 1868 and the Winter Washita campaign, serving on temporary duty with Company F under Thompson's southwestern wing. He accompanied the regiment on duty in the south, posted to various stations in Kentucky, during which time he was promoted to 1st Lt., Company H, on July 11, 1871, filling the vacancy created by the transfer of C.S. Ilsley. Upon posting to the Dakotas, he took part in the Yellowstone Expedition of 1873 the Black Hills Expedition of 1874. Counted amongst Custer's intimates, he fortuitously declined a transfer from Ft. Rice to a company vacancy at Ft. Lincoln under Custer just before the regiment took to the field on the Yellowstone campaign, thus surviving the massacre. During the battle, he temporarily commanded Company G on Reno's hilltop defense, following the death of Donald McIntosh. He again accompanied the regiment in the field during operations against the Nez Perce Campaign and following promotion to Capt. on February 5, 1880, remained on frontier duty in Kansas until June 1889. After a brief stint of detached recruiting duty, Frank "Gibby" Gibson, the popular and lighthearted officer, retired on disability on December 3, 1891, following a lengthy sick-leave. He died in New York City on January 17, 1919. *Highest rank achieved:* Captain, U.S.A.

Lee P. Gillette

Born in Kingsville, Ohio on April 21, 1832, the son of Col. G.G. Gillette. Appointed 1st Lt., Company D, 1st Nebraska Infantry in June 1861 at the outbreak of the Rebellion and took part in numerous engagements while attached to the Army of the Tennessee including the capture of Fort Donelson and Shiloh, where he was wounded in the arm in action against Gen. Beauregard's Confederate forces. With promotion to Capt. in September 1862, he served as Inspector and Chief of Cavalry from December 1863 to mid-1864, during which time his regiment was re-designated 1st Nebraska Cavalry. He remained under the Dept. of Missouri in operations against Indians on scouting and escort duties in Nebraska and Colorado and commanded the post at Ft. Kearney while serving on the Officer Commissioning Board. He was mustered out of the volunteers in July 1866.

Gillette joined the Seventh Regiment as First Lieutenant, assigned to Company L, on July 28, 1866, at the formation of the regiment and was amongst the many appointees from various state regiment, who had distinguished themselves during the war. Joining the regiment at Ft. Morgan, he served briefly as acting assistant quartermaster and was promoted to Captain on June 8, 1867, Company C, posted at Ft. Lyon. However, he went on detached posting at Ft. Reynolds commanding Company L in the absence of Capt. M.V. Sheridan through the remainder of the year. Although one of the few officers with actual experience fighting against Plains Indians, he appeared of little contribution to the success of the regiment. The following year, again posted to Ft. Lyon and Ft. Dodge, including a detail on staff of Gen. Sully in the latter half of 1868, records indicate a very poor performance. Seldom sober and generally disliked, scathing judgment by Custer describing him as, "utterly worthless and unfit to hold a commission," and pressure from his fellow officers fostered his resignation from service effective December 5, 1868, while the regiment was in the field on the Winter Campaign. He died in Lincoln, Nebraska, on May 13, 1894.

Highest rank achieved: Captain, U.S.A.

Gillette. *Yale Collection of Western Americana, Beinecke Rare Books and Manuscript Collection*

Edward Settle Godfrey

Born in Kalida, Ohio on October 9, 1843. Enlisting in Co. D, 21st Ohio Infantry in April 1861, he served until the regiment was disbanded and mustered out three months later, taking part at Scary Creek and operations near the Kanawha River. Godfrey enrolled at the United States Military Academy in July 1863, graduating class of 1867 with fellow Seventh Cavalryman J.M. Johnson.

Following his graduation, he was commissioned as Second Lieutenant, on June 17, 1867: the first of the Seventh Cavalry officer corps to be appointed directly from the Academy. Assigned to Company G shortly after his arrival, Godfrey, according to his company commander, had somewhat of an auspicious start. His marginal performance appears to have fallen under scrutiny, apparently finding frontier Cavalry duty somewhat disagreeable. He joined his company on escort of the Indian Peace Commission in October 1867 and was promoted to 1st Lt. February 1, Company K, 1868. He took part in the Winter Campaign of 1868, in which he commanded a platoon of West's Company K. During reorganization of the army, Col. Sturgis, unimpressed by his performance, recommended his "review" in front of the notorious "Benzine" Boards but fortunately escaped termination, eventually maturing into a reliable officer. He accompanied the regiment on duty in the south, posted to Yorkville, South Carolina. Upon deployment to the Dakotas, he took part in the Yellowstone Expedition of 1873, including the fight near the Yellowstone River on August 11, and the Black Hills Expedition of 1874. Godfrey accompanied elements from Ft. Rice to the South, commanding posts in Louisiana and Mississippi. After returning in spring of 1876, he marched with his regiment in the Yellowstone campaign and at the Battle of Little Big Horn while commanding Company K, he participated in Reno's hilltop defense. Promoted to Captain in December, he was transferred from his temporary position in Company L, to Company D to fill the vacancy created by the death of Thomas Weir. The following year, he took part in the Nez Perce campaign where wounded in the hip, he was awarded the Congressional Medal of Honor for his actions at Snake Creek (Bear Paw Mountain), on September 30, 1877. He details a dramatic episode during the opening action: "I saw an Indian taking aim at me – I was riding an Iron gray horse and my men were mounted on black horses. This, of course, made me a conspicuous target ... His rifle cracked and down went my horse, dead. The momentum threw me forward; and I lit on my head and shoulder ... but I turned a complete somersault and lit on my feet. I had my revolver in my hand and as soon as I recovered somewhat from the daze of my stun – I tried to raise my pistol found my arm was disabled." (Jerome Green, *Nez Perce Summer*).

> Captain, 7th U.S. Cavalry. "*Led his command into action when he was severely wounded At Bear Paw Mountain, Mont., 30 September 1877.*" (Committee on Veterans' Affairs, U.S. Senate, *Medal of Honor Recipients: 1863-1973*).

Godfrey*. L. Tom Perry Special Collections, Harold B. Lee Library, Brigham Young University*

Godfrey served primarily on frontier duty and as instructor at West Point from 1879 to 1883. With a brevet promotion to Major in February 1890 for gallantry at Bear Paw Mountain, he took part in the Sioux Campaign and the battles of Wounded Knee and White Clay Creek (Drexel Mission). He was severely injured in a train accident, which afterwards kept him out of the field. On December 8, 1896, he was promoted out of the regiment to Major, 1st U.S. Cavalry, but returned by transfer back to the Seventh the following year. He joined the regiment in Cuba in January 1899, and later accepted a promotion out of the regiment to Lt. Col., 12th Cavalry in February 1901. With service in the Philippines, he joined the 9th Cavalry as Colonel and in January 1907, was promoted to Brig. General, commanded the Dept. of Missouri. A distinguished career closed with Godfrey's retirement in October of that year. An avid writer, his "Reminiscences" chronicled the early history and campaigns of the regiment. Moreover, his recollection of the Big Horn Battle, published in 1892, is considered the most accurate of all white accounts. Godfrey died in Cookstown, New Jersey on April 1, 1932.

Highest rank achieved: Brigadier General, U.S.A.

John Chowning Gresham

Born in Lancaster, Virginia on September 25, 1851. Enrolled at the United States Military Academy in July 1872, graduating class of 1876. Among his classmates were fellow Seventh Cavalrymen Ernest Garlington, Loyd McCormick, Horatio Sickel, Hugh Scott, and Albert Russell. Following graduation, he was appointed 2nd Lt., 3rd U.S. Cavalry in June 1876, posted to frontier duty in the Dakotas.

Following the losses at Big Horn, Gresham transferred to the Seventh regiment as Second Lieutenant, Company M, effective June 25, 1876, to fill the vacancy created by the death of James Sturgis. Following the Sioux Campaign, he served with his company during the Nez Perce campaign in Benteen's battalion at Canyon Creek on Sept. 13. With promotion to 1st Lt. on June 28, 1878, he served on duty at various Dakota stations protecting the construction of the Pacific railroad and as Professor of tactics at the Virginia Agricultural College. Gresham took part in the Sioux campaign of 1890, where he was both commended for gallantry and "coolness" in action at White Clay Creek (Drexel Mission) and awarded the Congressional Medal of Honor for his action at the battle of Wounded Knee on December 29, 1890:

> First Lieutenant, 7th U.S. Cavalry. *At Wounded Knee Creek, S. Dak., 29 December 1890, he voluntarily led a party into a ravine to dislodge Sioux Indians concealed therein. He was wounded during this action.* (Committee on Veterans' Affairs, U.S. Senate, *Medal of Honor Recipients: 1863-1973*).

With a promotion to Capt. on May 8, 1892, he served on duty in Arizona and Texas and again returned to teaching as Professor of Military tactics at North Carolina College. After joining his regiment in Cuba, he was promoted to Major, 6th U.S. Cavalry on September 17, 1901. Serving in the Philippines, he was commended for services during the Malvar Campaign. In August 1903, he transferred to the 15th U.S. Cavalry, serving as Inspector General both stateside and abroad. In July 1906, he transferred to the 9th U.S. Cavalry, serving in Kansas. After promotion to Lt. Col., 14th U.S. Cavalry, serving both in the Northwest and in the Philippines, Gresham retired from active service in September 1915, advanced to the rank of Colonel and died in San Diego, California on September 2, 1926. *Highest rank achieved:* Colonel, U.S.A., Ret.

Owen Hale*

Born in Troy, New York on July 23, 1843, a descendant of American Patriot Nathan Hale. He enlisted in the 7th New York Cavalry in October 1861 serving on duty in Washington,

Top right
***Gresham**. Courtesy of Glen Swanson*

Right
***Hale**. L. Tom Perry Special Collections, Harold B. Lee Library, Brigham Young University*

D.C. until the regiment was disbanded and mustered out in March 1862. The cadre of the regiment merged with the 1st New York Mounted Rifles in April 1862 and re-designated the 7th New York Cavalry, in which he joining company B. In May 1863, he was commission 2nd Lt. of his company, serving in the Dept. of Virginia and North Carolina. He took part in numerous engagements including Bottom's Bridge and Suffolk and participated in Gen. Butler's Bermuda Hundred Campaign to the Peninsula, taking part at Drewry's Bluff. After promotion to 1st Lt. in October 1864 and brevet promotion to Capt., Vols. in March 1865 for gallantry and meritorious services during the war, his regiment was officially mustered out in July 1865. The cadre was absorbed into a conglomeration with another regiment, forming the 4th New York Provisional Cavalry, where he serving on duty in Virginia until mustered out in November 1865.

Hale was appointed to the Seventh Regiment as First Lieutenant, Co. M, on July 28, 1866, at the formation of the regiment. He accompanied the escort of the Indian peace commission at Medicine Lodge Creek in October 1867. After garrison at Ft. Harker, he joined the regiment in the field and took part in the winter campaign and the Washita Battle, serving under Elliot's northeastern wing. On March 1, 1869, he was promoted to Capt., Company K, where he would remain throughout his career. He accompanied the regiment on duty in the south, posted to Unionville and Spartanburg, South Carolina. After the regiment's deployment to the Dakota, he took part in the Yellowstone Expedition of 1873 and the Black Hills Expedition of 1874. Hale's detached duty with the Recruiting Service in St. Louis prevented his joining the regiment on the Yellowstone campaign and the Battle of the Little Big Horn. Rejoining his decimated regiment and own command at the conclusion of the Sioux campaign, he took part in the Nez Perce Campaign the following year commanding a battalion under Nelson Miles. At the battle at Snake River near Bear Paw Mountain, Hale, occupying the far right line, was killed in action by a shot in his throat on September 30, 1877, during a dismounted pistol charge (See J.W. Biddle).

Highest rank achieved: Captain, U.S.A.

Louis McLane Hamilton*

Born in New York, New York on July 21, 1844. Hailing from an affluent family, he was both the grandson of Alexander Hamilton, killed in the lauded duel with Aaron Burr in 1804,

Hamilton. *Courtesy of Glen Swanson*

and Louis McLane, Secretary of both State and Treasury in the Jackson Administration. He enlisted in the 22nd New York National Guard Militia in July 1862, which was organized for three months service and again enlisted for a brief time in the 14th U.S. Infantry in September 1862. With his family's influence, he received a commission as 2nd Lt., 3rd U.S. Infantry that same month, participating at Fredericksburg and Chancellorsville, where he was brevetted 1st Lt. in May 1863 for gallantry. His reward was a transfer to the staff of General Ayres who complimented his bravery as "perfect." In action at Gettysburg, he again distinguished himself, receiving a brevet rank of Captain in July 1863. With a promotion to 1st Lt. in May 1864, he took part in the campaigns in Virginia, distinguishing himself at the battles of Petersburg and Appomattox.

Although only twenty-two years of age, his exemplary war service won him a promotion to Captain, Seventh Regiment, Company C, effective July 28, 1866, at the formation of the regiment. Transferred to Company A, he joined the regiment on their first summer campaign of 1867. Hamilton, a favorite among the regiment and Custer and a highly competent company commander, was a "gentleman" steeped in the tradition of duty and honor. During the Sully

Expedition, he attempted to pursue hostiles who had captured lagging troopers, for which he was placed in arrest, along with Lt. A.E. Smith for "disobedience of orders." Although the issue was dropped, it further added to the plummeting morale and ultimate failure of the expedition. Following Custer's return, Hamilton took part in the winter campaign in November commanding a squadron at the battle of Washita, where he was killed in action on November 27, 1868. Leading the initial charge, witnesses reported he "... slowly came to a stop, sliding off his horse-dead from a shot in the chest." Following his death, and a posthumous brevet promotion to major for gallantry during the battle, a *New York Times* obituary eloquently exclaimed, "... his ever-flowing good humor and sparkling wit, quiet vivacity, and generous modesty made him one of the most loveable companions, and a favorite among his men." Col. West added to his eulogy, "unsullied honor and spotless fame with sparking wit and trusty warm heart." Attesting to his popularity, among his pallbearers were Gen. Sheridan, Lt. Col. Custer, Col. Schuyler-Crosby, Bvt. Lt. Col. Cooke, and Bvt. Lt. Col. T.W. Custer.
Highest rank achieved: Bvt Major, U.S.A.

Hare*. Little Big Horn Battlefield National Monument*

Luther Rector Hare
Born in Noblesville, Indiana on August 24, 1851. Enrolled at the United States Military Academy in September 1870, graduating class of 1874.

Hare was commissioned in the Seventh Regiment as Second Lieutenant, Company K, on June 17, 1874. He accompanied element of the regiment on duty in Colfax, Louisiana and McComb, Mississippi in 1874, returning north to the Dakotas in time to take part in the Yellowstone campaign. On duty under Varnum and his Indian Scouts, during the Battle of the Little Big Horn, he participated in the valley fight and at Reno's hilltop defense. He was promoted to 1st Lt. of Company I, effective June 25, 1876, to fill the vacancy created by the death of James Porter (the conclusion of the campaign, he took command of Company L). The following year he took part in the Nez Perce campaign and the battle of Canyon Creek, Sept. 13, 1877. On frontier duty at Ft. Lincoln, he served as Regimental Quartermaster from August 1886 to July 1887, and took part in the Sioux campaign of 1890, where he was promoted to Captain, effective December 29, 1890, to fill the vacancy created by the death of George Wallace. Following a yearlong leave, he served in Arizona and took part in operations against hostile Indians, including the Apache Campaign of 1896. While serving with the Seventh, he accepted appointment as Lt. Col., 1st Texas Volunteer Cavalry April 28, 1898, and Colonel, Vols., June 2, 1898, serving in Cuba. Mustered out in November 1898, Hare returned to Cuba with the Seventh, during which he was appointed Col., 33rd U.S. Volunteer Infantry in July 1899. Accompanying the regiment to the Philippines, he took part at San Fabian, Mangatani Bridge, San Jacinto, and San Quenton, Luzon, where he was awarded two Silver Stars for gallantry:

> "For gallantry in action against insurgent forces at San Jacinto, Luzon, November 11, 1899"
>
> "For gallantry in action in the pursuit of superior forces of the enemy under the insurgent General Tinio in Northern Luzon, December 4-18, 1899, through a most dangerous and difficult country, through hardships and exposure, thereby forcing the enemy to liberate 22 American prisoners held by him, December 18, 1899." (*Obituary*, Annual Report of Graduates, 1931)

With promotion to Brig. Gen. of Volunteers, he commanded the first District, Dept. of Luzon until discharge from the volunteers in June 1901. On July 16, 1903, Hare was promoted out of the Seventh Regiment to Major, 12th Cavalry, retiring on disability that same month. Following active duty, he was appointed professor of tactics at the University of Texas and advanced to the rank of Lt. Colonel upon his full retirement in 1916. He died in Washington D.C., on December 22, 1929.
Highest rank achieved: Brig. Gen., U.S.V., Lt. Colonel, U.S.A., Ret.

***Harrington**. Little Big Horn Battlefield National Monument*

Henry Moore Harrington*

Born in Albion, New York on April 30, 1849. Enrolled at the United States Military Academy in July 1868, graduating class of 1872. Among his classmates were fellow Seventh Cavalrymen Charles Varnum, George Wallace, and John Wilkinson.

Harrington was commissioned in the Seventh Regiment as Second Lieutenant, Company C, on June 14, 1872, filling the vacancy created by the promotion of James Porter. Joining his regiment on reconstruction duty in the south, he was posted to Charlotte, North Carolina, and various stations in South Carolina. In 1873, after deployment to the Dakotas, Harrington took part in the Yellowstone Expedition of 1873 and the Black Hills Expedition of 1874. Posted to Ft. Rice after a leave of absence, he rejoined the regiment in March, in time to take to the field on the Yellowstone campaign of 1876. Commanding Company C, he was killed in action at Little Big Horn on June 25, 1876. Although his body was not positively identified, it is presumed he perished with his troops at the northeast side of the ridge; his actions during the fight are an intriguing mystery. The owner of a unique Sorrel horse and one of the few "chiefs" clad in buckskin, he was refutably identified as what the Indians describe as the "bravest man they had ever seen."
Highest rank achieved: 2nd Lieutenant, U.S.A.

Verling Kersey Hart

Born in Wayne County, Indiana in 1838. Hart received appointment as Capt., 19th U.S. Infantry in October 1861, remaining with this regiment throughout the war. Serving with distinction, he took part in numerous campaigns and engagements while attached to the Army of Ohio and the Army of the Cumberland. He was brevetted Maj. in September 1863 for gallantry at Chickamauga and brevetted Lt. Col. in March 1865 for gallantry and meritorious service during the war. In September 1866, Hart transferred to the 37th U.S. Infantry on the Kansas frontier, posted to Ft. Hays with elements of his future regiment, the Seventh Cavalry. During the army's reorganization, he was again transferred to the 3rd U.S. Infantry in August 1869, where he remained in Kansas.

Hart transferred to the Seventh Regiment as Captain on January 1, 1871, assigned to Company C, in time to accompany the regiment on reconstruction and occupation duty in the south, posted to various stations in South Carolina. Upon deployment to the Dakotas, he took part in the Yellowstone Expedition of 1873, commanding a battalion, including the engagement on the Yellowstone River on August 11, and the Black Hills Expedition of 1874. Effective December 2, 1875, Hart was promoted out of the regiment to Major, 5th Cavalry and posted on detached duty to the International Exhibition until the end of 1876. Following his return to the field, he took part in operations against the Sioux and Northern Cheyenne, as well as the Nez Perce, commanding a battalion under W. Merritt. Stationed at various posts on the frontier, including Ft. Laramie, where he commanded the garrison, Hart died of a heart attack on February 17, 1883 while serving with his regiment at Ft. McKenny, Wyoming.

> *"... he was entrusted with various important commands in garrison and in the field, always discharging the duties devolving upon him with signal ability. His conduct during a long and meritorious career won him the confidence and respect of his superiors. By his manly and courteous conduct he was endeared to all with whom he was associated. As a tribute of respect to his memory, the usual badge of mourning will be worn by the officers of the regiment for thirty days, and the regimental standard will be draped in mourning for the same period. By order of Lt. Col. Compton, commanding."* (Verling K. Hart Obituary summary and Memorial Sketch)

Highest rank achieved: Bvt. Lt. Col., U.S.A.

***Hart**. Johnson County Public Library, Buffalo, Wyoming*

Benjamin Hubert Hodgson*

Born in Philadelphia, Pennsylvania on June 30, 1848. Enrolled at the United States Military Academy in July 1865, with fellow classmates William Craycroft and William Robinson. Found deficient in mathematics and withheld a year, he graduated with the class of 1870 among fellow Seventh Cavalrymen Charles Larned and Winfield Edgerly.

Hodgson was commissioned in the Seventh Regiment as Second Lieutenant, Company B, on August 9, 1870, to fill the vacancy left by the resignation of Charles Rea, joining his company in the field in Colorado. Following winter garrison at Ft. Leavenworth, he accompanied his regiment on duty in the south, posted to Columbia and Spartanburg, South Carolina until March 1873. Upon his posting to the Dakotas, he took part in the Yellowstone Expedition of 1873, and the Black Hills Expedition of 1874. Stationed at Ft. Rice, he accompanied elements of the regiment posted to the Dept. of the Gulf, where he served on duty in Shreveport, Louisiana. Hodgson,

***Hodgson**. Courtesy of Glen Swanson*

a fierce fighter of diminutive physical size, rejoined the command in the Dakotas in April 1876 in time to accompany the regiment on the Yellowstone Campaign, withdrawing his resignation papers for "the thrill of one last campaign." While on temporary duty as adjutant to Maj. Reno during the Battle of the Little Big Horn, he was killed in action in the valley fight, retreating back to high ground on June 25, 1876:

> *"I saw Lt. Hodgson's horse leap into the stream and saw him struggling as though wounded. I saw the Lt. disengage himself from the stirrups and grab the stirrup strap of a passing trooper and with that aid, make his way across the stream. No sooner had he reached the bank then it became apparent he had been wounded. But he pluckily held on and the trooper seemed to be trying to help him up behind him on the saddle but without daring to stop his horse. An instant later, Hodgson seemed to be hit again for he lost his hold, fell to the ground, staggered to his feet, and sought to reach another comrade who reigned in to aid him. And just as it seemed that he was saved, I saw the second trooper throw up his arms, reel in the saddle and fall heavily to the ground. Hodgson started to make his way toward the ravine, up which the command was disappearing, he staggered forward a few steps, stumbled, struggled to his feet again only to fall once more. He apparently decided that further effort to retreat was useless as I saw him turn and face the Indians, draw his revolver, and open fire. An instant later, three or four shots rang out from my side of the river, and I saw Hodgson reel and fall and I knew it was all over."* (Letter by Theodore Goldin, reprinted in *Indian Fights and Fighters,* Brady)

Highest rank achieved: Second Lieutenant, U.S.A.

Charles Stilliman Ilsley

Born in Portland, Maine on August 4, 1836. Enlisted in Co. C, 71st New York Militia in April 1861 for a ninety-day enlistment, serving until the unit was mustered out in July. He took part at Bull Run while attached to Burnside's Brigade, McDowell's army of Northeast Virginia. In December 1861, he was commissioned Capt., 15th Maine Infantry, participating in numerous engagements under the Dept. of the Gulf including Ship Island, Fort Pickens, Battle of New Orleans, and Thibodeaux. His performance won him an assignment

Ilsley. *Massachusetts Commandery, Military Order of the Loyal Legion Collection*

to the staff of Gen. Ransom in Texas where he took part in the capture of Fort Esperanza and later several engagements during Maj. Gen. N. Banks' Red River Campaign including Sabine Crossroads, Pleasant Hill, and Cane River. Both Gen. Francis Fessenden and Gen. Emory took notice of Ilsley's administrative abilities during the Campaign, and later found himself attached to their staff. In early summer 1864, his regiment moved operations to Virginia where he participated in the Shenandoah Valley Campaign and the battle of Opequon against Gen. Jubal Early's Confederate forces. In November 1864, Ilsley was transferred to the staff of Gen. Seward, and following an appointment to Capt., 5th New York Heavy Artillery Regiment in April, he was mustered out of the volunteer service in July 1865. He was later brevetted Captain in March 1867 for gallantry and service during the war. Faithful service with numerous recommendations landed Ilsley a post-war commission in the regular army as 1st

Lt., (immediate promotion from 2nd) 16th U.S. Infantry in February 1866. By December of the following year, he was on staff assignment with Gen. Pope, who commanded the Department of the Lakes.

During the reorganization of the army, following a brief assignment to the 1st U.S. Cavalry in December 1870, he transferred to the Seventh Regiment as First Lieutenant on December 23, 1870, assigned to Company H. Ilsley, remaining on detached duty with Gen. Pope and the Dept. of the Lakes until long after the loss at Big Horn, was one of several officers in the regiment whom held only a nominal position on the roster. On July 11, 1871, he was promoted to Captain, Company E, to fill the vacancy created by the death of Edward Myers. In August 1879, he was relieved of duties under the Dept. of the Lakes and joined the regiment in the Dakotas at Ft. Meade. On June 30, 1892, he was promoted out of the regiment to Major, 9th U.S. Cavalry. He was again promoted out of his regiment to Lt. Col., 6th Cavalry, in March 1899 and retired from service a month later. He died in Salt Lake City, Utah on April 17, 1899.

Highest rank achieved: Lt. Colonel, U.S.A.

Jackson. *Courtesy of Glen Swanson*

Henry Jackson

Born in Canterbury, England on May 31, 1837. Enlisting in the British army, he received a commission as 2nd Lt. and saw service in the Crimean War. After immigrating to America in 1863, he enlisted in Co. A, 14th Illinois Cavalry in December 1863. (He also held a simultaneous nominal position as Sergt Maj., 5th U.S. Colored Cavalry; also effective from December 1863). Serving under both the XXIII Corps, Dept. of Ohio, and the Sixth Cavalry Corps, Division of the Mississippi, he took part in the Atlanta Campaign. Discharged from the Illinois Volunteers in January 1865, he accepted a commission as 2nd Lt., 5th U.S. Colored Cavalry in May 1865 under the Dept. of Ohio and the Dept. of Arkansas. With promotion to 1st Lt. in December 1865, he was mustered out of service with his regiment in March 1866.

Jackson secured an appointment to the Seventh Regiment as Second Lieutenant, company G, effective July 28, 1866 at the formation of the regiment. After promotion to 1st Lt., Company F, on July 31, 1867, posted to detached duty the following year as engineering officer and Assistant Adjutant General within the Dept. of Missouri, Jackson began a series of assignments away from the regiment in the field. In August 1871, he was again posted as engineer with the Office of the Signal Corps in Washington, D.C., in which he remained until after the Yellowstone Campaign. Returning to his emasculated regiment in September 1876, he was promoted to Captain, Company C, effective June 25, 1876 to fill the vacancy created by the death of Tom Custer. One of several officers who had been absent on other duties, he too endured Benteen's caustic referrals, being deemed somewhat undeserving of the position of company commander (see J. Bell). At the conclusion of the Sioux campaign, he took part in operations against the Cheyenne and the Nez Perce the following year on scouting duty near the Black Hills. Jackson remained primarily in the field with the regiment and took part in the Sioux Campaign of 1890, where he was wounded at the Battle of Wounded Knee on December 29, 1890. Promoted out of the regiment to Major, 3rd Cavalry on August 27, 1896, he served on duty in Cuba, taking part at the battle of Santiago. After a brief promotion to Lt. Colonel, 5th Cavalry, he returned as commanding Colonel, 3rd U.S. Cavalry in April 1901. Advanced to Brig. General, Jackson retired a month later and died from throat cancer in Leavenworth, Kansas on December 9, 1908.

Highest rank achieved: Brig. Gen., U.S.A., Ret.

John Mitchell Johnson

Born in Linn County, Indiana on November 15, 1843. Enlisted in Co. B, 20th Iowa Infantry in August 1862 until October 1863, serving in Missouri and Arkansas. Attached to the 2nd Brigade, 2nd Division, Army of the Frontier, he participated at the Siege of Vicksburg, where he was commended for gallantry. With an endorsement from Gen. U.S. Grant, he left service to attend the United States Military Academy in November 1863, graduating class of 1867.

Johnson entered the Seventh Regiment as Second Lieutenant on June 17, 1867, assigned to Company A, joining his company at camp near Ft. Hays. Along with E. S. Godfrey, Johnson was among the first to be posted to the regiment directly from West Point. Promoted to 1st Lt., Company E on November 1, 1867, he took part in field operations the following year under Maj. Elliot and Sully's Expedition as well as the winter campaign and the battle of Washita, commanding Company E (Myers was incapacitated by snow blindness). In spring of 1870, his company was detailed to Ft. Wallace under Gen. C.R. Wood as guard to the construction of the Kansas Pacific Railroad, where he served as Adjutant General. Following posting at Ft. Leavenworth, he resigned from service on December 31, 1870. Fellow cavalryman E.S. Godfrey wrote, "… Johnson's record as a soldier was without a blemish, and he left his regiment with the hearty goodwill of all his comrades." (*Obituary,* Annual Report of Graduates, 1914). Following resignation, he became prominent in local politics, serving as a member of the Missouri Legislature and county attorney for Colorado. In 1899, he returned to duty with the National Guard, serving as Aide-de-Camp to Gen. C.S. Thomas and Inspector General of the Colorado National Guard. Johnson died in Colorado Springs, Colorado on June 23, 1913.

Highest rank achieved: 1st Lieutenant, U.S.A.

Johnson. *United States Military Academy*

Myles Walter Keogh*

Born in Carlow, Ireland on March 25, 1840. A devout Catholic, he joined the cause to preserve sovereign Papal States and was recruited to fight for the Vatican, posted to Ancona, Italy. When the Papal army was defeated, his garrison surrendered and he was thrown in jail. Following his repatriation, he was commissioned in the St. Patrick Battalion, Papal Guards in November 1860 known as the "Company of St. Patrick." In February 1862, he was recruited by American agents to come to America, receiving a commission as Capt., Volunteers, and appointed to the staff of fellow Irish-born Brig. Gen. J. Shields in April of that year. Transferred in July to the staff of Brig. Gen. Buford, he participated in the Maryland Campaign, taking part at South Mountain and Antietam, and the Fredericksburg, Chancellorsville, Gettysburg, and Mine Run campaigns, seeing action at numerous battles including Brandy Station, Gettysburg, and Mine Run. Following Buford's death, he transferred to the staff of Gen. Stoneman, where he would remain for the duration of the war. After promotion to Major, Volunteers in April 1864, he was captured with Stoneman's command near Macon, Georgia in July and released several months later. He took part in operations in Virginia and North Carolina and distinguished himself both at Saltsville, Virginia and Salisbury; personally leading the 11th Kentucky Cavalry in the capture of hundreds of Confederate prisoners. Brevetted Lt. Col. Vols. in March 1865, he was mustered out of the Volunteers in September 1865. Later in March 1867, he was brevetted Major for gallantry at Gettysburg and Lt. Col. for gallantry at Dallas, Georgia.

Keogh's distinguished and meritorious service in over thirty engagements won him a post-war appointment, assigned to the 4th U.S. Cavalry as 2nd Lt.. in May 1866. Recommendations on his behalf secured a Captaincy with

Company I, Seventh Cavalry, effective July 28, 1866 at the formation of the regiment. Despite legendary status within the history of the Seventh, he played little part in field operations with the regiment and service under Custer. After commanding the garrison at Ft. Wallace throughout 1867, Bvt. Gen. Sully recognized his talents and assigned him to his staff. Serving as Acting Inspector General during Sully's forgettable expedition, he remained on detached duty and did not take part in the regiment's Winter Campaign of 1868. He rejoined his command for scouting duty in 1870 and accompanied the regiment on duty in the south, posted to various stations in Kentucky. Following deployment to the Dakotas, he accompanied elements of the regiment on escort duty with the International Boundary Commission from 1873 to early 1874. After a yearlong leave of absence he again joined the regiment as it prepared for the upcoming campaign. Keogh, the quintessential "hard charging" and "hard drinking" cavalryman was killed in action with his company at Little Big Horn on June 25, 1876. Regarding his peculiarities, Custer gave him tacit respect in a letter written to his wife in 1871, confiding, "... I do think him rather absurd, but would rather have him stationed near us than many others." (Merrington, *The Custer Story*,) His body was found on the northeast side of Battle Ridge: evidence of his obvious stubborn defenses were testimony to his value as a soldier.
Highest rank achieved: Brevet Lt. Colonel, Vols., Bvt. Maj., U.S.A.

Keogh. *Villa Louis Collection, Wisconsin State Historical Society*

Charles William Larned

Born in New York City on March 9, 1850, the son of Paymaster William Larned. Enrolled at the United States Military Academy in July 1866, at the age of 16, graduating class of 1870. Among his classmates were fellow Seventh Cavalrymen Benjamin Hodgson and Winfield Edgerly. Following graduation, he was appointed 2nd Lt., 3rd U.S. Cavalry in June 1870.

While awaiting orders, Larned was transferred to the Seventh Regiment as Second Lieutenant, Company F, on October 10, 1870, joining the regiment just before winter garrison at Ft. Leavenworth. In spring, he accompanied his regiment on duty in the south, posted to Louisville, Kentucky. Deployed with his regiment to the Dakotas, he took part in Stanley's Yellowstone Expedition of 1873, where he participated in the fight against the Indians near the Yellowstone River on August 11. In December 1873, following a leave of absence, Larned went on detached duty as Aide-de-Camp for President Grant and the War Department until July 1874. Following duty in Washington, D.C., he was appointed Assistant Professor of Drawing at the United States Military Academy and from those tranquil surroundings read about the annihilation of his very own company a year later. Following the losses at Big Horn, a promotion to 1st Lt., Company F, effective June 25, 1876, filled the vacancy created by the promotion of Henry Jackson. Larned remained at the Academy and with an appointment to full professor of drawing; he resigned from the regiment and active service in September 1876. After years of faithful service, he was advanced to acting Colonel upon his retirement in June 1902 and died in New York City on June 19, 1911.
Highest rank achieved: Colonel, U.S.A., Ret.

***Larned**. Courtesy of Glen Swanson*

***Law**. Yale Collection of Western Americana, Beinecke Rare Books and Manuscript Collection*

Edward Law

Born in Philadelphia, Pennsylvania on November 30, 1847 to an affluent local family. Graduated in Law from Harvard and the University of Pennsylvania.

Law was commissioned in the Seventh Regiment as Second Lieutenant, assigned to Company K, on August 15, 1867, joining his company at Ft. Leavenworth, as the regiment went into winter garrison. He took part in field operations with the regiment the following summer as well as the winter campaign and battle of Washita, under West's squadron (center wing). With promotion to 1st Lt., assigned to Company G, on March 11, 1869, he filled the vacancy created by James Bell. Law applied for leave of absence in late 1869, during which time he resigned from service on March 22, 1870 to pursue a career in Law.

After military service, he was admitted to the bar and found work as an attorney. With the prominence of his family and host of influential acquaintances, he sought political office. In 1880, he won election for a seat in the Lower House of Legislation as Republican and one of the youngest members. Tragically, a year later he died on October 5, 1881 when his small boat capsized on the Schuylkill River in Philadelphia.

Highest rank achieved: 1st Lieutenant, U.S.A.

Rynd Edward Lawder

Born near Dayton, Ohio on June 30, 1837. Enlisted in Co. B, 11th Ohio Infantry in April 1861 and mustered out in August after a three-month enlistment. In December 1862, he was commissioned 1st Lt., 2nd Ohio Cavalry and took part in numerous engagements in Kentucky and east Tennessee, serving with fellow Seventh Cavalryman Albert Barnitz. In January 1864, Lawder was assigned Aide-de-Camp to Brig. Gen. Landers, after which he participated in numerous campaigns including Grant's Overland Campaign, Richmond-Petersburg, and Sheridan's Valley Campaign. Attached to the 3rd Brigade, 3rd Division, Army of the Shenandoah, he took part in numerous engagements including Wilderness, Winchester, Petersburg, Fisher's Hill, and Cedar Creek. Following promotion to Capt. in December 1864, he participated in the Appomattox Campaign, including action at Five Forks, Sayler's Creek, and Appomattox. In June 1865, his regiment was posted to Springfield, Missouri, where he served as Acting Assistant Inspector General, Division of Missouri on staff of Brig. Gen. J.W. Sprague. Following a promotion to Major in September 1865, he was mustered out later that month.

Lawder's conspicuous service record and numerous benefactors won him an appointment to the Seventh Regiment as Second Lieutenant, effective July 28, 1866, at the formation of the regiment. However, he resigned to civilian life effective April 4, 1867 before he could join his regiment on the frontier. Lawder died in Mexico, Missouri October 16, 1890.
Highest rank achieved: Major, Vols.

James Trotter Leavy
Born in Lexington, Kentucky on February 4, 1840. Enlisted in Co. H, 3rd Kentucky Cavalry in October 1861. With a commission as 2nd Lt. in April 1862, he took part in numerous actions attached to a Cavalry Brigade under the Army of Ohio in Tennessee, Mississippi and Kentucky, including Shiloh, serving on staff of Gen. P.A. Hackleman (killed at the battle of Corinth), Stones River, and the Siege of Knoxville. He took part in the numerous engagements during the Atlanta campaign, and saw action at Dalton and the surrender of Ft. Morgan. Attached to the 1st Brigade, Leavy participated in several engagements during the Savanna campaign, before being discharged in December 1864. In March 1867, he was brevetted 1st Lt. for gallantry at Shiloh, and Captain for gallantry at Savanna.

Leavy won appointment to the Seventh Regiment as Second Lieutenant, Company M, on January 22, 1867, joining the regiment in at Fort Hays. Promoted to 1st Lt., Company G on July 31, 1867, he took part summer operations with the regiment. Leavy was not a particularly stable or reliable individual. His fellow officers were subjected to his bouts of drunkenness and insubordination and he would simply "disappear from time to time." Regimental returns indicate he deserted while stationed near Ft. Hays in May 1868 and was subsequently dropped from the roster with arrest warrant to follow, as fellow officer Albert Barnitz mentions, he was several thousand dollars in debt. He was, however, reinstated to the roster when it became known he had been sick in Washington. Ordered before an examining board, he was judged to be insane and placed in an asylum, where he was relegated to the retired list, effective July 31, 1868. Released from the hospital in October 1868, records show his full retirement in July 1869.

In 1872, Leavy enlisted again in the 4th U.S. Artillery Regiment under the name of Robert Carey. After service in the Modoc war, he was discharged in 1874. Leavy died of heart failure in Washington, D.C. on July 8, 1893.
Highest rank achieved: Brevet Captain, U.S.A.

Oliver Watson Longan
Born in Lycoming County, Pennsylvania on March 29, 1840. Enlisted in the 13th Pennsylvania Cavalry in August 1862, serving under fellow Seventh Cavalryman J.M. Bell. Attached to the 1st Brigade, 2nd Division, VIII Corps, he was engaged in scouting operations around Leesburg and the Shenandoah and took part at the battle of Winchester. In late June 1863, while operating near Richmond, he was captured and sent to Libby Prison for a short time. Following his repatriation and discharge from the Volunteers in March 1864, he served as a government clerk of third-class in the Office of the Attorney General in Washington, D.C.

Through influential connections intervening on his behalf, Longan secured an appointment in the Seventh Regiment as Second Lieutenant, Company H on November 20, 1867. Longan held only a nominal position in the regiment as one of several officers to merely occupy the "paper" vacancies. He applied for a continuation of service east, assigned as detached duty and did not join the regiment in the field. In early 1869, he applied for leave to tender affairs at home and remained there until offering resignation from service on June 30, 1869. He remained with the Adjutant Generals office as a civilian clerk, working until medical retirement in 1890. Longan died in Washington, D.C. on May 18, 1892.
Highest rank achieved: 2nd Lieutenant, U.S.A.

Thomas Jefferson March
Born in Lawrenceville, Pennsylvania on February 16, 1844. Enrolled at the United States Military Academy in July 1864, graduating class of 1868.

March was commissioned Second Lieutenant, Seventh Regiment, on June 15, 1868, the third officer assigned directly from West Point. Assigned to Company G, he joined the regiment in October at camp near Ft. Dodge as they prepared for the winter campaign. Under Elliot's northeast wing he was wounded in the hand during the battle of Washita. The following year, while commanding Company G on scouting duty in July 1869 (in the absence of Barnitz), he took part in a brief "skirmish" with Indians near the Saline River. Following

the conclusion of offensive operations in 1869, he went on detached duty serving on the Schofield tactics board until November 1870. Returning to duty at Ft. Lyon, Colorado, he applied for leave in March 1871 during preparations for deployment to the south, submitting his resignation effective on March 10, 1872. March died in Pottstown, Pennsylvania on February 8, 1909.
Highest rank achieved: 2nd Lieutenant, U.S.A.

***March**. United States Military Academy*

Edward Gustave Mathey
Born in Besancon, France on October 27, 1837. As a young man, Mathey studied for the Priesthood, but came to America in 1845. After gaining his citizenship in 1859, he enlisted in Co. C, 17th Indiana Infantry at the outbreak of war. Commissioned 2nd Lt., May 1862, he served in operations in West Virginia and Kentucky until August of that year. In September 1862, following his resignation from the 17th infantry, he was appointed 2nd Lt., 81st Indiana Infantry at the formation of the regiment. While attached to the 3rd Brigade, 1st Division, XIV Army Corps, he took part in operations in Tennessee, including the battle at Stone's River. Following promotion to 1st Lt. in March 1863, he took part in numerous campaigns and engagements including Liberty Gap and Chickamauga. In November 1863, he was promoted to Captain and participated in the Atlanta Campaign, including the engagements at Resaca, Kenawsaw Mountain, Atlanta, Jonesboro and Tunnel Hill. After promotion to Major in September 1864, he commanded his regiment in the campaign battles of Franklin and Nashville, until being mustered out in June 1865.

Mathey joined the Seventh Regiment as Second Lieutenant, Company H, on September 24, 1867. Joining the regiment at Camp Alfred Gibbs, he took part in scouting with the regiment until transferred to Company A. He took part in the Winter Campaign of 1868 and at the Battle of Washita, while incapacitated from "snow blindness," he exchanged places with Capt. Hamilton's pack-train detail, allowing Hamilton to lead his company into battle, during which he was killed. Mathey, although by most accounts considered competent, never rose above mediocrity. Sharing the misfortune of several other officers, he was subjected to Sturgis' review and subsequent attempt to have him cashiered. Spared by the intervention of Custer, who obviously saw his better qualities, he escaped the dubious "Benzine" boards. Following promotion to 1st Lt., Company B, May 10, 1870, he accompanied his regiment on duty in the south, posted to Unionville and Spartanburg,

***Mathey**. Yale Collection of Western Americana, Beinecke Rare Books and Manuscript Collection*

South Carolina. Upon deployment to the Dakota, he took part in Stanley's expedition in 1873, the Black Hills Campaign of 1874, and the 1876 Yellowstone Campaign and the Battle of Little Big Horn, where he participated in Reno's hilltop defense commanding the pack train. At the conclusion of the Sioux campaign temporarily commanding Company C, he took part in the Nez Perce campaign the following year, serving temporarily under Capt. McDougal's Company B. Effective September 30, 1877, he was promoted to Captain, Company K, filling the vacancy created by the death of Owen Hale. Mathey remained in the field with the regiment, participating in various scouting and escort duties including the campaign against the Northern Cheyenne in 1878 and the Sioux campaign of 1890. One of the few who served with the regiment through the conclusion of the Plains Indian wars, he retired from active service on disability with the rank of Major on December 11, 1896. Following a brief stint as Professor of Military Science at Baylor University from 1901 to 1903, he retired with the rank of Colonel. Mathey died in Denver, Colorado on July 17, 1915.
Highest rank achieved: Colonel, U.S.A., Ret.

McCormick. *Villa Louis Collection, Wisconsin State Historical Society*

Loyd Stone McCormick
Born in Beverly, Ohio on November 18, 1854. Enrolled at the United States Military Academy in September 1872, graduating class of 1876. Among his classmates were fellow Seventh Cavalrymen Ernest Garlington, John Gresham, Hugh Scott, Horatio Sickel, and Albert Russell. Following graduation, he was commissioned Second Lieutenant, 10th Cavalry in early June, posting to Ft. Lincoln.

McCormick, one of many officers to enter the Seventh Regiment as a result of the Big Horn Battle, transferred to the regiment, Company L, effective June 25, 1876, filling the vacancy created by the resignation of Charles Braden. At the conclusion of the Sioux campaign, he applied for sick leave in May 1877 suffering from pneumonia and did not accompany the regiment against Chief Joseph in the Nez Perce Campaign. With promotion to 1st Lt., June 30, 1878, Company D and transfer to Company C in June 1879, he took part in field operations in the Dakotas, Nebraska, Missouri, and Kansas. From September 1887 to September 1891, he served as regimental adjutant to Col. Forsyth and took part in the Sioux campaign of 1890 and the battle of Wounded Knee and White Clay Creek (Drexel Mission). Following promotion to Capt. on July 17, 1895 and duty in Kansas and Arizona, McCormick applied for duty with the Fifth Army Corps and following assignment to the 1st U.S. Volunteers "Rough Riders," served in Cuba, where he took part at the battles of Las Guasimas, San Juan, Ridge, and Santiago and was twice awarded the Silver Star:

> "For gallantry in action against Spanish Forces at Las Guasimas, June 24, 1898."
>
> "For gallantry in action against Spanish Forces at Santiago, Cuba, July 1, 1898." (*Obituary,* Annual Report of Graduates, 1929)

Following detached duty with the Subsistence Department in August 1902, he was promoted to Major on April 15, 1903, serving with the Seventh Cavalry in the Philippines. In 1907, he went on detached duty, detailed as Inspector General serving on various staff postings stateside. With promotions to Lt. Col. in March 3, 1911 and Colonel on September 25, 1911, he returned to the Philippines, serving on Staff in Manila. Upon his return stateside, he was transferred out of the regiment to the 10th Cavalry in August 1914, resigning the following month. "Old Mike" McCormick died at Ft. Leavenworth, Kansas on October 14, 1928.
Highest rank achieved: Col., U.S.A.

Thomas Mower McDougal

Born at Ft. Crawford (Prairie Du Chien), Wisconsin on May 21, 1845, the son of Brig. General Charles McDougal, Medical Corps. After attending a military prep-academy in New York, he volunteered as Aide-de-Camp to Gen. Hawkins in October 1863, where he participated in operations against Vicksburg, including Millikin's Bend, Goodrich Landing, and Lakeville, Mississippi, where he was wounded. In February 1864, he was appointed 2nd Lt., 10th Louisiana Colored Vol., under Hawkins' Negro division. In March, the regiment was re-designated the 48th U.S. Colored Regiment, where he took part in operations in Mississippi and Alabama until mustered out in June 1865. Appointed Capt., 5th U.S. Volunteer Infantry (ex-confederates) in June 1865, he was assigned to the District of the Upper Arkansas, serving only a short time until mustered out at Ft. Leavenworth in August 1865. McDougal secured a post-war commission in the regular army in May 1866 as 2nd Lt., 14th U.S. Infantry, posted near Ft. Laramie. Following a promotion to 1st Lt. in November 1866 as his regiment was re-designated the 32nd U.S. Infantry, and a brevet promotion to Capt. for faithful and meritorious service during the war, he took part in engagements with Indians at Aravipa Canyon, Tonto Point, Point of Mountain, and Rock Springs.

During the restructuring of the army in 1869, his regiment was consolidated with the 21st U.S. Infantry, leaving him unassigned. On December 30, 1870, he was reassigned to the Seventh Regiment as First Lieutenant, Company E, following the vacancy created by the resignation of J.M. Johnson. He joined the regiment while on duty in the south, posted to Spartanburg, South Carolina. Upon the regiment's deployment to the Dakotas, he took part in the Black Hills expedition of 1874. In 1875, he again was posted to the south with elements of the regiment on duty in the Gulf. Following a promotion to Capt., Company B, on December 15, 1875, he rejoined the regiment in the Dakotas in time for the Yellowstone Campaign, commanding the escort company to the pack-train during the battle of Little Big Horn and taking part in Reno's Hilltop defense. The next year, he joined the regiment in the field during the Nez Perce campaign under Major Lazelle on scouting duty. In May 1888, he went on sick leave from effects of Malaria, during which he retired on disability, advanced to Major on July 22, 1890. McDougal died in Brandon, Vermont on July 3, 1909.

Highest rank achieved: Major, U.S.A., Ret.

McDougal. *L. Tom Perry Special Collections, Harold B. Lee Library, Brigham Young University*

Donald McIntosh*

Born in Quebec, Canada on September 4, 1838. Of Scotch-Indian descent, his mother was a direct descendant of Six Nations Chief Red Jacket. Working as a civilian clerk with the quartermaster department since 1856, the outbreak of war landed him a position as clerk for Col.(*Gen.) Daniel Rucker, Quartermaster Dept.

With support from influential individuals, McIntosh procured a commission in the army, appointed Second Lieutenant, Seventh Regiment on August 17, 1867. Assigned to Company M, he joined the regiment at Ft. Harker in

McIntosh. *Little Big Horn Battlefield National Monument*

Merrill. *United States Military History Institute*

October. During field operations, he sustained an injury which kept him from participating in the winter campaign. Although considered both courageous and one of the most "beloved" officers, his efficiency report from Col. Sturgis was less complimentary, narrowly avoiding dismissal from the infamous review board by Custer's intervention. It read, "... if he were enlisted, he would pass as a malingerer." (Swanson, *Custer: His Life and Times*) Following a promotion to 1st Lt., Company G, on March 22, 1870, he accompanied the regiment on duty in the south, posted to various stations in South Carolina. Upon the regiment's deployment to the Dakotas, he took part in the Yellowstone expedition of 1873 and Black Hills expedition of 1874. McIntosh again was posted south to the Gulf with elements of his regiment stationed at Ft. Rice. Upon his return to the Dakotas, he accompanied the regiment on the Yellowstone campaign, which would be his last. On June 25, 1876, at Little Big Horn, "Tosh" McIntosh was killed in action while retreating back to Reno Hill. Details of his demise are somewhat cloudy. Eyewitnesses claim that as he hastily emerged from the thickets, he was either shot or thrown from his horse from a loose lariat.

Highest rank achieved: 1st Lieutenant, U.S.A.

Lewis Merrill

Born in New Berlin, Union County, Pennsylvania on October 28, 1834. Enrolled at the United States Military Academy with fellow Seventh Cavalryman Marcus Reno in July 1851, graduating class of 1855. Few vacancies in the army at that time allowed him only a brevet rank of 2nd Lt., 1st Dragoons in July 1855. Following a full commission as 2nd Lt. in the 2nd Dragoons in December 1855, he served on frontier duty in Kansas and Missouri, taking part in the Utah Expedition of 1858, as well as the Comanche and Kiowa campaigns. Promoted to 1st Lt. on April 1861, he took part in anti-guerilla operations in Missouri. Merrill was instrumental in the organization of the 2nd Missouri Cavalry and in August 1861, he was appointed its Colonel. the regiment became known as

"Merrill's Horse". In October 1861, the 2nd Dragoons were redesignated 2nd U.S. Cavalry and following promotion to Captain and brevet promotion to Major in September 1862, he took part in numerous campaigns and engagements including the Arkansas Campaign and the capture of Little Rock where he was brevetted Lt. Col. in September 1863 for gallantry. By summer 1864, commanding the Western Division of Cavalry Bureau, Merrill and his provisional brigade of Cavalry took part in the invasion of Missouri and participated in anti-guerilla operations in Georgia and Alabama. With brevet promotion to Brig. Gen., Vols. for gallantry and meritorious service during the war in March 1865, he was mustered out of the Volunteers in December 1865.

After the end of hostilities, Merrill served as Acting Assistant Inspector General of Dept. of the Platte until his promotion to Major, Seventh Regiment on November 11, 1868, filling the vacancy created by the death of Joel Elliot. Merrill, outspoken against Custer, soon established himself as an antagonist. In March 1871, he accompanied the regiment on duty in the south where was he praised for his services against Ku Klux Klan operations in South Carolina. Rejoining the regiment at Ft. Rice, Dakota Territory in September 1874 after a year-long sick leave, he commanded elements of the regiment south to the Dept. of the Gulf; commanding the District of Red River in Shreveport, Louisiana until February 1876. In March 1876, as the regiment prepared for the coming offensive, Merrill was assigned Chief of Military Staff to President Grant in Philadelphia and did not rejoin his command until November after the Battle of Little Big Horn. The following year, he took part in the Nez Perce campaign, where he was scrutinized and subjected to off-handed criticism for his actions during the campaign: Commanding a battalion during the battle at Canyon Creek, the lack of success of his advance was said to allow the delay necessary for Chief Joseph's band to "slip away." Years later, however, (1890) he did receive a brevet promotion to Brig Gen., U.S.A. for gallantry during that battle. Merrill remained on frontier duty in the Dakotas, commanding troops at various stations and on protection detail to the Northern Pacific Railroad until retirement from active service on May 21, 1886. In early 1891, he was appointed Lt. Col., 9th U.S. Cavalry, with reinstatement to active service, effective January 9, 1886, but retired just a few months later. Merrill died in Philadelphia on February 27, 1896.

Highest rank achieved: Brevet Brigadier General, U.S.A.

Morrow*. Brady-Handy Collection, Library of Congress*

Albert Payson Morrow

Born in Payson (Hatboro), Illinois on March 10, 1842. He enlisted in the 17th Pennsylvania Infantry in April 1861, posted in Virginia, for a ninety-day enlistment and was mustered out in August of that year. He enlisted again in the 6th Pennsylvania Cavalry in September posting near Washington D.C., and was commissioned 2nd Lt. in March 1862. During the Peninsula Campaign, engaging J. E. B. Stuart's Confederate forces, he was wounded in fierce close-quarters fighting near Bethesda Church on June 13, resulting in his capture. Following repatriation from Libby Prison in August and a promotion to 1st Lt. in November 1862, he participated in the Maryland campaign attached to a Reserve Brigade, Cavalry Corps, Army of the Potomac. Taking part at the battle of Chancellorsville, he was again captured and soon after exchanged. He returned to his command in the field and was captured for a third time by Col. Mosby's men in May and again sent to Libby Prison. Following parole in early June, he rejoined his regiment during the Gettysburg campaign and took part at Brandy Station and Gettysburg, and afterwards was again wounded near Greencastle, Pennsylvania. His actions did not go unnoticed by Gen. Buford, who assigned him as Aide on his staff, serving alongside fellow Seventh Cavalryman Myles Keogh. Following Buford's death, Morrow was promoted to Captain in February 1864, taking part in numerous campaigns including Grant's Overland campaign and Sheridan's Valley campaign. Following promotions to Maj., Vols. in February and Lt. Col., Vols. and brevet Colonel in March 1865 for "conspicuous gallantry in action," he took part in the Appomattox campaign including the battle at Dinwiddie Courthouse (Gravelly Run), where he was severely wounded. Morrow was mustered out of the volunteer service in August 1865.

His extraordinary courage and exceptional service record personified the ideal candidate for post-war appointment winning a vacancy in the Seventh Regiment as Captain, Company E, effective July 28, 1866. Joining his company at Ft. Dodge in late February, Morrow soon afterwards accepted promotion out of the regiment, thus depriving the Seventh Cavalry of what would have no doubt been a promising future. Appointed Major, 9th U.S. Colored Cavalry, known as the famed "Buffalo Soldiers" on March 6, 1867, Morrow served on frontier duty, taking part in numerous campaigns and engagements including the Sioux Campaign of 1876, and the Ute Campaign of 1878. In 1882, he was promoted to Lt. Colonel, 6th U.S. Cavalry and assigned detached duty to the staff of Gen. Sherman, Commander of the Army. In 1883, he rejoined his regiment in Arizona, serving until his promotion to Colonel, 3rd U.S. Cavalry in February 1891. Morrow retired from service in August 1892 and died on January 20, 1911. *Highest rank achieved:* Colonel, U.S.A.

***Moylan**. Courtesy of Glen Swanson*

Myles Moylan

Born in Amesbury, Massachusetts on December 17,1838. Enlisting in the 2nd Dragoons in June 1857, serving under fellow Cavalryman Lewis Merrill, he participated in the Utah expedition, including actions at Blackwater Springs. In August 1861, as his regiment was re-designated 2nd U.S. Cavalry, he took part in Gen. Lyon's Missouri campaign and actions at Wilson's Creek. The following year he took part in engagements near the Cumberland and Tennessee Rivers, including Ft. Henry, Ft. Donalson, and Shiloh. After taking part in operations and engagements near Corinth, he was commissioned 2nd Lt., 5th U.S. Cavalry in February 1863 and took part in the Gettysburg campaign and the engagements at Beverly Ford, Aldie, Middleburg, Snicker's Gap, Ashby's Gap, and Gettysburg. In October 1863, he was arrested for traveling without a pass and failure to appear on duty, resulting in his dismissal from service. In December of that year, he enlisted again in the 4th Massachusetts Cavalry under an assumed name and received a commission as 1st Lt. in January 1864, while his unit was attached to the Cavalry Division, Dept. of the Gulf and Army of Shenandoah. Following a promotion to Captain in December 1864 and a brevet promotion to Major, Vols. in April 1865 for gallantry during the Virginia campaigns, he was mustered out in November 1865.

After enlisting in the Mounted Service after the end of the war, Moylan entered the Seventh Regiment as a non-commissioned officer on August 20, 1866; the only one of the officer corps to do so. The persistence of Lt. Col. Custer on his behalf eventually yielded a commission as First Lieutenant in December, effective July 28, 1866 at the formation of the regiment. Almost immediately he was appointed regimental adjutant (replacing T.W. Custer from February 1867), occupying that position through the majority of duty on the southern plains, including the winter campaign and the battle of the Washita. Relieved of duty as adjutant in December 1870, he accompanied the regiment on duty in the south, posted to Bagdad, Kentucky with his Company I. On March 1, 1872, he was promoted to Captain, Company A, to fill the vacancy created by the resignation of Samuel Robbins. Upon deployment to the Dakotas, he took part in the Yellowstone expedition of 1873, including the engagements on August 4 and August 11, and the Black Hills expedition of 1874. Commanding Company A during the Yellowstone campaign of 1876 and the Battle of Little Big Horn, he took part in the fight in the valley under Maj. Reno, and at the hilltop defense. Following the conclusion of the Sioux campaign, he took part in the Nez Perce campaign of 1877 under Gen. Miles and the battle of Snake Creek on September 30, 1877, where he was both wounded in the thigh and awarded the Congressional Medal of Honor for actions:

> 7th U.S. Cavalry. At Bear Paw Mountain, Mont., 30 September 1877. *"Gallantly led his command in action against Nez Perce Indians until he was severely wounded."*(Committee on Veterans' Affairs, U.S. Senate, *Medal of Honor Recipients: 1863-1973*).

Moylan remained on frontier duty throughout his career with the regiment, serving at various posts in both Dakota Territory and Montana Territory and participating in several engagements including the fight against the Crow Indians in 1887 and the Sioux campaign and Battle of Wounded Knee in 1890. Following a brevet promotion in February 1890 for gallantry and service at Snake Creek (Bear Paw Mountain), he was promoted out of the regiment to Major 10th U.S. Cavalry on April 8, 1892. Moylan retired from service in April 1893 and died of cancer in San Diego, California on December 11, 1909.

Highest rank achieved: Major, U.S.A.

Edward Myers

Born in Prussia (Eastern Germany) in 1830. After immigrating to the United States in 1857, he enlisted in Co. H, 1st Dragoons in August of that year, posted to the northwest frontier. He took part in the Steptoe and Wright Expeditions against hostile Indians in the northwest and the Sturgis and Kearney Expeditions into New Mexico. With the regiment re-designated 1st U.S. Cavalry in 1861, he was commissioned 2nd Lt. in July 1862 and took part in the Peninsula campaign and the campaigns in Virginia the following year, including Gettysburg where he was slightly wounded. Promoted to 1st Lt. in Sept. 1863, Myers was appointed Aide-de-Camp to General W. Merritt in the Reserve Cavalry Brigade under the command of Gen. Sheridan, taking part in numerous engagements during Grant's Overland campaign including Todd's tavern, where he was brevetted Capt. for gallantry. Following the Shenandoah and Appomattox campaign and a brevet promotion to Maj. for gallantry at Five Forks and Lt. Col. for wartime service, he took part at Petersburg and afterwards joined Gen. Merritt in Texas on occupation duty until January 1866. After duty in New Orleans and Carlisle, Pennsylvania, he accompanied elements of his regiment to Dakota and Idaho Territory, taking part in both operations of Gen. Steele and Gen. Marshall against hostile Indians as well as operations in Nevada and Oregon including Gen. Crook's expedition against the Paiute Indians.

Myers was promoted to the newly formed Seventh Regiment as Captain, Company E, effective July 28, 1866 at the formation of the regiment, joining the regiment in early 1867. Although a competent and capable officer, he was often troublesome and difficult to get along with. Sometimes insufferable to subordinates, he was referred to as the "crotchety Prussian" who on numerous occasions found himself under arrest for drunkenness. In August 1867, he was placed under arrest for disobedience of orders from acting regimental commander Maj. Elliott, in which he refused to submit and then broke arrest. Following further similar infractions, he was court marshaled in December during winter garrison at Ft. Leavenworth and sentence to be cashiered. Fortunately for him, the Judge Advocate General overturned the sentence and to the astonishment of his fellow officers, he was returned to duty in July 1868. He took part in the Winter Campaign where he commanded the far-western wing during the Battle of Washita. In March 1871, Myers accompanied the regiment on occupation and reconstruction duty in the south, stationed in South Carolina. Already slightly feeble and weakened from a lengthy affliction of Phthisis Pulmonalis, he died from dysentery in Spartanburg on July 11, 1871.

Highest rank achieved: Brevet Lt. Colonel, U.S.A.

Andrew Humes Nave

Born in Knoxville, Tennessee on February 23, 1846. Enrolled at the United States Military Academy in July 1867, graduating class of 1871.

Commissioned Second Lieutenant, Seventh Regiment on August 15, 1871, and assigned Company I, he filled a long-standing vacancy in the company. Following graduation leave in Knoxville, he joined the company in Shelbyville, remained there until his brief assignment to Company D, stationed in Opelika, Alabama. In April 1873, upon the regiment's deployment to the Dakotas, he accompanied elements of the regiment on escort duty with the Northern Boundary Survey Commission from August to September 1873 and again in 1874. While stationed at Ft. Totten, he sustained an injury to his arm shortly after the Black Hills expedition. He applied for leave of absence in July 1874, during which time he taught at East Tennessee University. He remained there until after the Battle of Little Big Horn, thus missing the annihilation of his company. Following those losses, Nave was promoted to 1st Lt., Company A, effective June 25, 1876, to fill the vacancy created by the death of A.E. Smith. Remaining at Ft. Lincoln on detached duty as Ordnance officer and post-adjutant during the Nez Perce campaign, he returned to field duty at various stations including Ft. Rice, Ft. Lincoln, and Ft. Meade until September 1880. Plagued by deteriorating health, he applied for sick leave, during which time he was promoted to Capt. January 16, 1884. He eventually retired from active service on disability on September 23, 1885. Following his service, he returned to teaching at the University of Tennessee as Professor of Military Tactics and died at home in Knoxville on December 7, 1924.

Highest rank achieved: Captain, U.S.A.

Nave. *Courtesy of Glen Swanson*

William John (Jones) Nicholson

Born in Washington, D.C. on January 16, 1856, the son of Capt. Somerville Nicholson, United States Navy. One of several officers to be appointed to the regiment following the wake of Little Bighorn, he entered the Seventh Regiment as Second Lieutenant assigned to Company B on August 15, 1876 to fill the vacancy created by the promotion of W. Robinson. At the conclusion of the Sioux campaign, he transferred to Company G and took part in the Nez Perce campaign, serving in Benteen's battalion at Canyon Creek, Sept. 13, 1877. With promotion to 1st Lt. on January 16, 1884, he remained on the frontier throughout the Indian wars stationed at various posts in Dakota Territory and Kansas and took part in the Sioux uprising and operations at Pine Ridge in 1890. With promotion again to Captain on August 27, 1896, he took part in operations against renegade Apache Indians in

Nicholson. *Villa Louis Collection, Wisconsin State Historical Society*

Arizona Territory. In July 1898, he was appointed Major and Chief Ordnance officer, U.S. Volunteers during the Spanish War. After his discharge from the volunteers the following year, he accompanied his regiment to Cuba in 1899. In April 1901, Nicholson was transferred to the 12th U.S. Cavalry at the organization of the regiment serving in Texas and afterwards, accompanying the regiment to the Philippines. With promotion to Major in January 1905, he transferred back to the 7th Cavalry, serving in Manila until returning stateside in 1907. Promoted to Lt. Col. in January 1912 and to Colonel of Cavalry in September of that year, he commanded the regiment stateside and during their return to the Philippines. With America's involvement in the First World War, Nicholson was appointed Brig. General, commanding the 157th Infantry Brigade, American Expeditionary Forces. In an extraordinary set of circumstances, Nicholson, after a successful forty-year career that spanned operations against Sitting Bull and Poncho Villa, was awarded the Distinguished Service Cross for extraordinary heroism in action near the Bois-de-Beuge, Montfaucon, France, September 29, 1918.

> *157th Infantry Brigade, 79th Division, A.E.F. General Orders No. No. 15, W.D., 1923*
> *General Nicholson established and maintained his brigade post of command on an exposed elevation near the Bois-de-Beuge, in order that he might effectively direct the attack of his brigade upon the Madeleine Farm and its surrounding woods. Realizing the important of increased artillery support, he personally visited the division post of command behind Montfaucon to seek such support. In his absence the brigade post of command open to enemy observation was swept by a concentration of enemy machinegun and artillery fire. In the face of this terrific fire, General Nicholson, with great coolness and with complete disregard for his own safety, rode forward on horseback to his brigade post of command to issue orders for the renewed attack upon the Madeleine Farm, supervising the formation for attack, and by his brave and gallant example inspired the men of his command with renewed courage and determination, which enabled them to reach their objective and hold it against repeated enemy counterattacks.* (Arlington National Records)

Retiring after the War, Nicholson died in Washington, D.C. on December 20, 1931.
Highest rank achieved: Brigadier General, U.S.A.

Henry James Nowlan
Born in Island of Corfu, Ireland on June 18,1837. Following graduation from the Royal Military Academy at Sandhurst, he was commissioned in the 41st Welsh Regiment in August 1854. Serving during the Crimean War, he was decorated for gallantry at Sevastopol. After arriving in America in 1862, he was commissioned 1st Lt., 14th New York Cavalry (1st Metropolitan Cavalry) in January 1863 at the organization of the regiment. His regiment was deployed to the Gulf, where he took part in the Siege of Port Hudson and the Red River campaign. In June 1863, he was captured and sent to the notorious prison at Andersonville, eventually escaping in early 1865 to take part in the Carolinas Campaign attached to the XV Corps. Rejoining his regiment in May, he was transferred to the 18th New York Cavalry in June 1865, also stationed in New Orleans, and took part in the Yorktown Expedition into

***Nowlan**. Courtesy of Glen Swanson*

Texas, during which he was severely wounded. Following promotion to Captain in January 1866, he was mustered out with his regiment in May 1866.

Nowlan accepted a commission in the Seventh Regiment as Second Lieutenant, Company F, effective July 28, 1866, at the formation of the regiment. Promoted to 1st Lt., Company G on December 3, 1866, he was posted to Ft. Harker. In November 1867, appointed Regimental Commissary, he remained in garrison throughout 1867 and 1868 and did not take part in field operations with the regiment. In July 1870, he was released from commissary duty and the following year accompanied the regiment to duty in the south, during which time he was appointed Regimental Quartermaster in March 1872, remaining in this capacity through service in the Dakotas. Nowlan accompanied the regiment from Ft. Lincoln on the Yellowstone Campaign of 1876. However, detached as quartermaster with Terry's staff, he remained at the supply depot at the mouth of the Powder River and did not join his regiment into the Big Horn Valley. Following the losses, he was promoted to Captain, Company I, effective June 25, 1876 to fill the vacancy created by the death of Myles Keogh. Nowlan, promoted to command a company, was subjected to unfair scrutiny, along with several others officers for what was deemed an unfair promotion (See H. Jackson). At the conclusion of the Sioux campaign of 1876 and duty as quartermaster, he took part in the Nez Perce Campaign in Merrill's battalion and the battle at Canyon Creek on Sept. 13, 1877. He remained on frontier duty for the reminder of his career, with a brevet promotion to Maj. for gallantry at Canyon Creek in February 1890 and Major of Cavalry on July 17, 1895. While on leave from the regiment, Nowlan died in Hot Springs, Arkansas on November 10, 1898.
Highest rank achieved: Major, U.S.A.

Otis. *Courtesy of Glen Swanson*

Elmer I. Otis

Born in Westfield, Massachusetts on February 27, 1830. Enrolling at the United States Military Academy in July 1849 with classmates George Crook and Henry Slocum, Otis graduated class of 1853. Among his fellow graduating classmates were James McPherson, John Schofield and Phillip Sheridan. Few vacancies and slow promotion in the army allowed him only a brevet rank of 2nd Lt., assigned to the 1st Infantry. In February 1855, following duty in Kentucky and Texas, he was commissioned 2nd Lt., 4th Infantry but transferred to the 1st U.S. Cavalry in March of that year, taking part in the Sioux Expedition of 1855. Promoted to 1st Lt. in February 1856, he served at various stations on the frontier and took part in both the Utah Expedition of 1858 and actions against the Kiowa Indians in 1860. Promoted to Capt. in May 1861, Otis transferred to the 4th U.S. Cavalry in August 1861 and commanded his regiment during the advance into Kentucky and the battle of Perryville. Commanding a brigade in the Army of the Cumberland, he took part in the Tennessee Campaign, the Battle of Stone's River, and Murfreesboro. In September 1863, Otis began a series of detached assignments in which he would fill for the next thirteen years, serving as special Inspector of Cavalry for Dept. of West Virginia, the Army of the Potomac, Division of Mississippi, Division of Missouri, and Districts of Nevada and the Lakes. In June 1864, he was promoted out of the regiment to Maj., 1st U.S. Cavalry, brevetted Lt. Col. in October 1864 "for zeal and faithful service," and Colonel in April 1865 for meritorious service during the war.

Following the losses at Little Big Horn and the death of George Custer, Otis was promoted to Lieutenant Colonel,

Seventh Regiment, effective June 25, 1876. At that time he was on frontier duty in Washington State and did not join the regiment until after leave of absence at the end of the year. Following his arrival, he went on the sick list at Ft. Rice, and did not accompany his command in the Nez Perce Campaign of 1877. After commanding the regiment at various stations in Dakota Territory, he was promoted out of the regiment to Colonel, 8th U.S. Cavalry on April 2, 1883. Commanding his regiment in Texas and again in the Dakotas, he retired from service in February 1891 and died in San Diego, California on August 18, 1897.
Highest rank achieved: Colonel, U.S.A.

Satterlee Clark Plummer
Born at Fort Winnebago, Wisconsin in June 1844, the son of Brig. Gen. Joseph Bennett Plummer, U.S. Volunteers and Col., 11th Missouri Infantry. Enrolled at the United States Military Academy in July 1861, graduating class of 1865. Following graduation, Plummer was commissioned 2nd Lt. and 1st Lt, 17th Infantry in June 1865, garrisoned in New York, and served as Acting Assistant Inspector General of the Department of Washington. Stationed in Texas on frontier duty, he was transferred to the 26th Infantry in September 1866 where he served as chief signal officer. With a promotion to Captain in June 1868, he served in the District of Columbia and New Mexico until June 1869.

Unassigned in 1869 during reorganization of the army, a peculiar but not uncommon exchange of officers was orchestrated and approved between Mathew Berry (see M. Berry) and Plummer. Assigned Capt., Company C, Seventh Regiment on August 9, 1869, he joined the regiment at garrison at Ft. Leavenworth in November 1869. Posted to Ft. Wallace, he took part in scouting duty in Kansas and Colorado until September 1870. While in winter garrison at Ft. Harker, he resigned from service and was discharged on December 12, 1870. In May 1876, he reapplied for appointment in the army, accepting a commission as 2nd Lt., 4th U.S. Infantry, where he served on frontier duty in the Dakotas and took part in the Yellowstone Expedition of 1876 and the campaigns against the Sioux. In July 1877, he was dismissed from service, but again applied for reappointment. Receiving a commission as 2nd Lt. 15th U.S. Infantry, he served until his death in Washington D.C. on November 14, 1881.
Highest rank achieved: Captain, U.S.A.

***Plummer**. Massachusetts Commandery, Military Order of the Loyal Legion Collection*

James Ezekiel Porter*
Born in Strong, Maine on February 2, 1847. Enrolled at the United States Military Academy in September 1864. Found to be deficient in mathematics after his first year, he was held back to commence again the following year, graduating class of 1869. Among his classmates were fellow Seventh Cavalrymen Charles Braden and Charles Rea.

Following graduation, Porter was commissioned Second Lieutenant, Seventh Regiment on June 15, 1869, assigned to Company E. Returning from leave he joined the regiment in October at Ft. Leavenworth. Following posting at Ft. Wallace and Ft. Harker, he accompanied the regiment on duty in the south, posted to Chester, South Carolina, Ruthefordton and Lincolnton, North Carolina, during which he was promoted to 1st Lt., Company I on March 1, 1872, and Shelbyville, Kentucky. Upon deployment to the Dakotas, he served on escort duty with the National Boundary Survey Commission in 1873 and 1874. "Jimmy" Porter joined the regiment from

Porter. *Courtesy of Glen Swanson*

Rea. *United States Military Academy*

Ft. Totten on the Yellowstone Campaign of 1876, and was killed in action on June 25, 1876. Although his body was never positively identified, he most likely died with Keogh, his company commander on the northeast side of Battle Ridge.
Highest rank achieved: 1st Lieutenant, U.S.A.

Charles Henry Rea

Born in Oxford (Philadelphia), Pennsylvania in January 1848. Enrolled at the United States Military Academy in July 1864. Found to be deficient in mathematics after his first year, he was held back to commence again the following year, graduating class of 1869. Among his classmates were fellow Seventh Cavalrymen John Aspinwall, James Porter, and William Robinson.

Following graduation, Rea was commissioned Second Lieutenant, Seventh Regiment on June 15, 1869, assigned to Company B, joining his company at winter garrison at Ft. Leavenworth. As the companies were deployed in springtime, he was posted to Ft. Hays in May 1870. In July, he applied for leave of absence, during which time he resigned from service on September 14, 1870. Rea died in Woodland, Illinois on June 27, 1908.
Highest rank achieved: 2nd Lieutenant, U.S.A.

William Van Wyck Reily*

Born in Washington, D.C. on December 12, 1853, the son of Naval officer William Reily, who died aboard the U.S.S. *Porpoise* in a Typhoon off the coast of Formosa in 1854. Leaving Georgetown University, he accepted an appointment to the United States Naval Academy, attending from September 1870 to October 1872. Found deficient in math and science, he was dismissed. Returning from employment abroad, Reily was commissioned 2nd Lt., 10th U.S. Cavalry in October 1875, posted to the frontier.

Reily. *Villa Louis Collection, Wisconsin State Historical Society*

Reno. *L. Tom Perry Special Collections, Harold B. Lee Library, Brigham Young University*

Reily transferred to the Seventh Regiment as Second Lieutenant, Company E on January 26, 1876, filling the vacancy created by the promotion of William Craycroft. Joining the regiment in February as they prepared for the upcoming campaign, he left Ft. Lincoln with the column, purportedly still learning to ride a horse. At the Battle of Little Big Horn on June 25, 1876, Reily was killed in action while temporarily serving with Company F, under George Yates. His battered body was found at the crest of the hill among the rest of the command: the handsome features of his dashing persona no longer recognizable.

Highest rank achieved: 2nd Lieutenant, U.S.A.

Marcus Albert Reno

Born in Carrollton, Illinois on November 15, 1834. Enrolled at the United States Military Academy in September 1851 with fellow Seventh Cavalryman Lewis Merrill but was absent from February 1854 for ill health. Following his reappointment in 1855 and a brief suspension in 1856, he eventually graduated among the class of 1857. At that time, slow army promotion afforded only a brevet rank of 2nd Lt. 1st Dragoons in July 1857. In June 1858, Reno was commissioned 2nd Lt., serving on frontier duty in the Pacific Northwest. In May 1861, he was promoted to 1st Lt. as his regiment was re-designated 1st U.S. Cavalry. He took part in numerous engagements during the Peninsula campaign including Yorktown, Williamsburg, Beaver Dam Creek, Gaines' Mill, Glendale, and Malvern Hill. He took part in the Maryland Campaign attached to the Army of the Potomac, commanding the regiment at South Mountain and Antietam/Sharpsburg. In October, he took part in the Rappahannock campaign where he was brevetted major in March 1863 for gallantry at Kelly's Ford. Following an injury sustained during the battle, he recuperated while on detached duty with the Cavalry Bureau and as Inspector General of the 1st Cavalry Division, assigned chief of staff to Gen. W.F. Smith and the Pennsylvania Volunteers. After his return to the field, Reno participated in the Richmond campaign during the summer of 1864, taking part at Enon Church and Trevillian Station. Appointed chief of Staff of Cavalry in August during the Shenandoah campaign under Sheridan, he took part in numerous engagements including Cedar Creek, where he was brevetted Lt. Col. for gallantry. In January 1865, he was appointed Col., 12th Pennsylvania Cavalry, engaged in operations in Virginia. Mustered out in July of that year, he was later brevetted Col., U.S.A. and Brig. Gen., Vols. "for gallant and meritorious service" during the war.

Following various assignments after the War, Reno was appointed Major, Seventh Regiment, effective December 26, 1868, filling the vacancy created by the death of A. Gibbs. After serving as acting Assistant Inspector General, Dept. of Columbia, he joined the regiment at winter garrison at Ft. Hays in December 1869 and served on scouting duty in Kansas and Colorado. In July 1871, he accompanied the regiment on duty in the south, posted to Spartanburg, South Carolina where his company was praised for services against Ku Klux Klan operations. In August 1872, he was assigned to New York on the Board of Small Arms, rejoining his regiment in the Dakotas. Garrisoned at Ft. Totten, he commanding the escorts of the Northern Boundary Survey Commission and he did not take part in the expeditions with the regiment. Following a leave of absence, he joined his regiment on the Yellowstone Campaign of 1876 where he commanded a battalion at the Battle of the Little Big Horn. Although undoubtedly a courageous officer, he did not perform well at Big Horn with success at the hilltop defenses chiefly attributed to the calm and collective leadership of his subordinate, Capt. Frederick Benteen. While posted to Ft. Abercrombie, Reno underwent court marshal in February 1877 as the army sought accountability for the defeat and testimony against him brought to light his intense dislike for Custer. A sentence of suspension for two years with loss of rank and pay signaled the beginning of the end for Reno. Severe scrutiny from both his superiors and subordinates, compounded with recent personal tragedy caused him to deteriorate both mentally and physically, inducing heavy drinking. Posted to Ft. Meade upon his return to the regiment, he was placed in arrest for intoxication and objectionable behavior. Court marshaled for "Conduct to the prejudice of good military order and discipline," he was dismissed from service on April 1, 1880. (Years later, his status was changed to indicate honorable discharged effective the same date.) Reno died in Washington D.C., on March 30, 1889.
Highest rank achieved: Brevet Brigadier General, Vols., Bvt Col., U.S.A.

Samuel Marshall Robbins

Born in New York on February 2, 1832. After attending school in Illinois, he was commissioned Capt., 1st Colorado Infantry in November 1861, serving in Colorado and New Mexico. Participating in Canby's 1862 campaign under P.E. Connor, he distinguished himself at Apache Canyon and again at Pigeons Ranch in March 1862 against Gen. Sibley's Texas Volunteers. In November 1862, the regiment was re-designated 1st Colorado Cavalry and afterwards served as acting engineering officer in Colorado and Kansas. He was

***Robbins**. Courtesy of Glen Swanson*

appointed district commander, Chief of Colorado Cavalry in which he served until mustered out in October 1865.

A solid and reputable record won him an appointment to the Seventh Regiment as First Lieutenant, assigned Company D, effective July 28, 1866, at the formation of the regiment. Commanding Company D during the Hancock Expedition and the summer operations of 1867, he successfully repulsed an Indian attack on his train-column near the Republican River in June. Robbins, although having a close relationship with the Custers, also had a fondness for alcohol and gambling. A notorious drunkard from the beginning, he found himself under arrest for absence without leave and drunkenness during winter garrison at Ft. Leavenworth. Following the winter campaign and the Battle of Washita, he was promoted to Captain, Company A on November 27, 1868 to fill the vacancy created by the death of Louis Hamilton. In March 1870, he was again under arrest for drunkenness, fighting, and lewd behavior but intervention from Custer on his behalf again saved his commission. In 1871, with the regiment on reconstruction duty in Elizabethtown, Kentucky, another infraction occurred of similar charge, including assault and cavorting with prostitutes, resulting in his court marshal in November. According to Elizabeth Custer, Robbins was afforded considerable latitude by his commanding officer for his many indiscretions. Inevitably, even Custer had had enough and his unfavorable character testimony fostered a sentence of dismissal. However, before sentence could be passed, he tendered his resignation on March 1, 1872. Robbins died from yellow fever in Baton Rouge, Louisiana on September 25, 1878 (other record show death July 8, 1893).

Highest rank achieved: Captain, U.S.A.

William Penn Robeson, Jr.

Born in Belvidere, New Jersey on July 8, 1837. Commissioned 1st Lt., 3rd Regiment, New Jersey Infantry in May 1861, where under Gen. Kearny's 1st Brigade, he took part in numerous engagements including Bull Run, Munson's Hill, Gaine's Farm (Mill), Charles City Crossroads, and Malvern Hill. Promoted to Capt. in August 1862, he participated in numerous engagements during campaigns in Virginia while attached to the 1st Brigade, 1st Division, VI Corps including Manassas, Chantilly, Crampton's Gap, Antietam, Fredricksburg, Salem Church, Gettysburg, Fairfield, Funktown, Rappahannock, and Mine Run. Following his resignation in January 1864 after his regiment was reorganized, he was appointed Maj., 3rd New Jersey Cavalry in January 1864 at the formation of the regiment. With promotion to Lt. Col. in December 1864, he took part in numerous campaigns in Virginia including Sheridan's Valley campaign and the Appomattox campaign under Custer's Cavalry Corps, Army of the Potomac. In March 1865, he was brevetted Col. and Brig. General, Vols. for distinguished and meritorious service at Five Forks, where he was wounded, and South Side Railroad.

Robeson. *Massachusetts Commandery, Military Order of the Loyal Legion Collection*

Mustered out of the Volunteers in August 1865, Robeson's achievements and distinguished record won him an appointment as Captain, Seventh Regiment, effective July 28, 1866, assigned to Company B at the formation of the regiment. Never joining the regiment in the field, he resigned from service on June 8, 1867 and died in Camden, New Jersey on September 15, 1881.

Highest rank achieved: Brevet Brigadier General, Vols.

William Wallace Robinson, Jr.

Born in Amhearst (Berea), Ohio on April 21, 1846. Enlisted in Co. E, 7th Wisconsin Infantry in March 1865 under his father,

Col. W.W. Robinson of the famed Wisconsin Iron Brigade, serving in Washington and Kentucky until June of that year. After the end of hostilities, with the help of his father who was acting as Consol to Madagascar and other influential connections, he enrolled at the United States Military Academy in July 1865, graduating class of 1869. Among his classmates were fellow Seventh Cavalrymen Charles Rea, James Porter, Charles Braden and William Craycroft. Following graduation, Robinson was appointed 2nd Lt., 3rd U.S. Cavalry, serving on frontier duty in New Mexico, Arizona, Wyoming, and Utah scouting against the Ute Indians and participating in several engagements with the Apache Indians.

After duty in Nebraska and Dakota Territory, Robinson transferred to the Seventh Regiment as Second Lieutenant, Company B, effective June 25, 1876 to fill the vacancy created by the death of Benjamin Hodgson. Leaving post at Ft. McPhearson, he joined the regiment in September in Bismarck, during which time he was promoted to 1st Lt., Company F on August 14, 1876. He took part in the Nez Perce campaign of 1877 under Col. Sturgis. While serving at various posts in the Dakotas and Kansas, he was appointed regimental quartermaster from November 1883 to November 1887. He took part in the Sioux campaign of 1890 and participated at Wounded Knee and White Clay Creek (Drexel Mission) in December, 1890, where he was cited for efficient services by Gen. J.W. Forsyth. On June 1, 1891, Robinson was promoted out of the regiment to Captain, Assistant Quartermaster, serving in the Dept. of Texas and the Dept. of Colorado. He remained in the Quartermaster Department with promotion to Major, both Vols, and Quartermaster, U.S.A in late 1900, Lt. Col., Deputy Quartermaster in January 1904, and Colonel, Assistant Quartermaster General, U.S.A. in February 1910. Following duty in Hawaii and the Philippines, Robinson retired in April 1910 with the rank of Brig. General. Outliving his beloved son, Capt. Edward W. Robinson, 10th U.S. Cavalry, who died in 1912, "Rob" Robinson died in Seattle, Washington on March 23, 1917.
Highest rank achieved: Brig. Gen., U.S.A., Ret.

Robinson. *Courtesy of Glen Swanson*

Albert Judson Russell

Born in Wayne County, Ohio on March 1852. Enrolled at the United States Military Academy in September 1872, graduating class of 1876. Among his classmates were fellow Seventh Cavalrymen Ernest Garlington, John Gresham, and Loyd McCormick. Following graduation, he was commissioned 2nd Lt., 10th U.S. Colored Cavalry effective June 15, 1876, posted to Ft. Lincoln.

Before he could join his regiment, Russell was transferred to the Seventh Regiment as Second Lieutenant, Company H, effective June 25, 1876, to fill the vacancy created by the promotion of Charles DeRudio. Following the conclusion of the Sioux Campaign, he took part in the Nez Perce Campaign in Benteen's battalion at Canyon Creek on Sept. 13. He remained with the regiment in the Dakotas with promotion to 1st Lt. on November 30, 1881, but suffering from deteriorating health, applied for several leaves of absence and missed most of the regiment's field operations. Following detached recruiting duty and posting in Kansas, he applied for sick leave in May 1895, during which time he retired on disability, advanced to the rank of Capt. on April 23, 1896. Russell died in Sierra Madre, California on April 15, 1900.
Highest rank achieved: Captain, U.S.A., Ret.

Russell*. United States Military Academy*

Scott*. United States Military Academy*

Hugh Lenox Scott

Born in Danville, Kentucky on September 22, 1853. Enrolled at the United States Military Academy in July 1871, but was suspended for one year in July 1872 (as per M.A.O. No.7). Reinstated in the third class, he graduated with the class of 1876. Among his classmates were fellow Seventh Cavalrymen Horatio Sickel, Albert Russell, and Loyd McCormick. Commissioned 2nd Lt., 9th Cavalry after graduation, he was posted to frontier duty at Ft. Lincoln.

As were several others, Scott was transferred to the Seventh Regiment as Second Lieutenant, effective June 25, 1876, before he could join his assigned regiment. Assigned to Company E to fill the vacancy created by the death of William V.W. Reily, he arrived at Ft. Lincoln in September. The following year, he joined the regiment in the field during the Nez Perce Campaign, but was on assignment to the Big Horn Battlefield during the engagements in September. Promoted to 1st Lt. on July 28, 1878, he participated in several geological surveys and served at various posts in the Dakotas and Oklahoma including Ft. Totten, Ft. Meade, and Ft. Sill. While stationed at Ft. Sill, Scott became active in Indian affairs in Oklahoma Territory and was involved with the various regional tribes during the ""Messiah Dance" influence in 1890. Following the uprising, he organized and commanded Company L, which had been redesignated an all-Indian company (consisting of Kiowa, Comanche, and Apache Indians) and received a subsequent promotion to Capt. on January 24, 1895. Overseeing Geronimo's captured band, his skill of diplomacy and keen understanding of Indian culture found him detailed to the Military Information Bureau, where he was active in development of sign language. In 1897, Scott was appointed Maj., Vols., and Assistant Adjutant General, and following the outbreak of the Spanish War, served as Adjutant General, I Corps. With promotion to Lt. Colonel, Vols., he served as Adjutant General, Dept. of Cuba. In February 1903, he was promoted out of the regiment to Maj., 3rd Cavalry, and again to the 14th Cavalry a month later, serving in the Philippines as Governor of Sulu Archipelago until July 1906. Scott again returned to the field, active in Indian affairs. After a series of promotions, he achieved the rank of Maj. Gen. in April 1915. Scott was instrumental assisting in preparations against the Germans in World War I and was awarded the

Distinguished Service Medal for his work. After a long and successful career, he retired in September 1917 and died in Washington D.C., April 30, 1934.
Highest rank achieved: Major General, U.S.A.

Jacob Henry Shellabarger
Born in Lycoming County, Pennsylvania on February 3, 1845. Enlisting in the Pennsylvania Volunteers, he served with the Quartermaster Department in Pittsburgh.

With the influence of his uncle, Ohio Congressman and Hon. Samuel Shellabarger, he secured an appointment in the Seventh Regiment as Second Lieutenant on August 12, 1867, narrowly passing the physical entrance exam. Assigned to Company L, he was posted to Ft. Reynolds to fill the vacancy created by the promotion of Henry Abell. Shellabarger, often in arrest for drunkenness, was by most accounts, an unsavory and less-than-mediocre officer. In June 1867, he was court marshaled for drunkenness on duty while posted to Ft. Harker, but insufficient evidence found him not guilty. Promoted to 1st Lt., Company M on March 1, 1869, to fill the vacancy created by the promotion of Owen Hale, Shellabarger was posted to Ft. Lyon where in July, he again found himself under court marshal for drunkenness and fighting with a superior officer. Barring charges of "Conduct Unbecoming an Officer," as well as "drunkenness on duty," failing to attend his own second general court martial sealed his fate and he was summarily dismissed on September 18, 1869. He later tried unsuccessfully to clear his name, claiming he was "robbed of his commission," and vindictively blamed his misfortune solely on Lewis Merrill, the officer who preferred the charges.
Highest rank achieved: 1st Lieutenant, U.S.A.

Michael Vincent Sheridan
Born in Somerset, Ohio on May 24, 1840. After attending St. Joseph's College, he volunteered for duty as Aide-de-Camp to his older brother, General Philip Sheridan from July 1862 until September 1863, participating in the campaigns in Kentucky and Tennessee and taking part at Perryville and Stone's River. In September 1863, he was appointment 2nd Lt., 2nd Missouri Infantry, where he took part at Chickamauga and Missionary Ridge. In May 1864, he was appointed Capt., Volunteers and A.D.C, taking part in numerous campaigns and Cavalry engagements on staff of General Sheridan including

Sheridan. *Courtesy of Glen Swanson*

the Richmond campaigns, the Shenandoah campaigns and the Appomattox campaign. Following a brevet promotion to Maj., Vols. in March 1865 for "gallant and meritorious" service during the war, he was mustered out of Volunteer service in August 1865, but remained on staff with Gen. Sheridan when transferred in May 1865 to the Department of the Gulf until August 1866. Later in March 1867, he was brevetted Major for gallantry at Opequon and Lt. Col. for "gallantry and meritorious" service at Fisher's Hill.

Sheridan won a post war appointment as 2nd Lt., 5th U.S. Cavalry in February 1866, but again with the influence of his brother, he secured an appointment as Captain, Seventh Regiment, effective July 28, 1866, at the formation of the regiment. Joining the regiment in early 1867, he was posted to Ft. Morgan with Company L, where he commanded the post through early summer. As his company was dispatched to Ft. Reynolds in June 1867, he went on detached duty from the Seventh Cavalry again appointed A.D.C to his brother in July 1867. He remained with his brother through most of his career with promotion to Lt. Col., Aide-de-Camp on August 1, 1870. Although he did not take part in field operations with the regiment, he did however unfortunately accompany the detail returning to the Little Big Horn battle site to rebury the dead.

In April 1878, he was appointed Military Secretary to Gen. Sheridan and promoted to Colonel, Aide-de-Camp in June 1888, where he served as Adjutant General, Dept. of the Platte. In August of that year, he was appointed Lt. Col., Assistant Adjutant General and with promotion to Col. in January 1897, he served as Assistant Adjutant General, Dept. of the Missouri and Commanded the Dept. of the Lakes. At the outbreak of the Spanish War, Sheridan was appointed Brig. Gen., Vols., in May 1898, serving in Georgia until mustered out of the Volunteers in May 1899. He retired in April 1902, advanced to Brig. Gen., and died in Washington D.C., on February 21, 1918.
Highest rank achieved: Brig. Gen., U.S.A., Ret.

Sickel. *Civil War Library and Museum, MOLLUS Collection*

Horatio Gates Sickel, Jr.
Born in Philadelphia, Pennsylvania on January 15, 1854, the son of Brig. Gen. Horatio Gates Sickel, Col. 3rd Penn. Vols. Enrolled at the United States Military Academy in September 1872, graduating class of 1876. Among his classmates were fellow Seventh Cavalrymen Albert Russell, Ernest Garlington, and H.L. Scott. Following graduation, he was commissioned 2nd Lt., 14th U.S. Infantry in June 1876, posted to the frontier.

While on duty in the field during the campaign against the Sioux, he was transferred to the Seventh Regiment as Second Lieutenant, assigned to Company C, effective June 25, 1876 to fill the vacancy created by the death of Henry Harrington. Joining his regiment at Ft. Lincoln in November, he was posted to Ft. Totten, Dakota Territory. The following year, he accompanied the regiment in the field on campaign against the Nez Perce, on scouting duty near the Black Hills. He took part in scouting and field operations from Ft. Meade and Ft. Sisseton, where he commanded a detachment of Indian scouts. With promotion to 1st Lt. on December 17, 1882, he remained on the frontier, on duty in Oklahoma and Kansas. Joining the regiment in the Sioux campaign of 1890, Sickel took part in the battles of both Wounded Knee, where he was commended for gallantry and distinguished service, and White Clay Creek (Drexel Mission). After duty in Missouri, serving as Regimental Adjutant, he was promoted to Capt. on May 23, 1896, posted to Arizona, Alabama, and Georgia. During Cuban occupation, he was posted to Havana, Cuba in 1899 with the regiment until October 1901. In July 1903, "Tiny" Sickel was promoted out of the regiment to Major, 12th U.S. Cavalry and posted to the Philippines, commanding garrisons at Laguna and Manila. After service in the Dakotas, Nebraska, New Mexico and Texas and promotions Lt. Col. and Colonel, he went on leave of absence, during which he was retired from service in January 1918. Suffering from depression and despondency, Sickel committed suicide in St. Louis, Missouri on September 9, 1918.
Highest rank achieved: Colonel, U.S.A.

Herbert Jermain Slocum
Born in Cincinnati, Ohio on April 25, 1855, the son of Col. Joseph Jermain Slocum, U.S. Vols. Slocum attended the United States Military Academy from July 1872 to June 1876, but was dismissed his last year for deficiencies in Engineering. With various recommendations, he received an army commission as 2nd Lt., assigned to the 25th Infantry in June of that year until a transfer to the 2nd U.S. Cavalry.

Following the losses from the Big Horn Battle, Slocum was transferred to the Seventh Regiment, assigned to Company

F, effective September 20, 1876 to fill the vacancy created by the resignation of Charles Larned. At the conclusion of the Sioux campaign, he took part in the Nez Perce campaign the next year, serving in Merrill's battalion at the battle of Canyon Creek, Sept. 13, 1877. Promoted to 1st Lt. on September 22, 1883, he remained on frontier duty with his regiment throughout the Indian Wars and in February 1890, was brevetted 1st Lt. for gallantry at Canyon Creek. Promoted to Capt. on August 26, 1896, he traveled to South Africa as a guest of the British government to observe the British campaign against the Boers. At the outbreak of the Spanish war, he was appointed Maj., Inspector General of Volunteers in May 1898, until discharge in May 1899. In 1900, while stationed in Cuba, he served as Acting Chief Quartermaster and Chief Disbursing Officer of Cuban Customs under the Dept. of Western Cuba. Returning stateside, while stationed at Governor's Island, New York under the Dept. of the East, his wife was killed in an automobile accident in March 1910. Slocum was promoted through the ranks to Colonel, commanding the 13th U.S. Cavalry, stationed in New Mexico during the Mexican Revolution. Following the army expedition into Vera Cruz, his command was attacked by Poncho Villa's forces in March 1916, while garrisoned at Columbus, New Mexico. Unprepared for the attack, the Mexicans eluded his command after chase across the border, prompting the forthcoming and well-known expedition under "Black Jack" Pershing into Mexico. Slocum died in Connecticut on March 29, 1928.

Highest rank achieved: Colonel, U.S.A.

***Slocum**. United States Military Academy*

Algernon Emory Smith*

Born in Newport, New York on September 17, 1842. After attended Hamilton College, he enlisted in Co. K, 7th U.S. Infantry in June 1862 and was quickly commissioned 2nd Lt., 117th New York Inf. in August 1862 at the formation of the regiment. In April 1863, his regiment was ordered to Virginia, where he participated at Suffolk against Longstreet's Confederate forces and on into the Carolinas, where he participated in the operations against Charleston including Ft. Wagner and Ft. Sumter. Following a promotion to 1st Lt. in April 1864, he participated in the Bermuda Hundred Campaign including Drury's Bluff and Cold Harbor, and the Petersburg

***A.E. Smith**. United States Military History Institute*

Campaign, taking part at Richmond and Fort Gilmer. After the engagement at Darbytown Road, Smith was promoted to Capt. in October 1864 and assigned Aide-de-Camp to Gen. Alfred Terry (also served on the staff of General Ord, Ames, and Sully). In December, he took part in the expedition against Ft. Fisher, where he was severely wounded in the shoulder while leading a charge against the Confederate forces of Gen. R. Hoke. After recuperation and brevet promotion to Major, Vols. for "gallantry and meritorious service" at Ft. Fisher in March 1865, he was mustered out of service in May 1865. Later in August 1867, he was brevetted 1st Lt., for gallantry at Drury's Bluff and Captain for gallantry at Ft. Fisher.

Smith received appointment as Second Lieutenant, assigned to Company F, Seventh Regiment on August 9, 1867, joining the regiment in November at Leavenworth. Known as "Fresh" Smith (to differentiate between H.W. Smith), he took part in the failed Sully Expedition under his old commander. During the winter campaign of 1868 and the battle of Washita, Smith served as regimental commissary, and after which promoted to 1st Lt. on December 5, 1868. In April 1869, he was appointed regimental quartermaster in the absence of James Bell, until July 1869. Although popular in regimental social circles and counted among Custer's "family," Sturgis, on the other hand, though less of him professionally. Relieved of quartermaster duties for questionable practices, Smith endured a shaky review in front of the "Hancock" review board. Transferred to Company A, he accompanied the regiment the following year on duty in the south, posted to Elizabethtown, Kentucky. After deployment to the Dakotas, he took part in the Yellowstone Expedition of 1873 including the engagement on the Yellowstone River on Aug. 11, and the Black Hills Expedition of 1874, served as acting (field) Quartermaster and Commissary. On the Yellowstone campaign as acting Regimental quartermaster in the absence of Henry Nowlan and temporarily commanding Company E, Smith was killed in action on June 25, 1876 at Little Big Horn. His mutilated body was found near the crest of Last Stand hill.

Highest rank achieved: Brevet Major, Vols.

Andrew Jackson Smith

Born in Bucks County, Pennsylvania on April 28, 1815. Enrolled at the United States Military Academy in July 1834, attending with numerous notable names as Meade, McClellan, Sully, Sherman, Early, Armistead, and Hooker, graduating class of 1838. His fellow classmates included P.T. Beauregard and Irvin McDowell. After graduation, he was commissioned 2nd Lt., 1st Dragoons in July 1838, serving on frontier duty in Kansas and Colorado. After promotion to 1st Lt. in March 1845 and service in the War with Mexico, he was promoted to Capt. in February 1847, where he took part in various scouting expeditions and engagements in the Northwest Territories including Cow Creek, Oregon, and both Harney Lake and Owyhee River, Washington. In May 1861, he was promoted to Major in the newly re-designated 1st U.S. Cavalry, serving with fellow Seventh Cavalryman Edward Myers. In October 1861, he was briefly appointed Col., 2nd California Volunteer Cavalry but resigned later that year to serve under academy classmate Gen. H.W. Halleck as Chief of Cavalry. Appointed Brig. Gen., Vols. in March 1862, he commanded a division at Chickasaw Bluffs as well as the XIII corps during the Vicksburg Campaign. In May 1864, with promotion to Maj. Gen. Vols., he commanded XVI and XVII Corps in Tennessee, Mississippi, and Missouri, and successfully led troops in engagements against forces of Gen. N.B. Forrest and J.B. Hood. In April 1864, he was brevetted Col., U.S.A. in April 1864 for gallantry at Pleasant Hill and the following month,

***A.J. Smith**. Library of Congress*

received a nominal promotion in the regular army to Lt. Col., 5th U.S. Cavalry. In 1865, he commanded the XVI Corps in the campaign against Mobile and with brevet promotions to Brig. Gen., U.S.A. for gallantry at Tupelo and Maj. Gen. for "gallantry and meritorious service" at Nashville, he was mustered out of the Volunteers in January 1866.

Smith was handpicked for command of the new regiments and appointed Colonel, Seventh Regiment, effective July 28, 1866. However, his service with the regiment was limited. Upon arriving at Ft. Riley in February 1866 from leave of absence, his associated duties as commander of District of Upper Arkansas kept him away from the regiment's operations. Following Hancock's removal, he took over command of the Dept. of Missouri temporarily during Sheridan's absence until March 1868, when he applied for leave of absence. Smith, an immensely popular, amiable, and able commander, apparently no longer shared the enthusiasm of his younger officers he resigned his commission after a yearlong leave on June 5, 1869. After brief appointment commanding a brigade of Missouri Militia, he was wholly retired from service on January 1, 1889. Smith died on January 30, 1897 in St. Louis, Missouri.

Highest rank achieved: Colonel, U.S.A., Brevet Major General, U.S.A., Brevet Major General, Vols.

H.W. Smith*. Daniel Potochniak Collection*

Henry Walworth Smith

Born in Groton, Connecticut on January 6, 1827. An adventurous spirit landed him employment for several years in the Merchant Marines, serving as Shipmaster. Upon his return from abroad, he enlisted in the Massachusetts Volunteers at their organization at the age of thirty-six. He quickly procured a commission as 2nd Lt., company L, 4th Massachusetts Cavalry by the end of the month and took part in the operations in the Dept. of the South. After his regiment was deployed to Virginia, under the Dept. of Virginia and North Carolina, he participated in the Bermuda Hundred and Richmond campaigns. Promoted to 1st Lt., in December 1864, he remained in Virginia under the XXV Army Corps. With a promotion to Captain, Company G, in June 1865, he was mustered out of the Volunteers in November 1865.

Smith won appointment as Second Lieutenant, Company D, in the Seventh Regiment at the organization of the regiment, accepting the appointment August 17, 1867. Joining his company at winter garrison at Ft. Leavenworth, he was placed almost immediately in arrest for drunkenness and absence-without-leave. The following year, he took part in the winter campaign and the battle of Washita, temporarily assigned to Company H. During duty at Ft. Leavenworth, he was promoted to 1st Lt., Company C on September 18, 1869. Undisciplined, unscrupulous and often in arrest, "Salt" Smith, as he was known, made little contribution to the success of the regiment. Charged with embezzlement and certain punitive severity, Smith deserted from the regiment in December 1870 and disappeared. He was dropped from the roster effective January 9, 1871.

Highest rank achieved: 1st Lieutenant, U.S.A., Capt., Vols.

James Garland Sturgis*

Born in Albuquerque, New Mexico on January 24, 1854. Enrolled in the United States Military Academy in July 1871, graduating class of 1875. The son of Colonel Samuel Sturgis, he was appointed Second Lieutenant on July 3, 1875, Company M, Seventh Regiment, filling the vacancy created by the death of R.H.L. Alexander. The youngest officer in the regiment, he joined his company at Ft. Rice in October after returning

J.G. Sturgis. *Western History Department, Denver Public Library*

S.D. Sturgis. *Brady-Handy Collection, Library of Congress*

from graduation leave. When the opportunity arose, young Sturgis, desiring to serve near his father, eagerly accepted the transfer to a vacancy at Ft. Leavenworth. Accompanying the regiment on the Yellowstone campaign, "Jack" Sturgis was killed in action of June 25, 1876 serving with Company E at the Battle of the Little Big Horn. Although a grave marker was established for the sake of his visiting mother, his body was never positively identified. He most likely died near cemetery ravine with the majority of his company.
Highest rank achieved: 2nd Lieutenant, U.S.A.

Samuel Davis Sturgis

Born in Shippensburg, Pennsylvania on June 11, 1822. Enrolled in the United States Military Academy in July 1842, graduating class of 1846. Fellow classmates and cadets included George McClellan, A.P. Hill, and Ambrose Burnside. After graduation, minimal vacancies afforded only a brevet appointment to 2nd Lt., 1st Dragoons, until he received a full commission as 2nd Lt. in February 1847. Serving in the War with Mexico, Sturgis was captured before Buena Vista and released following the battle. On frontier duty in Kansas and Missouri, he was promoted to 1st Lt. in July 1853 and again to Capt. in March 1855 (re-designated the 1st U.S. Cavalry). Sturgis participated in numerous expeditions and engagements as a young officer, including operations and skirmishes against the Apaches in 1854-1855, the 1857 Cheyenne and 1858 Utah Expedition, and the Kiowa and Comanche campaigns in 1860, while commanding the southern column. In May 1861 at the outbreak of the Civil War, he was promoted to Major, taking part at Wilson's Creek and was brevetted Lt. Col., U.S.A. for gallantry. In August 1861, as his regiment was re-designated 4th U.S. Cavalry, he was appointed Brig. Gen., Volunteers. Attached to Pope's Army of Virginia, he took part in numerous campaigns, commanding troops in Maryland and Northern Virginia including the battle of Second Manassas, where he was brevetted Col., U.S.A., South Mountain, Antietam, Fredericksburg, and Sharpsburg. In October 1863, he was promoted Lt. Col., 6th U.S. Cavalry, with a subsequent appointment of Chief of Cavalry, Department of Ohio. Following expeditions and operation in the Carolinas and Tennessee, Sturgis' command was defeated by Confederate forces under Gen. N.B. Forrest at Brice's Cross Roads, near Guntown, Mississippi in June 1864. Although exonerated from charges of inefficiency and cowardice, his reputation was damaged. He sat for the remainder of the war "awaiting further orders," while on duty with the 6th Cavalry in both Texas and at the Cavalry School. Following brevet promotions to Brig. Gen., U.S.A. for gallantry at South Mountain, and Maj. Gen., U.S.A. for gallantry at Fredericksburg in March 1865, he was mustered out of volunteer service in August 1865.

Sturgis remained in Texas commanding his regiment until his promotion to Colonel, Seventh Regiment on May 6, 1869. Replacing the aging Andrew Smith, Sturgis joined the regiment in October at Ft. Leavenworth. His arrival coincided with the incoming Grant administration's "Army Appropriation Act of 1869," and the so-called "Hancock" qualification Boards. Obliged with the unsavory task of "trimming" the officer corps, his recommendations naturally gained him some degree of unpopularity. In 1871 he accompanied the regiment to the south on occupation duty, posted to Louisville, Kentucky. As the regiment received orders to the Dakotas, Sturgis went on detached duty with both the Mounted Service and the Mounted Recruiting Office, and did not take part in field operations. In October 1874, he was again posted away from the regiment to St. Louis commanding the Cavalry Depot, in which he occupied until after his son marched to his death on the Yellowstone campaign. Sturgis, a devastated and broken father, rejoined the regiment at Ft. Lincoln in October 1876: Grief at the loss of his young son Jack was reflected in scathing criticism of Lt. Col. Custer. In the absence of Elmer Otis, Sturgis took command of the regiment in the field in the closing operations against the Sioux and Cheyenne as well as the Nez Perce campaign and the battle of Canyon Creek on Sept. 13. In 1878, he was assigned command of the Middle District, Dept. of Dakota until 1881 and the United States Old Soldiers home until 1885. Following a leave of absence, he retired from service on June 11, 1886 and died in St. Paul, Minnesota on September 28, 1889.

Highest rank achieved: Brevet Major General, U.S.A., Brig. Gen., Vols.

William Thompson

Born in Fayette County, Pennsylvania on November 10, 1813. (Records also show 1818) Practicing law in Ohio, he moved to Iowa where he became active in politics, winning election to both the House of Legislative Assembly in 1843 and as

***W. Thomspon**. Courtesy of Glen Swanson*

Democratic Representative in Congress (first district) in 1847. A prominent local citizen and owner of the Burlington Gazette, he helped raise a company of volunteers in Davenport at the outbreak of the Rebellion and was subsequently appointed Capt., Company E, 1st Iowa Cavalry in July 1861. Participating in operations in the Dept. of Missouri while attached to both Freemont's Army of the West and 1st Brigade, 3rd Division, Army of the Frontier, Thompson took part in the campaigns in Missouri and Arkansas and following promotion to Major in May 1863, he took part in operations around Little Rock. Following the retirement of his predecessor, Thompson was promoted Colonel in June 1864, taking part in operations in Missouri and numerous campaigns including the Camden Expedition and Price's Missouri Expedition and was brevetted Brig. Gen., Vols. in March 1865 for gallantry and meritorious service. Following the end of the War and his regiment's posting to Texas, he served under Custer in Alexandra during the well publicized "mutiny" of several of the state regiments. Ardently critical, his open opposition to Custer's perceived "malicious" treatment toward the enmity of the northerners created a virulent antagonism. When Custer's staff was eventually mustered out of service, Thompson, commanding 1st Battalion, served under another future fellow seventh cavalry commander Samuel Sturgis until mustered out himself in March 1866. Later in March 1867, he was brevetted Maj. for gallantry at Prairie Grove, Ark and Lt. Col. for gallantry at Bayou Metoe, Arkansas.

Thompson applied for a post war appointment in the cavalry, and to his chagrin, was appointed Capt., Seventh Regiment under Custer, effective July 28, 1866, at the formation of the regiment. At the likely awkward introduction with his new commanding officer, as Elizabeth Custer states, past hostilities were graciously forgotten; the penitent Thompson eventually becoming a close confidant of Custer. Assigned to Company B, he joined the regiment at Ft. Dodge. Commanding the garrison, his command took part in engagements against hostile Indian attacks and bore the brunt of the cholera epidemic ravaging through the region. At age fifty-four and the oldest officer in the regiment, he took part in the winter campaign commanding the southern wing at the battle of Washita. In March 1871, he accompanied the regiment on reconstruction duty in the south, posted to Unionville and Spartanburg, South Carolina. But as did the infirmity of Maj. Gibbs' before him, Thompson's age kept him away from the field and operations in the Dakotas. He retired from service at sixty-two on December 15, 1875, prior to the Yellowstone campaign and died of old age in Tacoma, Washington on October 7, 1897.

Highest rank achieved: Bvt. Brig. Gen., Vols., Bvt. Lt. Col., U.S.A.

John A. Thompson

Born in Ohio, he was commissioned 2nd Lt., 1st Dragoons in June 1855, posted to the frontier. Elements of the regiment were consolidated into the newly formed 1st U.S. Cavalry in August 1855 in which he transferred to, serving under fellow Seventh Cavalrymen Samuel Sturgis and Elmer Otis. After taking part in the various campaigns of the regiment, Thompson was promoted to 1st Lt., in January 1861 and Captain in May of the same year, after which his unit was re-designated 4th U.S. Cavalry in August 1861. Thompson took part in numerous engagements with the regiment, serving in Tennessee during the Stone's River campaign, Alabama, and Arkansas and was brevetted Maj. in June 1863 for Gallantry at Hoover's Gap during the Tullahoma Campaign. Following the capture of Macon, his regiment remained in Georgia until November 1865, when it was transferred to San Antonio, Texas.

As an active-duty officer, a creditable service record procured promotion to the vacancy of Major, Seventh Regiment, in which he accepted on August 25, 1867. While stationed at Ft. Mason awaiting duty orders to his new posting, Thompson was shot in the head and killed on November 14, 1867 by refuted members of the Taylor gang in Mason County, Texas.

Headquarters 5th Military District
Office Asst. Adj General
Austin, Texas, October 31st

Proclamation
A reward of 500 dollars ($166 2/3 dollars each) will be paid for the arrest of;

P.G. Taylor (alias doughboy)
J. Hays Taylor
R.W. Spencer

Charged with the murder of the late Maj. J.A. Thompson, 7th U.S. Cavalry.

This reward will be paid on delivery on the parties to the commanding officer at San Antonio or upon the production of evidence satisfactory to him that said parties were killed in the attempt to capture them.

The protection of the U.S. government is guaranteed to the parties who may perform the above service.

By command of Brevet Maj. Gen. J.J. Reynolds
Sighed S. Roberts
Captain, USA
ADC and AAAG
(Marcus A. Coker, *Spencer Tracks in the 19th Century,*)

Highest rank achieved: Major, U.S.A.

Joseph Green Tilford

Born in Georgetown, Kentucky on November 26, 1828, the son of Col. Alexander Tilford Jr., who served in the War of 1812. Enrolled at the United States Military Academy in July 1847, attending with notable names J.E.B. Stuart and Eugene Carr, graduating class of 1851. Few vacancies allowed only a brevet 2nd Lt., Mounted Rifles in July 1851 following graduation. With a full commission in January 1853, he served on frontier duty in Texas and took part in the Utah Expedition of 1858 during which he was promoted to 1st Lt. in June and the Navaho expedition of 1860. Following a promotion to Capt. in July 1861 and the re-designation to 3rd Cavalry at the outbreak of the Rebellion, Tilford participated in operations in New Mexico under Gen. Canby, including Valverde, where he was brevetted Maj. in February 1862, Albuquerque, Peralta, and Parugo. He participated in Sheridan's expedition to Chattanooga, taking part in the engagements at Cherokee Station, Tuscumbia, Alabama, Chattanooga, Lookout Mountain, and Missionary Ridge. Following service in Arkansas until the close of the War and a brevet promotion to Lt. Col. in March 1865 for "faithful and meritorious service", he went on detached duty as Acting Inspector General, both to VII Corps and the Dept. of Arkansas.

Tilford's distinguished service record won promotion to Major, Seventh Regiment on November 14, 1867, filling the staff vacancy created by the death of Wickliffe Cooper. Posted to Ft. Reynolds, Colorado until leave-of-absence in October 1868, he returned to field duty at Ft. Hays and Ft. Harker, commanding the garrison until March 1871. The following month, he accompanied the regiment on duty in the south, stationed in Chester, South Carolina, various stations in Kentucky until December 1872, and Jackson Barracks, Louisiana until the end of March 1873. After deployment to the Dakotas, Tilford was posted to Ft. Rice, where for unknown reasons, developed a keen dislike towards Custer. Plagued by poor health, he applied for frequent sick-leaves and did not join the elements of Ft. Rice to stations in the Gulf. He did however take part in the Black Hills Expedition of 1874 as second in command, where differences in command styles and a rebuke by Custer over a wagon detail, widened the rift between them. In October 1875, he went on leave-of-absence and did not join the regiment on the Yellowstone Campaign. Returning in October 1876, he served for the remainder of his career in a series of post commands, commanding Ft. Rice in 1876, Ft. Lincoln in 1877 during the Nez Perce campaign, and Ft. Buford in 1882 after which he received promotion to Lt. Col. on September 22, 1883. On April 11, 1889, he was promoted out of the regiment to Colonel, 9th U.S. Cavalry, posted to Ft. Robinson, Nebraska. Retiring from service in 1891 and advanced to the rank of Brigadier General, Tilford died from pneumonia in Washington D.C., on February 24, 1911.

Highest rank achieved: Brigadier General, U.S.A., Ret.

Tilford*. Villa Louis Collection, Wisconsin State Historical Society*

John Eaton Tourtellotte

Born in Windham, Connecticut on July 3, 1833. Graduated from Brown University. Leaving a law practice for fortunes of war, he enlisted in Co. H, 4th Minnesota Infantry in September 1861 and shortly afterwards secured a commission as Capt. by the end of the year. With promotion to Lt. Col. in September 1862, he took part in the campaigns in Mississippi attached to 1st Brigade, 3rd Division, Army of Mississippi, including Iuka and Corinth. In March 1863, he participated in Grant's campaigns against Vicksburg, where he took part at Jackson, Raymond, Baker's Creek (Champion Hill), Missionary Ridge, and the battle of Vicksburg with XVII Corps. Promoted to Colonel, Vols. in October 1864, he commanding a brigade during the Franklin/Nashville Campaign and was severely wounded at the battle of Allatoona. Tourtellotte distinguished himself in operations against Atlanta and the Carolinas and was brevetted Brig. Gen., Vols. in March 1865 for gallantry and meritorious service. He was mustered out of the Volunteers in June 1865. Later in March 1867, he was brevetted Maj., U.S.A. for gallantry at Vicksburg, Lt. Col. for gallantry at Allatoona, and Col., U.S.A. for gallantry at Bentonville.

Recommended by Sherman for a post-war position, Tourtellotte was commissioned Capt., 28th U.S. Infantry in July 1866. During the reorganization of the army, he was reassigned to the Seventh Regiment as Captain, Company G, on December 15, 1870. By January 1871, already earmarked by Gen. Sherman, he went on detached duty with appointment as Colonel, Aide-de-Camp, during which time he served in varying staff capacity until February 1884. In his absence, he was promoted to Major in the regiment on September 22, 1883. On March 20, 1885, he retired from service on disability and died from heart disease in LaCrosse, Wisconsin on July 22, 1891.

Highest rank achieved: Brevet Brig. Gen., Vols., Col., A.D.C., Bvt. Colonel., U.S.A.

Tourtellotte. *Roger D. Hunt Collection*

Charles Albert Varnum

Born in Troy, New York on June 21, 1849. Enrolled at the United States Military Academy in September 1868, graduating class of 1872. Among his classmates were fellow Cavalrymen George Wallace, John Wilkinson, and Henry Harrington.

Following graduation, Varnum was commissioned Second Lieutenant, Company A, Seventh Regiment on June 14, 1872. Filling the vacancy created by the promotion of Frank Gibson, he joined his company after leave on duty in the south, posted to Huntsville, Alabama and Elizabethtown, Kentucky. Deployed to the Dakotas with his regiment, he took part in the Yellowstone Expedition of 1873, including the engagements with hostile Indians on both August 4 and August 11, and the Black Hills Expedition of 1874. In October 1874, Varnum accompanied elements of the regiment again south to the Gulf, posted in Livingstone, Alabama with his company. Returning to the Dakotas in May 1875, he was stationed at Ft. Randall and then on to Ft. Lincoln, where he took part in the Yellowstone campaign of 1876. Commanding a detachment of scouts at the battle of the Little Big Horn, he took part in Reno's collapsed attack and was slightly wounded during the hilltop defense. Following the battle and the conclusion of the campaign, he was promoted to 1st Lt., Company C, effective June 25, 1876, to fill the vacancy created by the death of James Calhoun. Following appointment as regimental quartermaster in November 1876, he took part in the Nez Perce Campaign in 1877 and Canyon Creek, Sept. 13, occupying that position until October 1879. After duty at Ft. Sill, he was promoted to Capt., Company B, on July 22, 1890, afterwards joining his regiment in the Sioux campaign of 1890. Varnum participated in the

Varnum. *Courtesy of Glen Swanson*

battles at both Wounded Knee, where he was commended for gallantry, and White Clay Creek, (Drexel Mission) where he was awarded the Congressional Medal of Honor:

> Captain, Company B, 7th U.S. Cavalry. At White Clay Creek, S. Dak., 30 December 1890. "*In command of Troop B and part of E, 7th U.S. Cavalry, the regiment then retiring by detachment before superior force of hostile Indians. While executing an order to withdrawal, Capt. Varnum saw that a continuance of the movement would result in exposure of another troop of his regiment to being cut off and surrounded. Disregarding orders to retire, he place himself in front of his men, led a charge upon the advancing Indians, regaining a commanding position that had just been vacated, and thus insured the safe withdrawal of both detachments without further loss.*" (Committee on Veterans' Affairs, U.S. Senate, *Medal of Honor Recipients: 1863-1973*).

Following posting at Ft. Sheridan, Illinois, he went on detached duty as Professor of Military Science at the University of Wyoming in 1895 until the outbreak of the Spanish war, where he served in the U.S. Volunteer Cavalry. He rejoined his regiment as it sailed for Cuba in January 1899, but returning stateside shortly afterwards on sick leave, he was assigned Adjutant General, Dept. of Colorado. With promotion to Major on February 2, 1901, Varnum transferred out of the regiment in September 1904 to the 9th U.S. Cavalry, serving in Washington State and Kansas. Transferred again in April 1905 with promotion to Lt. Col., 4th U.S. Cavalry, he served in the Philippines as well as commander of the Department of Dakota, after which he retired from active service on disability in 1907. He wholly retired in 1918, advanced to the rank of Colonel. Varnum, referred to by fellow cavalryman and friend Frederick Benteen as a soldier "of magnificent courage," died in San Francisco, California on February 26, 1936.
Highest rank achieved: Colonel, U.S.A., Ret.

George Daniel Wallace*
Born in York County, South Carolina on June 29, 1849, the son of South Carolina Congressman Alexander Stewart. Enrolled at the United States Military Academy in September 1868, graduating class of 1872. Among his classmates were fellow Seventh Cavalrymen Charles Varnum and Henry Harrington.

Following graduation, Wallace was commissioned as Second Lieutenant, Company G, Seventh Regiment, on June

***Wallace**. L. Tom Perry Special Collections, Harold B. Lee Library, Brigham Young University*

14, 1872. Filling the vacancy created by the resignation of T.J. March, he joined his company in the south, posted at Laurens Court House and Newberry, South Carolina until March 1873. After deployment to the Dakotas, he took part in the Yellowstone Expedition of 1873 and the Black Hills Expedition of 1874, commanding a detachment of scouts. In September 1874, he accompanied elements of the regiment to the Dept. of the Gulf, serving in Shreveport and New Orleans, Louisiana as Acting Assistant Adjutant General, District of Red River. He rejoined his regiment at Ft. Lincoln in May 1876, in time to take to the field in the Yellowstone Campaign of 1876 and the battle of Little Big Horn. In the absence of acting company commander McIntosh, killed in the valley fight, he commanded Company G at Reno's hilltop defense. Following the battle, he was promoted to 1st Lt, effective June 25, 1876 and appointed Regimental adjutant, in which he served until June 1877. Wallace took part in the Nez Perce Campaign in 1877 in Benteen's battalion at the battle at Canyon Creek on Sept. 13. He remained in the field with the regiment, promoted to Capt., Co. L, on September 23, 1885 serving in Kansas, Montana, and Missouri. During the Sioux campaign of 1890,

Wallace was killed in action at the battle of Wounded Knee on December 29, while leading a dismounted charge – the last of the cadre who served under Custer to die in battle.
Highest rank achieved: Captain, U.S.A.

David W. Wallingford

Born in Vermont in 1836. Enlisted in Kansas City in June 1861 for a three-month stint in Co. C, 2nd Kansas Infantry until mustered out in August of that year. Finding no substantial employment, Wallingford procured commission as 2nd Lt., Company A, 15th Kansas Cavalry in August 1863, at the organization of the regiment at Ft. Leavenworth. He served on duty in the Dept. of Missouri and Kansas in the defense of the frontier until his dismissal by court martial in April 1865 for "outrages" against civilians. After the War, the influence of several prominent Kansas politicians including Gov. Samuel Crawford allowed his reinstatement to reflect an honorable discharge as well as an endorsement for a commission in the new regiments being formed.

After failing his initial examination for appointment, he passed the second attempt, winning an appointment to the Seventh Regiment as Second Lieutenant, effective July 28, 1866, at the formation of the regiment. Assigned to Company E, he was posted to Ft. Dodge. Promoted 1st Lt on June 8, 1867 while posted to Ft. Hays but transferred to Company B again at Ft. Dodge, he temporarily commanded Company C in the absence of Capt. Gillette. It is no surprise, based on his ignominious appointment and murky past, that Wallingford was another of the regiment's unsavory officers. His service while in the regiment was un-notable, and he was for the most part, genuinely disliked by his fellow officers. Despite numerous arrests and discredit, he took to the field with the regiment in the winter campaign, where he participated at the battle of Washita under Capt. Thompson's squadron. Unfortunately, in September 1869 he was again in trouble; court marshaled for "Conduct Unbecoming an Officer" and cavorting with lewd women. Although Wallingford's support during Custer's own court martial won him unaffectionate camaraderie among Custer's intimates, his flaws were beyond defending and he was ultimately dismissed on May 10, 1870. After his military service, he landed in Lansing Penitentiary in Kansas for "misappropriation of U.S. Property." Serving a term of one year, he was discharged in October 1872. Incarceration obviously left little impression, for he died ten years later on July 11, 1883, refutably again in prison.
Highest rank achieved: 1st Lieutenant, U.S.A.

***Wallingford**. Yale Collection of Western Americana, Beinecke Rare Books and Manuscript Collection*

Thomas Benton Weir

Born in Nashville, Ohio on September 28, 1838. After leaving the University of Michigan, he enlisted in the 3rd Michigan Cavalry in August 1861. Securing a commission as 2nd Lt. in October of that year, he took part in numerous engagements under the Cavalry brigade, Army of the Mississippi including New Madrid, Corinth, and Farmington. Promoted to 1st Lt. in June 1862, he was captured near Iuka later that month on reconnaissance, and released in January 1863, during which time he received promotion to Captain, effective November 1862. For the remainder of the War, he took part in numerous campaigns and expeditions into Mississippi, Arkansas, and Alabama and was promoted to Maj. in January 1865. Following duty in Louisiana, his regiment was deployed to Texas in July 1865, where he was detailed as Acting Assistant Inspector General on Custer's staff. Following a promotion to Lt. Col. in November 1865, he was mustered out in February 1866. Later in July 1867, he was brevetted Maj., U.S.A. for gallantry at Farmington and Lt. Col., U.S.A. for gallantry at Ripley, Miss, against forces of Gen. N.B. Forest.

Endorsed by Custer, Weir was appointed to the Seventh Regiment as First Lieutenant effective July 28, 1866 at the

formation of the regiment. A close confidant of Custer, he was appointed Regimental Commissary in February 1867 in which he served until promotion to Captain, Company D, on July 31, 1867. Afterwards, he went on detached duty on Col. Smith's staff as Acting Assistant Adjutant General, department headquarters. Rejoining the regiment, he took part in the winter campaign and took over command of Hamilton's wing after his death at the battle of Washita. Weir took part in the Yellowstone campaign of 1876, and at Little Big Horn, commanded Company D, serving with distinction at Reno's hilltop defense. Fiercely loyal to Custer, he seemed to fall apart after the battle. Detailed to recruiting duty in the east, he died just six months after the battle of an unknown illness while on leave of absence at Governor's Island, New York on December 9, 1876.
Highest rank achieved: Bvt. Lt. Colonel, U.S.A.

Robert Mayhew West
Born in Newton, New Jersey on September 16, 1834. Enlisted in the 1st Mounted Rifles in April 1856 under fellow Seventh Cavalryman A. Gibbs, serving in New Mexico and Arizona until his discharge in February 1861. He was commissioned 1st Lt., Battery G, 1st Pennsylvania Light Artillery, in July 1861, which was a conglomeration of companies from the 1st Artillery and 43rd Volunteer Infantry, serving under the Pennsylvania Reserve Division. Promoted to Major in September of that year, he took part in actions and operations during the Peninsula campaign, attached to the Army of the Potomac. Promoted to Colonel, 1st Pennsylvania Light Artillery in July 1862, and took part in numerous engagements and operations in Virginia. In April 1864, transferred to the 5th Pennsylvania Cavalry (65th Penn. Volunteers) as commanding Colonel, he took part in numerous engagements during the campaigns in Virginia including actions at Petersburg, Weldon Railroad, where he commanded a brigade under Gen. Kautz, Malvern Hill, and Yellow Tavern. In December, his regiment participated in the engagement at Charles City Cross Roads against Longstreet's entrenched Confederate forces, receiving a commendation by his Departmental Commander. Joining Sheridan's command in early 1865, he distinguished himself again in several engagements during the Appomattox

Top right
***Weir**. United States Military History Institute*

Right
***West**. Library of Congress*

Campaign. Following a brevet promotion to Brig. Gen., Vols. in April 1865 for "gallantry and meritorious service", he was mustered out of the Volunteers in August 1865. Later in March 1867, he was brevetted Maj., U.S.A. for gallantry, Lt. Col. for gallantry at New Market Heights, and Col. for gallantry at Five Forks.

West's distinguished service record won him an appointment to the Seventh Regiment as Captain, Company K, effective July 28, 1866 at the formation of the regiment. From his arrival, his temperamental personality brought on a clash between himself and Lt. Col. Custer that would later manifest itself into a decade-long and well-known schism between the various factions of the regiment. Posted to Ft. Hays with his company, he took part in the Hancock Expedition and scouting operations in 1867, during which his timely arrival upon Robbin's besieged wagon train brought in needed reinforcement. Following Custer's arrest, which later resulted in court martial and suspension, West leveled additional charges at Custer for the shooting of deserters (which were troopers of his own Company K) and afterwards denying them proper medical treatment. Unsatisfied by the overall leniency of the court ruling, he later abetted charges of murder for the subsequent death of the wounded troopers, but it never did more than to embitter further relations. (Custer's trial in January for these offenses ended in acquittal). West, however, had his own share of problems. Occasionally incapacitated during field operations, alcohol excess ultimately proved his undoing, despite accounts of him as a "competent and polished" officer serving dutifully in the winter campaign and commanding a squadron at the Battle of Washita. In early 1868, he was placed in arrest for "consumption" during winter garrison at Leavenworth. Court marshal found him guilty and he was suspended for two months. He wisely opted to leave the regiment, resigning his commission on March 1, 1869. He unfortunately died just a few months later in Murray County, Oklahoma (near Ft. Arbuckle) on September 3, 1869.
Highest rank achieved: Brevet Brig. General, Vols., Bvt. Col., U.S.A.

John Francis Weston

Born in Louisville, Kentucky on November 13, 1845. With recommendations on his behalf, he was appointed 1st Lt., 4th Kentucky Cavalry in December 1861 at the age of 17, serving under fellow Seventh Cavalryman Wickliffe Cooper. With promotion to Capt. in February 1863 and Maj. in November of the following year, he took part in numerous engagements

***Weston**. Courtesy of Glen Swanson*

while attached to the 1st Division, Cavalry Corps, Army of the Cumberland. Weston took part in the Atlanta campaign and the Franklin/Nashville campaign, and following operations with Sherman's army in Georgia, his regiment was deployed to Alabama, where he took part in Wilson's Expedition into Alabama and Georgia. During operations and the fighting near Montgomery, he was awarded the Congressional Medal of Honor for his actions on April 13, 1865, near Wetumpka, Alabama:

> Major, 4th Kentucky Cavalry. Near Wetumpka, Ala., 13 April 1865. *"This officer, with a small detachment, while en route to destroy steamboats loaded with supplies for the enemy, was stopped by an unfordable river, but with 5 of his men swam the river, captured 2 leaky canoes, and ferried his men across. He then encountered and defeated the enemy, and on reaching Wetumpka found the steamers anchored in midstream. By a ruse obtained possession of a boat, with which he reached the steamers and demanded and received their surrender."* (Committee on Veterans' Affairs, U.S. Senate, *Medal of Honor Recipients: 1863-1973*).

Mustered out of the Volunteers in August 1865, his application for post-war assignment yielded a position as Second Lieutenant, Seventh Regiment on August 9, 1867. Assigned to Company C, Weston joined the regiment in October at Ft. Lyon. Posted to Trinidad, Colorado with a detachment of his company, he was promoted to 1st Lt., Company D on November 27, 1868, to occupy the vacancy created by the promotion of Samuel Robbins. In January, he was appointed Regimental Quartermaster, occupying the position until February 1872, during which time he joined the regiment in the south, posted to various stations in South Carolina. After the regiment's deployment to the Dakotas, he transferred to Company L, taking part in Stanley's Yellowstone Expedition, including the engagement on August 11 near the Yellowstone River in which Custer would later write he preformed with "characteristic perseverance and energy." Fortunately for Weston, Custer accepted with reluctant approval, being deprived of further services of this able officer, his request for transfer out of the regiment to promotion on November 24, 1875. Promoted to Capt., Commissary Dept., he missed the annihilation of his company at Big Horn. For the rest of his career, Weston served primarily with the Commissary Dept., promoted steadily through the ranks of the army, eventually achieving the rank of Brig. Gen., Vols. during the Spanish American War in 1898 and Brig. Gen., Commissary General, U.S.A., in 1900. After commanding the Dept. of Luzon, Philippines in 1906, he retired from service on Nov 13, 1909. Weston died in Briarcliff Manor, New York on August 3, 1917.

Highest rank achieved: Brigadier General, Commissary General, U.S.A.

John William Wilkinson

Born in Platte County, Missouri in February 1847. Enrolled at the United States Military Academy in July 1868, graduating class of 1872. Among his classmates were fellow Seventh Cavalrymen George Wallace, Henry Harrington, and Charles Varnum. Following graduation, he was commissioned 2nd Lt., 8th U.S. Cavalry in June 1872, serving on frontier duty in New Mexico, Texas, and Dakota Territory.

Following the losses at Big Horn and the reorganization of the regiment, Wilkinson transferred to the Seventh Regiment as Second Lieutenant, effective June 25, 1876 to fill the vacancy created by the promotion of George Wallace. Joining his company on duty at Ft. Lincoln after the campaign, he was promoted to 1st Lt. shortly afterwards on December 9, 1876 while on leave of absence. After returning in April 1877, he accompanied the regiment in the Nez Perce campaign assigned to Merrill's battalion, commanding Company L at the battle at Canyon Creek. While serving at Ft. Lincoln and Ft. Meade, he was appointed Regimental Adjutant in November 1881 until August 1886. Wilkinson remained in Dakota Territory at various posts and scouting operations until summer of 1888, when he was appointed Professor of Military Tactics at the University of Ohio. Following a brevet promotion to Captain in February 1890 for gallantry at Canyon Creek, Sept. 13, 1877, he rejoined the regiment in the field, posted to Ft. Sill, Oklahoma in early 1891 and missed the Sioux Campaign of 1891. Wilkinson applied for sick leave at the end of the year, during which time he received promotion to Capt. on January 30, 1892. Unfortunately he did not recover from his illness and died just a few months later in Yuma, Arizona on March 22, 1892.

Highest rank achieved: Captain, U.S.A.

Wilkinson*. Courtesy of Glen Swanson*

George Wilhelmus Mancius Yates*

Born to a influential family in Albany, New York on February 26, 1843. After moving to Michigan in 1860, he enlisted in the 4th Michigan Infantry in June 1861, taking part in the Battle of Bull Run and the Seven Days before Richmond Battle, attached to Gen. Heinzelmann's Division. Commissioned 1st Lt., in September 1862, he took part at Beverly Ford, Antietam, and Fredericksburg. Convalescing at home from wounds received at Fredericksburg he met George Custer, developing a friendship that would last until their death together. Returning to duty in late spring 1863, he joined the staff of Gen. A. Pleasanton, serving with Custer in the campaigns of Chancellorsville and Gettysburg. In June 1864, his regiment was mustered out of service and he accepted a commission as 1st Lt., 45th Missouri Infantry in August, at the formation of the regiment. Shortly afterwards, Yates accepted an appointment as Capt., Co. G, 13th Missouri Cavalry in September 1864 at the organization of the regiment, serving in Missouri and Kansas. Following a brevet promotion to Maj., Vols. for wartime "gallantry and meritorious service" and Lt. Col., Vols., "for conspicuous gallantry" at Fredericksburg, Beverly Ford and Gettysburg in March 1865, he was mustered out of the Volunteers in January 1866.

With Custer's endorsement, he secured an appointed as 2nd Lt., 2nd U.S. Cavalry in March 1866 and served on frontier duty in Nebraska. He soon put in for a transfer to Custer's regiment and was accepted as Captain, Seventh Regiment, Company F, on June 12, 1867. After joined the regiment at Ft. Leavenworth in November for winter garrison, he commanded a detachment of his company on escort of the Indian Peace Commission in early summer 1867. He took part in the Sully Expedition in 1868 and the winter campaign of 1868, serving under Thompson's southwestern wing. In 1871, he accompanied the regiment on occupation duty in the south, posted to Meridian Mississippi, and Taylor Barracks, Kentucky. Upon deployment to the Dakotas, he took part in the Yellowstone Expedition of 1873 and the Black Hills Expedition of 1874. Yates joined the regiment on the Yellowstone campaign, where commanding the lead battalion under Custer at the battle of Big Horn, he was killed in action on June 25, 1876. His mutilated body was found near Custer on Last Stand Hill.

Highest rank achieved: Brevet Lt. Col., Vols., Captain, U.S.A.

Yates. *L. Tom Perry Special Collections, Harold B. Lee Library, Brigham Young University*

APPENDICES

CIVIL WAR RANKS (MAJOR THROUGH GENERAL) PRIOR TO APPOINTMENT IN THE SEVENTH CAVALRY

Maj. General
George A. Custer (Vols.)
Alfred Gibbs* (Bvt.)
Andrew J. Smith* (Bvt., U.S.A. and Vols.)
Samuel D. Sturgis* (Bvt.)

Brig. General
William S. Abert (Bvt., Vols.)
Alfred Gibbs*
Lewis Merrill (Bvt., Vols.)
Marcus A. Reno* (Bvt., Vols.)
William P. Robeson, Jr. (Bvt., Vols.)
Samuel D. Sturgis*
William Thompson (Bvt., Vols.)
John E. Tourtellotte (Bvt., Vols.)
Robert M. West (Bvt., Vols.)

Colonel
Frederick W. Benteen*
Wickliffe Cooper (Vols.)
Lewis Merrill (Bvt., Vols.)
Elmer Otis (Bvt.)
Marcus A. Reno* (Bvt.)

Lt. Colonel
Frederick W. Benteen* (Vols.)
Charles C. Cressen (Vols.)
Lewis M. Dayton (Bvt., Vols.)
David Fairly (Vols.)
Verling K. Hart (Bvt.)
Myles W. Keogh (Vols.)
Edward Myers (Bvt.)
Joseph G. Tilford (Bvt.)
Thomas B. Weir (Vols., Nov. 1865)
George W. M. Yates (Bvt., Vols.)

Major
Charles Brewster (Bvt., Vols.)
Frank Y. Commagere (Vols.)
Charles G. Cox (Vols.)
Thomas W. Custer (Bvt., Vols.)
John T. Daniel (Vols.)
Rynd E. Lawder (Vols., Sept. 65)
Edward G. Mathey (Vols.)
Myles Moylan (Bvt., Vols.)
Michael V. Sheridan (Vols.)
Algernon Emory Smith (Bvt., Vols.)
John A. Thompson
John F. Weston (Vols.)

*Held concurrent rank in both United States Army and Volunteers

SEVENTH CAVALRY OFFICERS WHO ACHIEVED THE RANK OF GENERAL OFFICER

William Stretch Abert, Brig. Gen., Vols. (Bvt.)
James Montgomery Bell, Brig. Gen., U.S.A.
Frederick William Benteen, Brig. Gen., U.S.A.
George Armstrong Custer, Maj. Gen., Vols., Maj. Gen., U.S.A. (Bvt.)
Winfield Scott Edgerly, Brig. Gen., U.S.A.
Ernest Albert Garlington, Brig. Gen., Ret., U.S.A.
Alfred Gibbs, Maj. Gen., U.S.A. (Bvt.)
Edward Settle Godfrey, Brig. Gen., U.S.A.
Luther Rector Hare, Brig. Gen., U.S. Vols.
Lewis Merrill, Brig. Gen., U.S.A. (Bvt.)
William John Nicholson, Brig. Gen., U.S.A.
Marcus Albert Reno, Brig. Gen., Vols. (Bvt.)
William P. Robeson, Jr., Brig. Gen., Vols. (Bvt.)
William Wallace Robinson, Jr., Brig. Gen., Ret., U.S.A.
Hugh Lenox Scott, Maj. Gen., U.S.A.
Michael Vincent Sheridan, Brig. Gen., U.S.A.
Andrew Jackson Smith, Maj. Gen., U.S.A. (Bvt.)
Samuel Davis Sturgis, Maj. Gen., U.S.A. (Bvt.)
William Thompson, Brig. Gen., Vols. (Bvt.)
Joseph Green Tilford, Brig. Gen., U.S.A., Ret.
John Eaton Tourtellotte, Brig. Gen., Vols. (Bvt.)
Robert Mayhew West, Brig. Gen., Vols. (Bvt.)
John Francis Weston, Brig. Gen., U.S. Vols., Brig. Gen., C.S.

SEVENTH CAVALRY OFFICERS WHO ACHIEVED THE RANK OF COLONEL

Edwin Proctor Andrus, Col., U.S.A.
Albert Trorillo Siders Barnitz, Col., U.S.A. (Bvt.)
Edwin Parker Brewer, Col., U.S.A.
Wickliffe Cooper, Col., Vols., Col., U.S.A. (Bvt.)
Lewis Mulford Dayton, Col., A.D.C., U.S.A.
John Chowning Gresham, Col., U.S.A., Ret.
Henry Jackson, Col., U.S.A.
Charles William Larned, Col., U.S.A., Ret.
Loyd Stone McCormick, Col., U.S.A.
Albert Payson Morrow, Col., U.S.A.
Elmer Otis, Col., U.S.A.
Horatio Gates Sickel, Jr., Col., U.S.A.
Herbert Jermain Slocum, Col., U.S.A.
Charles Albert Varnum, Col., Ret., USA

DIVISION OF THE MISSOURI UNTIL 1876

Established Jan 30, 1865 under Maj. Gen. J. Pope, it was merged on June 27 into the Military Division of Mississippi under Maj. Gen. Sherman. On August 6, 1866, it was redesignated Division of Missouri with command succeeded by Lt. Gen. Sheridan after March 27, 1869. The Division consisted of five Military Departments within:

Department of the Dakota
Created Aug 11, 1866, Headquarters, St. Paul, Minnesota, Bvt. Maj. Gen. A. Terry
May 18, 1869, Maj. Gen. W.S. Hancock, Dec 3, 1872, Bvt. Maj. Gen. A. Terry, as of 1876.

Department of the Platte
Created Mar 5, 1866, Headquarters, Omaha, Nebraska, Brig. Gen. George Crooke
Jan 23, 1867, Bvt. Maj. Gen. C.C. Augur, briefly discontinued in Nov 1871. Nov 18, 1871, Brig. Gen. E.O.C. Ord, Brig. Gen. G. Crook, as of 1876.

Department of the Missouri
Created Nov 9, 1861, Headquarters, Ft. Leavenworth, Kansas, Maj. Gen. H.W. Halleck
Sept 19, 1862, merged into Dept. of Mississippi. Sept. 19, 1862, re-established under Maj. Gen. S.R. Curtis, May 24, 1863, Maj. Gen. J.M. Schofield, Jan 30, 1864, Maj. Gen. W.S. Rosecrans, Dec 9, 1864, Maj. Gen. G.M. Dodge, July 21, 1865, Maj. Gen. J. Pope, Aug 20, 1866, Maj. Gen. W. S. Hancock, Sept 12, 1867, Maj. Gen. P.H. Sheridan, Sept. 13, 1867,, Bvt. Maj. Gen. A.J. Smith, March 2, 1868, Maj. Gen. P.H. Sheridan, March 20, 1869, Maj. Gen. J.M. Schofield, May 3, 1870, Maj. Gen. J. Pope, as of 1876.

Department of Texas
Created Oct 31, 1853, Headquarters, San Antonio, Texas, Bvt. Maj. Gen. D.E. Twiggs, abandoned 1861-1865, re-established under H.G. Wright on Jun 27, 1865, Aug 6, 1866, merged into Dept. of Gulf, Mar 31, 1870, re-created under J.J. Reynolds, Nov 1, 1871, Indian Territory north of Texas and south of, Kansas added, under Bvt. Maj. Gen. C.C. Auger, Dec 1, 1871, Camp Supply absorbed into Dept. of Missouri, Mar 11, 1875, Indian Territory absorbed into Dept. of Missouri, Mar 11, 1875, Brig. Gen. E.O.C. Ord, until 1876, north portion of Texas absorbed into Dept. of Missouri.

Department of the Gulf

Created Nov 1, 1871, Headquarters, New Orleans, Louisiana, Attached to Division of South, Bvt. Maj. Gen. W.H. Emory, Jan 4, 1875, Department transferred into Dept. of Missouri, Mar 27, 1875, Bvt. Maj. Gen. C.C. Augur, as of 1876.

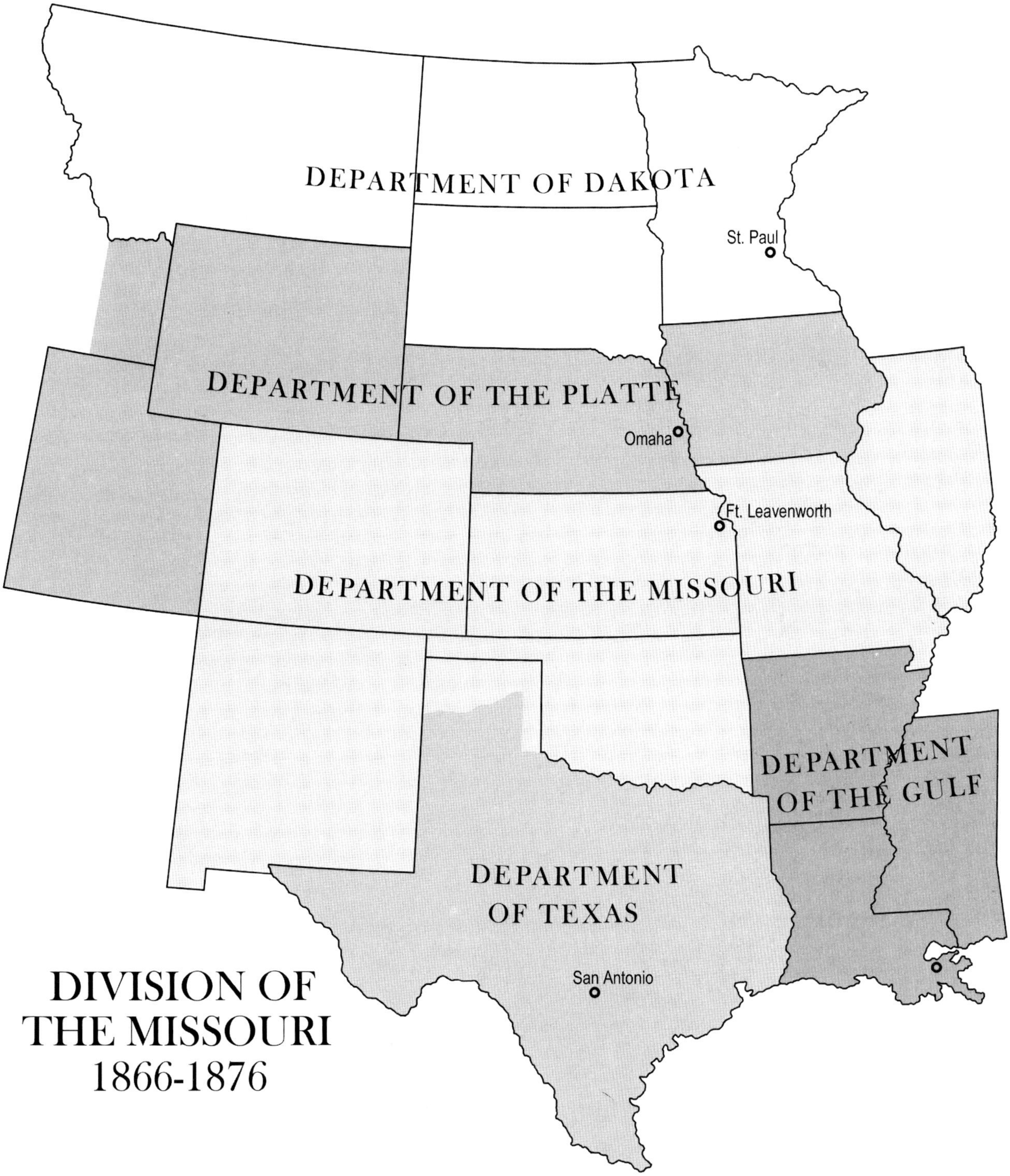

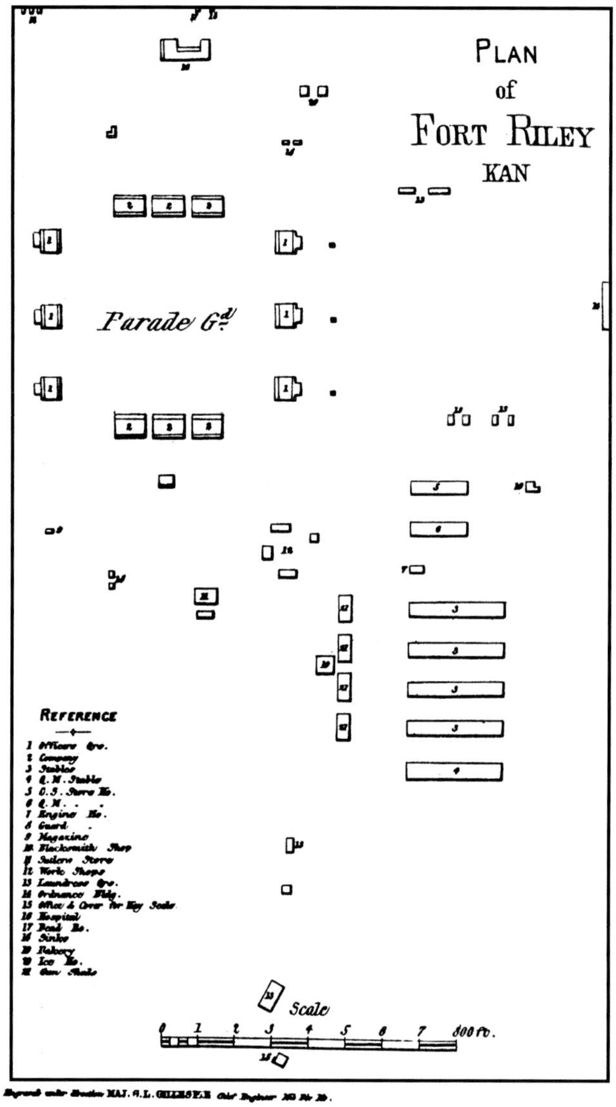

DEPARTMENT OF THE MISSOURI.

FORT RILEY, KANSAS.

Established in 1852. Lat. 39° 4′ 20″, long. 96° 47′. On the left bank of the Kansas River, at the junction of the Smoky Hill and Republican Forks. Postoffice and station of the Kansas Pacific Railroad at the post. Telegraph station at Junction City, three miles distant. Fort Leavenworth, Kan., 133 miles, and Kansas City, Mo., 137 miles distant by rail.

Buildings. Quarters for six companies, six buildings, 88×40 feet; gun sheds for four batteries of light artillery; officers' quarters, six buildings, 60×40 feet; chaplain's quarters, 43×40 feet; hospital, 57×40 feet, for forty-nine patients; guard house, 43×20 feet; all substantial stone buildings of two stories; chapel, one story stone; magazine, brick; two store houses, 149×40 feet, inferior frame structures; one store house, 119×18 feet, substantial, one-story stone building; five stables, 257×38 feet, 94 stalls, built of stone; two corrals, 277×277 feet, one with stables and one open, built of stone. Miscellaneous buildings, viz.: forage house, office, employes' quarters, bakery, laundress' quarters, blacksmith shops, saddler's and carpenter shops, etc., in good condition.

Supplies. Quartermaster's and subsistence stores furnished principally from depot at Fort Leavenworth. Hay and grain obtained in the vicinity, under contract. Water supplied from the river by means of water wagons, from cisterns at the principal buildings, and from wells at the post. Wood furnished by contract. Four months' subsistence kept on hand.

Indians. None in the vicinity. Indian reservation at Council Grove, about 30 miles distant.

Reservation. Declared by the President, May 5, 1855. Reduced as per act of March 2, 1867. Area, about nineteen thousand eight hundred and ninety-nine acres.

Description of Country, etc. The valley of the Kansas at this point has a width of about three miles. The bottom lands are very fertile and well watered. There are several gardens under cultivation at the post. Many varieties of grass, of good quality, grow well. Timber scarce and only useful as fuel. The climate, although subject to great and sudden variations of temperature, is healthy. In summer, owing to the dryness of the atmosphere, the heat is not oppressive. The winter months are pleasant, and there is little snow-fall. During March and the fall months, winds prevail. Settlements are being rapidly made.

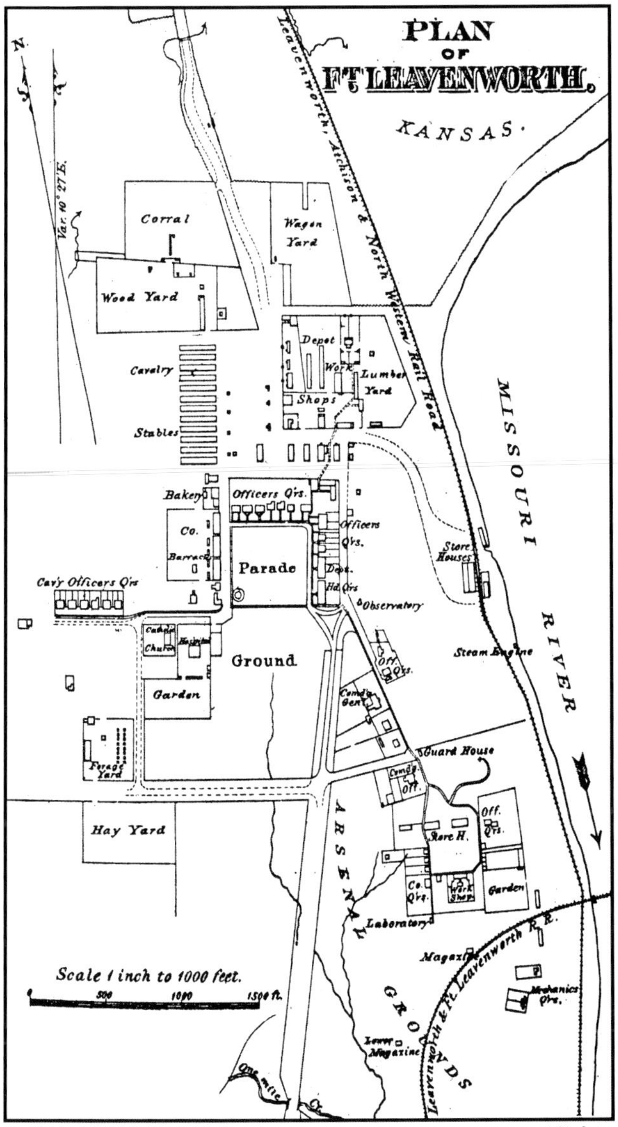

FORT LEAVENWORTH, KAN.

Established in 1827. Lat. 39° 21′, long. 94° 54′ 54″. On the right bank of the Missouri river, about two miles above Leavenworth city. Postoffice, railroad station, telegraph station and steamboat landing at the post. This post is the headquarters of the Department of the Missouri, and a supply depot.

Buildings. Quarters for six companies, band and non-commissioned staff, five frame buildings and one brick, with necessary out-buildings; officers' quarters, seven frame buildings and one brick, two story; post headquarters building, brick, one story; hospital, ten rooms, two story brick; guard house built of stone; post school and chapel, one story stone building; storehouse, bakery, laundress' quarters, workshops, etc., frame buildings; stable, frame, eighty stalls. Department headquarters building, and buildings of the supply depot, consist of thirteen frame buildings as quarters and offices; three storehouses built of stone, three story, 100×40 feet each, and two frame stables of seventy-eight stalls each, one of eighty-one stalls and one of 63 stalls; in use by depot and post quartermasters. All the buildings in fair condition.

Supplies. Quartermaster's and subsistence stores are furnished from the depot at the post; water is obtained from the Missouri river by means of a steam pump, and by cisterns at the quarters; wood supplied by contract.

Indians. None in the vicinity.

Reservation. Declared by the President October 10, 1854. Area, about ten square miles.

Description of Country, etc. The surrounding country is well adapted to agriculture; the soil is rich and well watered, and yields fine crops of corn, wheat, and all the productions of the temperate zone; grass excellent. The principal timber is the hard wood and cottonwood. Climate subject to sudden changes of temperature. Mean temperature about 51° F. The prevailing winds are from the south. Country well settled. A coal mine is on the reservation just north of Leavenworth city, which is being successfully worked by a company who have been granted the right to exclusive mining privileges, by Congress, for all coal or other minerals underlying the military reservation.

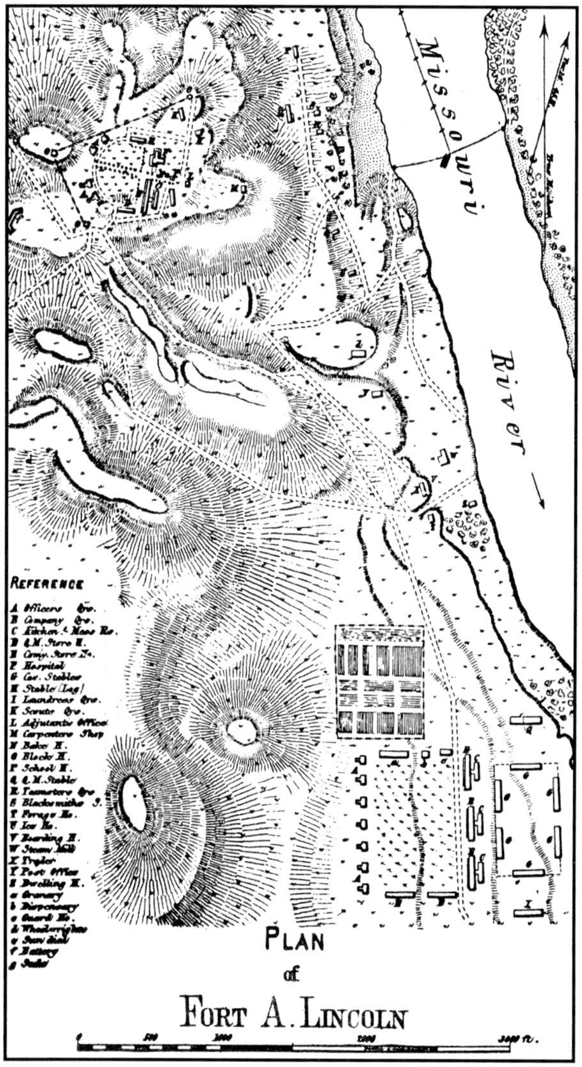

FORT ABRAHAM LINCOLN, D. T.

Established in August, 1872, as Fort McKeen. Name changed to Fort Abraham Lincoln, November 19, 1872. Lat. 46° 46′ 17″, Long. 100° 50′ 37″. On the right (west) bank of the Missouri river, opposite Bismarck, D. T. Postoffice and telegraph office at post. Bismarck, the present terminus of the Northern Pacific Railroad, 5 miles distant; Duluth, the eastern terminus of the road, 453 miles distant. Wagon roads on west bank to Fort Rice and Cheyenne Agency, and on the east bank to Forts Stevenson and Buford. Fort Seward 110 miles to the east. Fort Rice 25 miles by land. Fort Sully 303 miles by river. Fort Stevenson 70 miles by land and 94 miles by river.

Buildings. Cavalry barracks, situated on the low grounds; officers' quarters, seven buildings; quarters for six companies, three buildings, including kitchens. Non-commissioned staff quarters and band quarters, two buildings; laundress' quarters, one building; guardhouse, dispensary, granary, with capacity for 20,000 bushels; one commissary storehouse; one quartermaster's storehouse; six cavalry stables; one quartermaster's stable. All built of pine lumber, and (with the exception of the stables and storehouses) plastered. The buildings are in good condition. Infantry barracks, situated on the crest of the bluff. Quarters for three companies; officers' quarters, four buildings; one commissary storehouse and one quartermaster's storehouse; guard house; hospital, with capacity for 24 patients. All built of pine. Sawmill and shops built of cottonwood. Log buildings for laundresses and scouts. Two blockhouses of squared logs.

Supplies. Quartermaster's stores, etc., furnished from depot at Jeffersonville, Ind., by rail to Sioux City, and thence by boat. Subsistence stores from Chicago and Sioux City, by rail and river. Beef, hay and wood supplied by contract. Water hauled from the river in wagons. Twelve months' subsistence kept on hand.

Indians. The nearest Indians are on their reservation at Standing Rock Agency, between 50 and 60 miles from the post. Their number is estimated at 6,000, composed of different bands of Sioux. While rated as friendly, they are more or less constantly engaged, during the summer months in hostile expeditions. Fort Berthold Agency for the Rees, Gros Ventres and Mandans, 122 miles to the N. W. by river.

Reservation. Declared by the President February 11th, 1873. Enlarged by Executive order of December 17, 1875. Area 23½ square miles.

Description of Country, etc. The fort is surrounded, except on the river front, by ravines, broken and irregular bluffs, and hills. To the west and south are the "Bad Lands;" to the east, the valley of the Missouri River. The land generally is sterile, soil light, gravelly, alkaline and very dry. Outside the bottom lands no crops can be expected, as the average rain-fall is very small—13 inches. Timber is found in very limited quantities (mainly on the islands in the Missouri River and in the ravines) and consists of cottonwood, elm, ash and oak. Mean temperature, 43°. Prevailing winds, west and northwest. East and south winds bring rain during the warm months. The climate, though one of extremes, is very healthy. Coal (lignite) discovered in small quantities. The country to Red River is almost level.

Supplemental Biographies

The biographies listed below are among the replacement officers designated to the join the regiment following the Battle of Little Big Horn. Their transfers were cancelled and they remained with their respective regiments.

Andrus. U.S. Army Recruiting News XI, 6

Edwin Proctor Andrus

Born in Metuchen, New Jersey on November 17, 1851. Graduating from the United States Military Academy, class of 1875, he was appointed 2nd Lt., 5th Cavalry in June 1875 and took part in the engagement at Buffalo Station, Kansas in October 1875. Following the losses at Little Big Horn, Andrus was transferred to the Seventh Cavalry in July 1876 and assigned to Company K, designated to fill the vacancy created by the promotion of Luther Hare. At that time he was in the field scouting near Ft. Wallace. The regimental returns indicate he was en route to the regiment, but the transfer never materialized and he remained with his old regiment.

Andrus, throughout his duty on the frontier took part in numerous campaigns and engagements, including the Powder River Expedition and the fight at Bates Creek, the Nez Perce campaign, the Ute campaign and the Sioux campaign. He served in the Philippines with the 3rd Cavalry, in Arizona, Montana, and Minnesota with the 2nd Cavalry, and as Colonel, 11th Cavalry in Colorado. After retiring from active duty in December 1912, Andrus served in command of a recruiting depot throughout the First World War. He died in Washington D.C. on September 27, 1930.

George Francis Chase

Born in Illinois on July 29, 1848. Graduating from the United States Military Academy, class of 1871, he was appointed Second Lieutenant, 9th Infantry in June 1871. Transferred to the 3rd Cavalry, he took part in the Yellowstone Expedition of 1876. Following the losses from Little Big Horn, Chase was transferred to the Seventh Cavalry and assigned to Company I, designated to fill the vacancy created by the promotion of A.H. Nave. At the time, he was in the field with his regiment until October 1876. The regimental returns indicate that he was en route to the regiment but never arrived and his transfer was cancelled. Chase remained on the frontier, serving in Arizona and Texas and took part in the Ute Expedition. Posted to the Philippines, he participated in numerous campaigns and operations including the capture of Bongobong and San Fernando de Union in November 1899, and the battles at Taboatin Bridge, San Isidro, Manoeg, Aringay, and Tangaden Hill and was awarded two Silver Stars: For "gallantry in action against insurgent forces at Pao, Pangasinan Province, Luzon, Philippines, Nov. 14, 1899" and for "gallantry in action against insurgent forces at San Fernando de Union, Luzon, Philippines, Nov. 20, 1899." Chase did join the 7th Cavalry in February 1901 for several years, accompanying them to Cuba. Afterwards, he served with the 12th Cavalry and as Colonel,

15th Cavalry. He retired with the rank of Brig. Gen in July 1912 and died in Washington, D.C., December 13, 1925.

Chase. United States Military Academy

George Oscar Eaton

Born in Maine on May 14, 1848. Graduating from the United States Military Academy, class of 1873, he was appointed Second Lieutenant, 5th Cavalry, serving on frontier duty in Arizona and taking part in the engagement at Jarvis Pass, Arizona. Following the losses at Little Big Horn, Eaton was transferred to the Seventh Cavalry and assigned to Company C, designated to fill the vacancy created by the death of Henry Harrington. At that time he was on leave of absence from duty at Ft. Hays, Kansas. The regimental returns indicate that he was en route to the regiment but never arrived and his transfer was cancelled. He remained with the 5th Cavalry for the remainder of his career, serving primarily on the frontier and in the field with his unit. Following several lengthy sick leaves, he resigned from service and eventually died of old age in Ft. Myers, Florida on September 12, 1930.

Eaton. United States Military Academy

Daniel Crosby Pearson

Born in Cambridge, Massachusetts on May 19, 1845. Pearson left Dartmouth College and enrolled at the United States Military Academy, graduating class of 1870. Commissioned 2nd Lt., 2nd Cavalry in June 1870, he served on frontier duty at various posts in Wyoming. Following the losses from Little Big Horn, Pearson was transferred to the Seventh Cavalry and assigned to Company D, to fill the vacancy created by the promotion of Winfield Edgerly. At that time, he was in the field serving with his regiment on the Yellowstone Expedition. The regimental returns indicate that he was en route to the regiment, but he never arrived and his transfer was cancelled. Following frontier duty in Montana, Washington State, Idaho, Arizona, and New Mexico and brief appointment as Professor of Military Science and Tactics at Pennsylvania State College, he served with his regiment in Cuba and the Philippines. Pearson eventually found his way to the Seventh Regiment as Lt. Col, ironically filling the vacancy created by the promotion again of Winfield Edgerly. He retired a year later in 1905 and died at home in Cambridge on August 25, 1920.

Charles Brewster Schofield

Born in Freeport, Illinois on June 26, 1849, the brother of Lt. Gen. John M. Schofield. Graduating from the United States

Military Academy, class of 1870, he was commissioned in the 2nd Cavalry, serving on frontier duty in Montana where he was detailed as escort to Northern Pacific railroad surveyors and participated in the engagement with Indians at Pryor's Creek. Following the losses from Little Big Horn, Schofield was transferred to the Seventh Cavalry and assigned to Company F, designated to fill the vacancy created by the promotion of Charles Larned. At the time, he was on the Yellowstone/Sioux Campaign until September 1876. The regimental returns indicate he was en route to the regiment, but he never arrived and his transfer was cancelled. After duty on the frontier in the Nez Perce campaign and the battle of Muddy Creek, he was appointed Aide-de-Camp to his brother, where he remained for the duration of his career. While posted to Cuba, he died from heart disease on February 1, 1901 at Santa Clara Barracks.

Pearson. *United States Military Academy*

Schofield. *United States Military Academy*

GLOSSARY OF FORTS AND FORTIFICATIONS MENTIONED WITHIN THE TEXT

Camp Supply, Indian Territory

Built near the junction of the Wolf and Beaver Creek (Canadian River), it was established in November 1868 as a supply depot for the forthcoming winter offensive. It was not until 1872 that solid, permanent structures were erected. The camp garrisoned troops throughout the campaigns of 1870s and 1880s and was eventually abandoned in 1895.

Fort Abraham Lincoln, Dakota Territory

The fort, located on the west banks of the Missouri River, was originally established as an infantry post named Ft. McKeen, in honor of Col. Boyd McKeen killed at Cold Harbor in August 1872. As Cavalry units were added to the garrison, the post was renamed Ft. Abraham Lincoln in November of 1872. After the Seventh cavalry arrived in 1873, the small cavalry garrison was expanded to house nine cavalry companies. The fort was eventually abandoned in 1891.

Fort Dodge, Kansas

Ft Dodge was established in 1864 by order of Maj. Gen. G. Dodge, who commanded the department. Built on the left bank of the Arkansas River to guard the mail routes through the region, it housed a large garrison of troops included several companies of the Seventh Cavalry during operations in 1868-69. Ft. Dodge was decommissioned in 1882.

Fort Harker, Kansas

Ft. Harker was established as Fort Ellsworth in 1864. Declared by the president in 1866, it was renamed Ft. Harker after Brig. Gen. Charles Harker, killed at Kenasaw Mountain. The post provided protection to traffic along the Kansas stage lines and Smokey Hill trail and served as a supply depot for the region. Housing several companies of the Seventh Cavalry, Harker bore the majority of suffering during the cholera epidemic in 1867. The fort was abandoned in 1872.

Fort Hays, Kansas

Built in 1865 on Big Creek, a tributary of the Smokey Hill Fork of the Kansas river, it was originally designated Fort Fletcher. Utilized as a main western supply depot, the fort served as protection of the Smoky Hill Route and construction of the Union Pacific Railway. The post was renamed Ft. Hays in 1867 after Brig. Gen. Hays, killed at the Wilderness, and in addition to housing several companies of the Seventh Cavalry, it was home to the 5th, 9th and 10th Cavalry. Fort Hays was abandoned in 1890.

Fort Larned, Kansas

The fort was first constructed as a small military outpost in 1858 on the right bank of the Pawnee River (fork), and shortly after named Camp Alert. The post was redesignated Ft. Larned in 1868, after Paymaster Gen. B. F. Larned In addition to offering protection for traffic along the routes, it served as an Indian Bureau agency and also as the base of operations for various campaigns. The post was abandoned in 1878.

Fort Leavenworth, Kansas

Established on the Missouri River in 1827 by Col. Henry Leavenworth, it was constructed to protect both the Santa Fe and Oregon Trails. The fort served as the center for military operations in the region during early operations against the Cherokee Indians, as well as the Mexican War, the Civil War, and the war against the Plains Indians. Home to the Seventh Cavalry in 1868 through 1871, it also served as the headquarters for the Dept. of Missouri. It is the oldest fort west of the Missouri and is still active today.

Fort Lyon, Colorado Territory

The fort was originally built as a stockade by fur traders in 1826 named Fort William or "Bent's Fort," after Col. William Bent. A newer 1853 fortification was built on the banks of the Arkansas River and later leased by the government as Ft. Wise. In 1862, it was redesignated Ft. Lyon, in honor of Gen. Nathaniel Lyon, killed at Wilson's Creek. In the summer of 1866 the river undermined the fort, and on June 9, 1867, the new Fort Lyon was established on the north bank of the Arkansas near the fork of the Purgatory River. Built to protect travel along the Santa Fe Trail, the fort housed several companies of the Seventh Cavalry and played an active role during Sheridan's winter campaign of 1868. The fort closed in 1889.

Fort McPherson, Nebraska

Established in 1863 on the south side of the Platte River, it was originally named "Cantonment McKean." Later changed to "Cottonwood Springs," the post was renamed Ft. McPherson in February 1866, in honor of Gen. J. B. McPherson, killed at Atlanta. Built to quarter five companies, it served to protect travel along the Oregon Trail until abandoned in 1880.

Fort Morgan, Colorado Territory

Established as Camp Junction near the South Platte River in 1864 and later Camp Wardell, it served to protect the region and the route to Denver. Completed in 1866, the post was renamed Ft. Morgan in honor of Col. C.A. Morgan. As the railroad shifted traffic north, the post was abandoned in 1868.

Fort Reynolds, Colorado Territory

Established in 1867 on the right bank of the Arkansas River, it was declared by the president in 1868. Less than fifty miles from the Rocky Mountains, it was a small garrison, built only to house eighty men, including a company of the Seventh Cavalry. The fort was abandoned in 1872.

Fort Rice, Dakota Territory

Established in 1864 on the west side of the Missouri River by Brig. Gen. Alfred Sully during his 1864 campaign against the Sioux, it was declared by the president in 1867. Named after Brig. Gen. James Rice, killed at Laurell Hill, Virginia, the post was built to quarter four companies and served to protect both overland routes and travel along the Missouri River. The fort was decommissioned in 1878, and abandoned the following year.

Fort Riley, Kansas

Established in 1852 as Camp Center at the junction of the Smokey Hill and Republican Rivers (forks), it was renamed Fort Riley in May 1853, after Col. Bennett Riley, "Hero of

Cerro Gordo." The original home of the Seventh Cavalry at it's formation in 1866, the fort served to protect overland routes and defense of the population, as well as the construction of the Kansas Pacific Railroad. Later, Ft. Riley became a center for Cavalry units and is still active today.

Fort Sedgwick, Colorado Territory

Established as Camp Rankin, it was built in 1864 at the mouth of Lodgepole Creek. After the sacking and burning of a nearby town by Indians, the fort was rebuilt and named Ft. Sedgwick, after Gen. John Sedgwick, killed at Spottsylvania. The fort was the central point from which garrisoned troops would protect the construction of the Union Pacific Railroad. It was abandoned in 1871.

Fort Sill, Indian Territory

The fort, near Medicine Bluff Creek, was established in 1868 as Camp Wichita by Gen. Sheridan for use in the winter campaign of 1868. After the first troops arrived in early 1869, the post was renamed Ft. Sill in honor of Gen. J.W. Sill, killed at Stone's River. The fort served as garrison for troops during various campaigns against the Comanche, Southern Cheyenne, Kiowa, and Apache Indians. It later became the United States Field Artillery School and is still in use today.

Fort Totten, Dakota Territory

The fort was established in 1867 and declared by the President in 1870. Built to quarter four companies, it was named after Brig. Gen. Joseph Totten, U.S. Engineers and served as a garrison to guard overland routes. After decommission in 1890, the fort became property of the Bureau of Indian Affairs and later served as an Indian boarding school and health-care facility.

Fort Wallace, Kansas

Ft. Wallace was originally established as a military encampment for the Pond Creek Stage, and aptly named Camp Pond Creek. On the left bank of the Smokey Hill River, the post was redesignated Fort Wallace in 1866, named in honor of W.H.L. Wallace, killed at Shiloh and declared by the President in 1868. Quartered for four companies, the fort served to protect the western portion of the Smoky Hill Trail to Colorado until decommissioned in 1882.

ENDNOTES

Introduction

[1] Robert Utley, *Frontier Regulars* (New York: Macmillan Publishing, 1973). The act also introduced new geographic divisional and departmental boundaries of command, as well as the addition of Indian scouts and the Veteran Reserve Corps.

[2] Utley, *Life in Custer's Cavalry* (Lincoln: University of Nebraska Press, 1987), 12; Utley, *Frontier Regulars, 21.*

[3] Following the war, a board of officers was convened in 1866 to assess the entitlement of brevet ranks, in which hundreds were liberally and casually awarded. However, ambiguity and disagreement of title regarding corresponding regular army rank versus Civil war brevet rank in the new post war army led to misuse and confusion. By 1869, the army imposed restrictions upon both the wearing of brevet rank and addressing of brevet titles; henceforth awarding brevet promotions (between the years 1867 to 1890) solely for significant achievement and battlefield heroism.

[4] William Davis, *Commanders of the Civil War* (London: Chrysalis Books, 1989), 170. Custer is often misidentified as being the youngest brigadier general in US military history. That distinction actually went to Galusha Pennypacker, who reached that rank at twenty-one years of age. Custer does, however, hold the distinction of being the youngest major general, which he achieved at the age of twenty-five.

[5] Elizabeth Custer, *Tenting on the Plains* (Santa Barbara: The Narrative Press, 2003), 224.

[6] Melbourne Chandler, *Of Garryowen in Glory* (Annandale, Virginia: Turnpike Press, 1960), 3. Both incoming personnel as well as the Second Cavalry remained locked in garrisoned at Ft. Riley as the winter season set in; Clayton K.S. Chun, *Army in the Plains Indian Wars*, (Oxford: Osprey Publishing, 2004), 21. Not until the early 1870s did Sherman introduce advanced schools for the incoming officers, offering more specific and advanced instruction.

[7] Custer, *Tenting on the Plains, 234.*

[8] A more serious and sinister division between the officers later developed, beginning with the shooting of members of West's K company in June 1867 and the abandonment of Elliot's command at the battle of Washita, which overshadowed these common and mostly harmless differences between Custer loyalists, and as author Utley refers to officers excluded from the "Royal Family."

[9] Utley, *Frontier Regulars, 21 24.*

[10] Utley, *Life in Custer's Cavalry, 125.*

[11] Custer, *Tenting on the Plains, 217.*

[12] Alice O'neil, *Military Discipline Under General George A. Custer* (New york: Arrow and Trooper Publishing, 1998), 9. She references the Adjutant General's Report to the 40th Congress.

Operational History of the Seventh Cavalry, 1866-1876

[1] Utley, *Frontier Regulars, 20.*

[2] The primary difference between the two was the addition of a regimental Chaplain.

[3] Chandler, *Of Garryowen in Glory, 3-5.*

[4] *Ibid., 3-6.* The term "company" is also referred to. The Cavalry service referred to their companies, unofficially, as troops, to differentiate themselves from infantry companies. However, it was not until 1883 that "troop" became the official designation.

[5] Dee Brown, *Bury My Heart at Wounded Knee* (New York: Henry Holt and Company, 2001), 149. Southern Cheyenne bands left the confines of boundaries established in 1865 to utilize the land between the Smokey Hill River and the Republican River. Fueled by the earlier success of Northern Cheyenne and Teton Sioux defiance, retaining Powder River Territory, they aim was to all but eliminate the white presence in the region.

[6] James Dixon, "Across the Plains with General Hancock." In *Eyewitness to the Indian Wars,* ed. Peter Cozzens, 29-32 (Mechanicsburg, Pennsylvania: Stackpole Books, 2003). Although accompanying the column, Col. Smith was on detached duty commanding Dept. of Upper Arkansas; Theodore Davis, "A Summer on the Plains." 33-52, *Ibid.*

[7] Evan S. Connell, *Son of the Morning Star* (New York: Harper-Collins, 1984), 178. The Sand Creek massacre, as it became known, was a sad chapter in the establishment of the west. Assured of absolute safety by their own agents, Southern Cheyenne Chief Black Kettle and his band, in compliance with ultimatums presented by representatives from Ft. Lyon, remained camped near Sand Creek. On November 28, 1864, elements of the 3rd Colorado volunteers, under the command of the fanatical Col. Chivington, attacked the Indian encampment, killing mostly women and children as they huddled around an American flag; erected to show their good intentions.

[8] Utley, *Life in Custer's Cavalry*.

[9] Marvin Garfield, "Defense of the Kansas Frontier," *Kansas Quarterlies*, August 1932, No. 4: 326, 451.

[10] Minnie Dubbs Milbrook, The West Breaks in General Custer," *Kansas Quarterlies,* Summer, vol. 36, No. 2,1970: 114-118. Ft. Wallace was in poor shape and neither Sheridan nor Hancock was present. Awaiting orders and needing supplies for his exhausted troopers, Custer left his men to go to Ft. Harker. In addition, he had heard about the devastating floods and that his wife was amidst a cholera outbreak. Libby Custer had been at Ft. Riley and Custer, believing his wife to be at Ft. Harker during the cholera epidemic, left with several officers, leaving the regiment unauthorized. With a small detachment of men, he proceeded to Ft. Harker. During his forced march with about seventy-five of his men, the group lost two soldiers, in which Custer was accused of not ascertaining there whereabouts or well being, including spending of otherwise good horses.

[11] Milbrook, 117-140.Custer was plagued by desertion throughout the expedition. Ordering several deserters from West's K Company apprehended during which several were shot. This was certainly not outside the parameters of the rules, and in fact had been a standing order from Sherman. In addition, for whatever reasons, he made a public display of refusing the wounded men medical attention, although privately acquiescing to the regimental doctor. This episode naturally had an impact on relations between several officers, chiefly West, and Custer, whom remained from then on estranged. Desertions were rampant, not just for Custer, but in the army as a whole. Statistics show there were over 13,000 desertions from the army in 1867 alone.

[12] David Dixon, *Hero of Beecher Island* (Lincoln: University of Nebraska Press, 1994), 54. Hancock' removal was partly due to the failure of his expedition. However, Sheridan's appointment as department commander was also a punitive move by President Johnson, as Sheridan's opposition to reconstruction policy landed him at odds with the administration.

[13] Edward S. Godfrey, "Some Reminiscences, Including an Account of General Sully's Expedition Against the Plains Indians, 1868." *Eyewitness to the Indian Wars,* ed. Cozzens, 240-246.

[14] Anthony Rallya, "Fighting Indians from an Ambulance." In *Eyewitness to the Indian Wars,* ed. Cozzens, 247-249.

[15] Godfrey, *Some Reminiscences, 159*. Whatever Sully thought of Custer personally, he knew and respected his capabilities, and although stinging from the rebuke, he not only asked for his additional men and horses, but for Custer to lead them.

[16] Robert Utley, *Cavalrymen in Blue* (New York: Macmillan Publishing, 1967); Horrace L. Moore, "An Indian Campaign," *Eyewitness to the Indian Wars,* ed. Cozzens, 263-279. The 18th Kansas Volunteer Cavalry, consisting of four companies, was formed at the request of the governor of Kansas for additional protection from Indian aggression for the railroad workers and through the trails of the Kansas frontier. Mustered into service in July 1867 at Ft. Harker, under the command of Horrace L. Moore, they took part in field operations with the Seventh Cavalry, and unfortunately suffered heavily during the cholera outbreak. Further outrages on the frontier and the need for additional forces for forthcoming winter operations in 1868 facilitated the organization of the 19th Kansas Cavalry, which was formed for that purpose. Mustered in to service in October 1868 under the command of Bvt. Brig. Gen. Samuel Crawford, they joined the Seventh Cavalry during the winter campaign.

[20] A dispute arose between Sully and Custer regarding who would command the column. Since both were Lt. Colonels, Sully insisted he be in command, based on his higher brevet rank. Sheridan, with fresh memories of Sully's last debacle, resolved the situation favoring Custer and sending Sully to command the District of the Upper Arkansas.

[21] Although listed as missing and presumed killed, he was not actually discovered until a return to the battlefield in mid December.

[22] Don Heinrich Tolzmann, *Frederick Whittaker's Complete Life of General George A. Custer* (Bowie, Maryland: Heritage books, 1993), 426-442; Utley, *Cavalier in Buckskin, 70-73*. Black Kettle's village, where the battle ensued, was on the western edge of a larger nest of encampments along the Washita River.

[23] George A. Custer, *My Life on the Plains* (Lincoln: University of Nebraska Press, 1966), 447-463; Chandler, *Of Garryowen in Glory,* 23-27. Despite promises made to cease attacks and surrender, Cheyenne "Dog Soldier" bands, under the collective leadership of Tall Bull, who succeeded Roman Nose after his death at Beecher Island, continued to hold out. It was not until July of that year at the battle of Summit Springs with the under E. A Carr's 5th Cavalry, did these obstinate bands finally acquiesce, effectively ending Cheyenne aggression.

[24] Maj E.A Garlington, Inspector General, "The Seventh Regiment of Cavalry." p. 251-267. In *The Army of the United States Historical Sketches of Staff and Line with Portraits of Generals-in-Chief*, ed. Theophilus F. Rodenbough, and William L. Haskin, 251-267. New York: Maynard, Merrill, & Company, 1896.

[25] The treaty of 1868, among the various articles, allotted land, including the black hills region, to be "set apart for the absolute and undisturbed use and occupation of the Indians…" (see US Statutes at Large, 15, 635-40); G.A. Custer, "Battling with the Sioux on the Yellowstone." In *The Custer Reader*, ed. Paul Andrew Hutton, 201-219. Lincoln: University of Nebraska Press, 1992. The expedition was actually a second attempt, with the first being unsuccessful as it was not afforded sufficient numbers for protection against continuous harassment from hostile Indians.

[26] Charles W. Larned, "Expedition to the Yellowstone River: Letters of a young Cavalry Officer." Hutton, *Custer Reader, 180-197.*

[27] Marguerite Merrington, *The Custer Story* (New York: Devin Adair, 1950), 252. The start of the expedition found Custer and Stanley at odds, as Custer's aggressive nature antagonized Stanley's authority. Inevitably, they clashed and a frustrated Stanley, aggravated by heavy drinking, placed Custer under arrest for disobedience of orders. Stanley's arrest of Custer was eventually rescinded, according to sources, "when Stanley sobered up." Afterwards, Stanley acquiesced to Custer's nature and allowed him relative freedom of command of his regiment; G.A. Custer, "Battling with the Sioux on the Yellowstone." In *The Custer Reader*, ed. Paul Andrew Hutton, 201-219. The column suffered three losses during the fight. Regimental Veterinary surgeon Honsinger and two others were killed by roaming Indians as they attempted to join Custer's forward Column.

[28] Charles W. Larned, "Expedition to the Yellowstone River: Letters of a young Cavalry Officer." Hutton, *Custer Reader, 180-197.*

[29] Garlington, 251-257.

[30] Donald Jackson, *Custer's Gold* (Lincoln: University of Nebraska Press, 1966), 49-53. In addition to the army engineering personnel, the team included notable scientists George Bird Grinnell,

Paleontologist of Yale University, University of Minnesota geologist Newton H. Winchell, botanist A. B. Donaldson, photographer William H. Illingsworth, several civilian minors, and newspaper correspondents, who by standing order, were prohibited from accompanying the expedition. Ibid., 120. Pressure and criticism from the public about the true motives for the mission, prompted the rebuttal from the army, claiming it was for "much needed reconnaissance" and was in fact *not* in violation of the 1868 treaty.

[31] The expedition's late start was attributed to delays in supply, as Custer wanted to wait for the newer 1873 model Springfield carbines.

[32] Jackson, *Custer's Gold, 3.* Several white explorers had already been through the regions, among them French explorers and the famous Jedadiah Smith, who was credited with being the first to record passage; *Ibid., 11.* Several members of the expedition had disputed the fact of actually finding gold, among them Winchell and Fred Grant, who had accompanied the regiment. Mostly at fault were the newspapers, which without credible evidence and based soley on Custer's ambiguous reports, completely sensationalized the findings. Nevertheless, whether planned or merely an act of exuberance, Custer's inconclusive yet positive finding aided in the military's plan to "retake" the region and other added benefits such as "stimulate trade" and "strengthen the position of the territories."

[33] The well-publicized story of "Rain-in-the-Face" derives from his arrest at the Standing Rock Agency at that time by Tom Custer. Swearing vengence, he purportedly made good on his intention to "cut out" the heart of the arresting officer. Tom Custer's body did suffer extreme malevolence following his demise, but whether "Rain-in-the-Face" got his prize, we can only guess.

[34] Up to the point of the Big Horn fight, negotiations still were ongoing, as the Indians still held the region of the Black Hills. However, after the fight, the army all but abandoned reasonable negotiations for the rights to the land.

[35] Brown, *Bury My Heart at Wounded Knee, 284.*

[36] The term "Sioux" refers to several bands including the Teton, Yankton and Santee. However, in discussing the Indians of the Dakotas, it refers to the Teton, or the western most band, which consisted of numerous smaller bands within, including the Brulé, Minneconjou, Hunkpapa, Sans Arc, and Blackfoot. The Oglala, also of the Teton band, incorporated smaller bands such as the Osage, the Bad Faces, and the Loafers.

[37] Poor weather and even poorer communications prohibited many of the "willing" to ever meet the deadline set forth by the government; Chandler, *Of Garryowen in Glory.* Crook also commanding the Dept. of the Platte.

[38] Frederic F. Van de Water, *Glory Hunter* (Lincoln: University of Nebraska Press, 1934), 275-279. Custer had been relieved of his position of command of the third column of the expedition for his damning testimony against the Grant administration concerning deplorable conditions at Indian reservations in spring of 1876. Lobbied by Sherman and Terry to utilize Custer's experience, he was allowed to join the expedition but was relegated to a subordinate position, commanding only his immediate regiment.

[39] Utley, *Cavalier in Buckskin, 242*; Brady, *Indian Fights and Fighters, 185-193.*

[40] Frazier and Robert Hunt, *I Fought with Custer: The Story of Sergeant Windolph* (Lincoln: University of Nebraska Press, 1974), 63-77. In addition, the reference made to "Stanley's Stockade" refers to the existing supply base, which had been used during Stanley's expedition of 1873.

[41] Utley, *Cavalier in Buckskin, 133-142.* During the conference aboard the Steamer, Custer declined both an offer to bring additional forces of the Second Cavalry, as well as a battery of Gatling Guns under Lt. Low. He reasoned they would both promote discord between the two regiments and the condemned horses used to pull the guns would impede his progress; Edward S. Godfrey, "Custer's Last Battle" *The Custer Reader*, ed. Hutton, 257-330.

[42] Chandler, *Of GarryOwen in Glory, 59.* Indians were well aware of the presence of military forces in the area, especially from participants in Crook's fight on June 17 who joined the village. Unknown to Custer's column, their presence also had been observed several days before from Indians enroute to and from the reservations.

[43] Hunt, *I Fought with Custer, 76.*

[44] Marquis, *Keep the Last Bullet for Yourself, 12.*

[45] *Ibid., 106.* His reference to the Creek is the Indian name. It is known to us as Reno Creek; Connell, *Son of the Morning Star, 43-51.* Reno at this point was beside himself, and he vacillated between orders to vacate the timbers. His orders were reportedly countered from Capt. French to remain. Noise from the battle and confusion as to what the orders actually were, resulted in a chaotic departure from the tree line. Many troopers never even heard the order and simply followed the others.

[46] Cyrus Townsend Brady, *Indian Fights and Fighters*, (Lincoln: University of Nebraska Press, 1971), 242. The regimental surgeon, Dr. DeWolf, was also killed here. Accounts of his death record his dramatic demise as "stopping and turning his horse, firing at the rushing Indians until he himself was shot and killed."

[47] Chandler, *Of GarryOwen in Glory, 61.*

[48] Katherine Gibson-Fougera, With Custer's Cavalry, (Caldwell Idaho: Caxton, 1942), 266-272. From letter from Francis Gibson following the battle, describing the events; Edward S. Godfrey, "Custer's Last Battle" *The Custer Reader*, ed. Hutton, 257-330.

[49] Godfrey,257-330.

[50] Utley, *Cavalier, 137-153;* Chandler, *Of GarryOwen in Glory, 45-51.* After Crook departed the column, he marched south where he engaged the hostiles again at the Battle of Slim Buttes.

[51] Marquis, *Keep the Last Bullet for Yourself, 87.* Crooks engagement was at that time unknown to Terry. It is possible that the trail found by Reno's detachment was that very group moving to join Sitting Bull's band. Nevertheless, even to the conservative strategist, Indian nature and their tendency to lodge in proximity to neighboring tribes made an accurate count near difficult at best.

[52] This blanket autonomy was not given lightly as Terry, actually commanding the column, specifically lobbied for Custer's experience and initiative during his removal from the campaign, requesting and charging Custer with actual field command of the expedition's third column.

[53] Marquis, *Keep the Last Bullet for Yourself, 104-119.*

[54] Gregory Michno, *The Mystery of E Troop* (Missoula, Montana: Mountain Press, 1994), 286.

BIBLIOGRAPHY, SOURCES AND CREDITS

Brady, Cyrus T., *Indian Fights and Fighters*, McClure, Philips & Company, 1904. Reprinted, University of Nebraska Press, Lincoln, 1971

Brewster, Charles, "Battle of Washita," *National Tribune*, May 18, 1899. Reprinted in Peter Cozzens, ed., *Eyewitness to the Indian Wars, 1856-1890: Conquering the Southern Plains, Volume III*, Mechanicsburg, 2003.

Brown, Dee, *Bury My Heart At Wounded Knee*, Holt, Rinehart and Winston, 1971. Reprinted, Henry Holt and Company, New York, 2001.

Carroll, John M., *They Rode with Custer*, J.M. Carroll & Company, New York, 1987.

—, Custer's Chief of Scouts: The Reminiscences of Charles A. Varnum, University of Nebraska Press, Lincoln, 1987.

—, *Ten Years with Custer Among the Indians: The Writings of John Ryan*, J. M. Carroll & Company, Bryan, Texas, 1980.

Chandler, Melbourne C., *Of Garryowen in Glory: History of the Seventh United States Cavalry Regiment*, Turnpike Press, Inc., Annandale, Virginia, 1960.

Chronological List of Actions with Indians; January 1, 1866-January, 1891, Office Memoranda, Adjutant General's Office, U.S. Army Military History Research Collection.

Chun, Clayton K.S., *US Army in the Plains Indian Wars*, Osprey Publishing, Oxford, 2004.

Committee of Veterans' Affairs, U.S. Senate, *Medal of Honor Recipients: 1863-1973,* Government Printing Office, Washington, D.C., 1973.

Connell, Evan S., *Son of the Morning Star*, Harper Perennial, New York, 1984.

Cozzens, Peter, *Eyewitnesses to the Indian Wars, 1865-1890, Volume Two, The Wars for the Pacific Northwest*, Stackpole Books, Mechanicsburg, Pennsylvania, 2002.

—, *Eyewitnesses to the Indian Wars, 1865-1890, Volume Three, Conquering the Southern Plains*, Stackpole Books, Mechanicsburg, Pennsylvania, 2003.

Cullum, George W., *Biographical Register of the Officers and Graduates of the United States Military Academy, 1802-1890, Volume III*, NOS 2001-3384, Houghton Mifflin & Co., New York, 1891. (Supplimental Sections 1901, 1910, 1920, 1930).

Custer, Elizabeth B., *Following the Guidon*, Harper & Brothers, New York, 1890. Reprinted, University of Nebraska Press, 1994.

—, *Tenting on the Plains: With General Custer from the Potomac to the Western Frontier*, C.L. Webster & Company, 1887. Reprinted, The Narrative Press, Santa Barbara, 2003.

—, *Boots and Saddles*, University of Oklahoma Press, Norman, 1961.

Custer, George A., *My Life on the Plains*, Lakeside Press, Chicago, 1952. Reprinted, University of Nebraska Press, Lincoln, 1966.

Davis, Theodore R., A Summer n the Plains, *Harpers New Monthly Magazine*, Vol. 36, 1868. Reprinted in Peter Cozzens, ed., *Eyewitness to the Indian Wars, 1856-1890: Conquering the Southern Plains, Volume III*, Mechanicsburg, 2003.

Davis, William C., *The Commanders of the Civil War, Rebels and Yankees Series*, Chrysalis Books, London, 1989.

Dillon, Richard H., *North American Indian Wars*, Chartwell Books, Inc., Secaucus, New Jersey, 1993.

Dixon, David, *Hero of Beecher Island: The Life and Military Career of George A. Forsyth*, University of Nebraska Press, Lincoln, 1994.

Donaldson, A.B., The Black Hills Expedition, *South Dakota Historical Collections*, Vol. VII, 1914.

Dyer, Frederick H., *Compendium of the War of the Rebellion, Volume I, Volume II, Volume III*, Dyer Publishing Company, Des Moines, 1908.

Elliot, Joel H., *Sully Expedition to the Canadian: A Huge Joke*, Miscellaneous Collection, Theodore R. Davis, Manuscript Department, Kansas State Historical Society, Topeka, Reprinted in Peter Cozzens, ed., *Eyewitness to the Indian Wars, 1856-1890: Conquering the Southern Plains, Volume III*, Mechanicsburg, 2003.

Ferris, Robert G., *Soldier and Brave: Historic Places Associated with Indian Affairs and the Indian Wars in the Trans-Mississippi West*, United States Department of the Interior, National Park Service, Washington D.C., 1971.

Frazer, Robert W., *Forts of the West*, University of Oklahoma Press, Norman, 1965.

Garfield, Marvin H., "Defense of the Kansas Frontier, 1866-1867," *Kansas Historical Quarterlies*, No. 4, August 1932.

Garlington, E.A., Maj., Inspector General, *The Seventh Regiment of Cavalry*, p. 251-267. Printed in Rodenbough, Theophilus F., Bvt. Brig. Gen., USA and, William L. Haskin, Maj. USA, eds. *The Army of the United States Historical Sketches of Staff and Line with Portraits of Generals-in-Chief*, Maynard, Merrill, & Company, New York, 1896.

Gibson Foguera, Katherine, *With Custer's Cavalry*, Caxton Printers, Caldwell, Idaho, 1942. Reprinted, University of Nebraska Press, Lincoln, 1986.

Gibson, Francis, "Our Washita Battle," Little Bighorn National Monument Library. Reprinted in Peter Cozzens, ed., *Eyewitness to the Indian Wars, 1856-1890: Conquering the Southern Plains, Volume III*, Mechanicsburg, 2003.

Godfrey, Edward S., "Some Reminiscences, Including an Account of General Sully's Expedition Against the Southern Plains Indians, 1868, *The Cavalry Journal,* Vol. 36, 1927. Reprinted in Peter Cozzens, ed., *Eyewitness to the Indian Wars, 1856-1890: Conquering the Southern Plains, Volume III*, Mechanicsburg, 2003.

, "Some Reminiscences, Including the Washita Battle, November 27, 1868," *The Cavalry Journal,* Vol. 37, No. 153, 1928.

—, "Custer's Last Battle," *Century Magazine*, January 1892.

Goplin, Arnold O., *The Historical Significance of Fort Lincoln State Park,* North Dakota Parks and Recreational Department, Bismark, 1988.

Green, Jerome A., *Nez Perce Summer, 1877: The US Army and the Nee-Me-Poo Crisis*, Montana Historical Society Press, Helena, 2000.

Hamersly, T.H.S., *Complete Regular Army Register of the U. S. for One Hundred Years, 1779-1879*, Hamersly Company, Washington, D.C., 1880.

Hancock, Winfield S., "The Indians," Army and Navy Journal 5, No. 3, 43, 1867. Reprinted in Peter Cozzens, ed., *Eyewitness to the Indian Wars, 1856-1890: Conquering the Southern Plains, Volume III*, Mechanicsburg, 2003.

Heitman, Francis B., *Historical Register and Dictionary of the United States Army*, 2 Vols. Washington, GPO 1903 Rpt., University of Illinois Press, Urbana, 1965.

Hunt, Frazier, and Robert Hunt, *I Fought with Custer: The Story of Sergeant Windolph, Last Survivor of the Battle of Little Big Horn*, University of Nebraska Press, Lincoln, 1947.

Hutton, Paul Andrew, *The Custer Reader*, University of Nebraska Press, Lincoln, 1992.

—, *Soldiers West; Biographies from the Military Frontier*, University of Nebraska Press, Lincoln, 1987.

Jackson, Donald, *Custer's Gold: The United States Cavalry Expedition of 1874*, University of Nebraska Press, Lincoln, 1966.

Josephy Jr., Alvin M., *The Nez Perce Indians and the Opening of the Northwest*, Yale University Press, New Haven, 1965. Reprinted, Houghton Mifflin, New York, 1997.

Lang, George, Raymond L. Collins and Gerard F. White, *Medal of Honor Recipients, 1863-1994. Two Volumes*, Facts on File, New York, 1995.

Langellier, John P., Kurt Hamilton Cox, and Brian C. Pohanka, B.C., *"Myles Keogh: The Life and Legend of an Irish Dragoon in the Seventh Cavalry,"* Upton & Sons Publishers, El Segundo, CA, 1991; 2nd Edition, 1998.

Marquis, Thomas B., *Keep the Last Bullet for Yourself*, Reference Publishing, Algonac, Michigan, 1976.

Michno, Gregory, *The Mystery of E Troop*, Mountain Press Publishing Co., Missoula, 1994.

Mills, Charles K., *Charles C. DeRudio,* Mattituck, New York, 1983.

—, *Harvest of Barren Regrets: The Army Career of Frederick William Benteen, 1834-1898,* Arthur H. Clark Company, Glendale, California, 1885.

Merrington, Marguerite, *The Custer Story: The Life and Intimate Letters of General Custer and His Wife Elizabeth*, Devin-Adair Company, New York, 1950.

Milbrook, Minnie Dubbs, "The West Breaks in General Custer," *Kansas Historical Quarterlies,* Vol. 36, No. 2, 1970.

—, "Diary of Rebecca Richmond," *Kansas Historical Quarterlies*, Vol. 42, No. 2, 1976.

Moore, Horace L., "The 19th Kansas Cavalry in the Washita Campaign," *Chronicles of Oklahoma*, Vol. 2, No. 4, 1924. Reprinted in Peter Cozzens, ed., *Eyewitness to the Indian Wars, 1856-1890: Conquering the Southern Plains, Volume III*, Mechanicsburg, 2003.

Nichols, Ronald H., *Men with Custer: Biographies of the 7th Cavalry*, Custer Battlefield Historical & Museum Association, Inc., Hardin, Montana, 2000.

O'neil, Alice T., *Military Discipline under General George A. Custer*, Arrow and Trooper Publishing, New York, 1998.

Record of Engagements with Hostile Indians within the Military Division of the Missouri; From 1868 to 1882, U.S. Army Military History Research Collection, General Staff College Library, Chicago, 1882.

Reedstrom, E. Lisle, *Custer's Seventh Cavalry: From Fort Riley to the Little Big Horn*, Sterling Publishing Company, Inc., New York, 1992.

Robertson, William Glen, Jerold E. Brown, William M. Campsey, Scott R. McMeen, *Atlas of the Sioux Wars*, Combat Studies Institute, U.S. Army Command and General Staff College, Ft. Leavenworth, Kansas.

Rodenbough, Theophilus Francis, and William L. Haskin, *The Army of the United States: Historical Sketches of Staff and Line With Portraits of Generals-in-Chief*, : Maynard and Merrill, New York, 1896.

Sheridan, *Outline of Posts*, The Old Army Press, Fort Collins, Colorado, 1972.

Spurr, Dick and Wendy, *Historic Forts of Colorado*, Centennial Publications, Grand Junction, Colorado, 1994.

Starr, Stephen Z., *The Union Cavalry in the Civil War, Volumes I-III*, Louisiana State University Press, Baton Rouge, 1979.

Swanson, Glenwood J., *The Life and Times Of George Armstrong Custer*, Swanson Productions, Inc., Agua Dulce, California, 2004.

Tolzmann, Don Heinrich, *Frederick Whittaker's Complete Life of General George Armstrong Custer, Major General of Volunteers, Brevet Major US Army and Lieutenant Colonel Seventh US Cavalry*, Heritage Books, Inc., Bowie, Maryland, 1993.

US Army Registry of the United States, Department of the Army, US Government Printing Office, Washington, D.C., 1867.

US Army Uniforms and Equipment, 1889: Specifications for Clothing, Camp and Garrison Equipage, and Clothing and Equipage Material, Published by the Direction of the Quartermaster General of the Army, Reprinted, University of Nebraska Press, Lincoln, 1986.

Utley, Robert M., *Cavalier in Buckskin*, Salamander Books, Ltd., London, 2001.

—, *Custer's Chief of Scouts: The Reminiscences of Charles A. Varnum,* University of Nebraska Press, Lincoln, 1982.

—, *Life in Custer's Cavalry: Diaries and Letters of Albert and Jennie Barnitz, 1867-1868*, University of Nebraska Press, Lincoln, 1987.

—, *Frontiersmen in Blue: The United States Army and the Indian, 1848-1865*, Macmillan Publishing Co. Inc., New York, 1967.

—, *Frontier Regulars: The United States Army and the Indian, 1866-1891*, Macmillan Publishing Co. Inc., New York, 1973.

Van de Water, Frederic, *Glory Hunter: A Life of General Custer*, University of Nebraska Press, Lincoln, 1934.

Warner, Ezra J., *Generals in Blue; Lives of the Union Commanders*, Louisiana State University Press, Baton Rouge, 1964.

—, *Generals in Grey; Lives of the Confederate Commanders*, Louisiana State University Press, Baton Rouge, 1959.

Williamson, James J., *Mosby's Rangers: A Record of the Operations of the Forty-Third Battalion, Virginia Cavalry*, Ralph B. Kenyon Publishers, New York, 1896.

Sources and Credits

A large assortment of sources were referenced and used for biographical information to complete this project; with several more predominant and popular compilations providing the framework. The decision as to how to credit this huge assortment of varying sources was vexing. In the end, in order to avoid redundancy and pedantic documentation, I've chosen to list all sources in essay form, citing both the bulk of compiled information as well as to distinguish the single or more abstract sources. As mentioned prior, foundations for the biographical data on the officer corps of the Seventh Cavalry and the groundwork in which this project lay derived from several dominant and well-known sources, including Heitman's meticulously compiled *Historical Register and Dictionary of the United States Army, US Army Registry of the United States*, Department of the Army, as well as the wonderful preliminary biographical sketches *Men with Custer: Biographies of the 7th Cavalry,* by Ronald Nichols and *They Rode with Custer* by John Carroll (original works compiled by Kenneth Hammer in 1972). These provided the foundation of biographical data, chiefly of the 1876 corps roster.

In the cases of those members of the regiment buried there or at least affiliated, Arlington National Cemetery Records are referenced regarding Andrus, Commagere, Morrow, Nicholson, Plummer, Schofield, Scott, Sheridan, Sickel, and Weston. Data from graduates and attendees of West Point derived from several Academy publications including *Biographical Register of the Officers and Graduates of the United States Military Academy, 1802-1890, Volume III, IV, V, and VI,* by George W. Cullum. Data was also generated from *Annual Reports of Graduates, United States Military Academy* from the years 1891(Wallace), 1896(Merrill), 1897(Smith), 1900(Russell), 1901(Schofield), 1908(Craycroft), 1909(March), 1912(Larned), 1914(Johnson), 1917(Robinson), 1919(Braden, Sickel), 1921(Pearson), 1927(Chase, Gresham), 1929(Fuller, McCormick), and 1931(Edgerly, Hare). For all individuals, the outline for all biographical data was drawn primarily from several chief sources: *Letters Received, Regimental Returns* from various military posts as well as several National Archives Records including *Regimental Returns of the Seventh Cavalry*, Records Group 94, *Advancements, Commissions and Promotions,* AGO, 1871-1894, and U.S. Government Pension Index, Series T288 and *Records of the Record and Pension Office (RPO) of the War Department, 1784-1919,* all located at the National Archives, Washington D.C. Data specifically extracted and transposed within the biographical essay is indicated within, crediting the particular file number.

In addition to the bulk sources, various other single-source abstracts and publications including memorial sketches, periodicals, obituaries, Civil War Regimental histories and U.S. Census records, between the years 1840 through 1930, have been referenced: *Memorial sketch for Rynd Edward Lawder,* Military Order of Loyal Legion, Commandery of the State of Missouri Records 1885-1931; Missouri State Archives Circular no. 3 whole no. 6 January 20, 1891, "Captured by Mosby's Guerrillas," Brevet Major Charles Brewster, Capt. and C.S., U.S.V. Missouri Mollus, Sketches of War History, 1861-1865, Volume I; *Spencer Tracks in the 19th Century, From North Carolina to Texas,* by Marcus A. Coker; *Who's who in Iowa Politics*; Prison File No. 355, Series 1, David W. Wallingford, Lansing Prison Ledger A, Lansing, Kansas; *Sturgis Family Papers*, Wisconsin Historical Society, Villa Louis, Prairie du Chien, Wisconsin; *Letters Received and Post Returns*, Fort Hays, for E.P. Eckerson; Charles Cresson Obituary, *Washington Post, March 16, 1906*; *Obituary, Capt L. M Hamilton*, Printed Ephemera Collection, Portfolio 236, Folder 31a, Library of Congress, reprinted in the Army and Navy Journal, January 2, 1869 and Louis Hamilton Obituary and Louis Hamilton Obituary, *New York Evening Post*; Verling Hart obituary summary and Memorial sketch, Ft. Laramie; Edward Law Obituary, *Philadelphia Inquirer,* October 1881; and John F. Weston Obituary, *Washington Post*, August 6, 1917. Supplemental military records were accessed from *Chronological List of Actions with Indians; January 1, 1866-January, 1891,* and *Record of Engagements with Hostile Indians within the Military Division of the Missouri, 1868 to 1882*, both published by the army. Civil War biographical data through was accessed through regimental histories and numerous other sources including; *The Union Army: A History of Military Affairs in the Loyal States 1861-65*, *History of the Army of the United States,* by Rodenbough, which references histories of the 2nd and 6th Ohio Cavalry, 3rd Massachusetts Volunteer Heavy Artillery Regiment, 4th Massachusetts Cavalry, 40th Massachusetts Infantry, 1st Colorado Cavalry, 3rd New Jersey Cavalry, 7th Indiana Cavalry, 1st Nebraska Cavalry, 1st Iowa Cavalry, 10th Maryland Infantry, 3rd Kansas Battery, 15th Kansas Cavalry, 3rd and 4th Kentucky Cavalry. In addition, *The Fourth Regiment of Cavalry*, compiled by the office of the Military Service Institution, *History of Pennsylvania Volunteers, 1861-65*, by Bates, with references to the 73rd Pennsylvania Infantry, and the 5th and 6th Pennsylvania Cavalry, and *The Union Cavalry in the Civil War, Volumes I-III,* by Starr were also referenced. Historical information in regards to the participants of the Bighorn Battle and the following Nez Perce campaign was drawn from personnel and publications from associations including the Little Bighorn National Monument and Friends of Bear Paw, Big Hole, Canyon Creek Battlefields. Finally, biographical data derived from numerous books and publications including *Life in Custer's Cavalry: Diaries and Letters of Albert and Jennie Barnitz, 1867-1868, Frontier Regulars: The United States Army and the Indian, 1866-1891*, and *Custer's Chief of Scouts: The Reminiscences of Charles A. Varnum,* written by Robert Utley; *I Fought with Custer: The Story of Sergeant Windolph, Last Survivor of the Battle of Little Big Horn*, by Frazier and Hunt; *Mosby's Rangers*, by James Williamson; *Boots and Saddle* and *Tenting on the Plains: With General Custer from the Potomac to the Western Frontier,* both written by Elizabeth Custer;

George A. Custer; His Life and Times, by Glenwood Swanson; *Custer: The Civil War Years*, by Gregory Urwin; *Soldiers West; Biographies from the Military Frontier;* and various excerpt and accounts within several compilations including *The Custer Reader* by Hutton; Peter Cozzens complilation *Eyewitnesses to the Indian Wars, 1865-1890; Volume Three, Conquering the Southern Plains,* including accounts of the Washita Campaign by Charles Brewster, Edward Godfrey, Horrace Moore, and Francis Gibson, accounts of the Sully Expedition by Joel Elliot and accounts of Sully's campaign and the Yellowstone Campaign by Edward Godfrey; *Charles C. DeRudio* and *Harvest of Barren Regrets: The Army Career of Frederick William Benteen,* both by Charles K. Mills; *"Diary of Rebecca Richmond,"* Kansas Historical Quarterlies; *Medal of Honor Recipients, 1863-1994,* compiled by Lang, Collins, and White and *Medal of Honor Recipients: 1863-1973*, compiled by the Committee on Veterans Affairs; *"Myles Keogh: The Life and Legend of an Irish Dragoon in the Seventh Cavalry,"* by Langellier, Cox, and Pohanka; *With Custer's Cavalry,* by Katherine Gibson Foguera; *Nez Perce Summer*, by Jerome Greene; *Indian Fights and Fighters*, by Brady; *The Mystery of E Troop*, by Gregory Michno; and *Hero of Beecher Island: The Life and Military Career of George A. Forsyth*, by David Dixon.